Teaching Critically About Lewis and Clark

Teaching Critically About Lewis and Clark

Challenging Dominant Narratives in K–12 Curriculum

Alison Schmitke
Leilani Sabzalian
Jeff Edmundson

TEACHERS COLLEGE PRESS

TEACHERS COLLEGE | COLUMBIA UNIVERSITY
NEW YORK AND LONDON

Published by Teachers College Press,® 1234 Amsterdam Avenue, New York, NY 10027

Copyright © 2020 by Teachers College, Columbia University

Cover painting: Jaune Quick-To-See Smith, *State Names,* 2000, oil, collage and mixed media on canvas, Smithsonian American Art Museum, Gift of Elizabeth Ann Dugan and museum purchase. Map of Lewis and Clark's expedition courtesy of the Library of Congress.

Library of Congress Cataloging-in-Publication Data is available at loc.gov

ISBN 978-0-8077-6370-4 (paper)
ISBN 978-0-8077-6371-1 (hardcover)
ISBN 978-0-8077-7848-7 (ebook)

Printed on acid-free paper
Manufactured in the United States of America

We call upon all those who have lived on this Earth
Our ancestors and our friends,
Who dreamed the best for future generations,
And upon whose lives our lives are built,
And with thanksgiving, we call upon them to
Teach us and show us the way.

This blessing was read by Chinook Nation Chairman Gary Johnson on November 18, 2005, at the dedication of the Confluence Project site at Cape Disappointment. This was 200 years to the day from the arrival of the Corps of Discovery.

Contents

PART IV: TEACHING RESOURCES

Acknowledgments

We extend our gratitude to our families for supporting us, and to all who contributed to this project. Thank you to the teachers willing to teach drafts of the lesson plans and provide significant feedback—Brittany Dorris, Jenny Henke, Rachel Hsieh, Grace Groom, Tristan Moore, Heidi Sawitzke, and Julia Von Holt. We thank Greg Archuleta and Chris Remple, both members of the Confederated Tribes of Grand Ronde, for sharing their expertise about native plants for the trading card activity. We thank Rachel Cushman (Chinook) for sharing expertise about Canoe Journeys and the Chinook Indian Nation, and for her story "We Don't Need Those Anymore." We thank Courtney Yilik and Colin Fogarty at the Confluence Project. We thank Stephanie Wood and Dick Basch (Clatsop, Nehalem) with Honoring Tribal Legacies. We extend our gratitude to Renée Watson. Thank you also to Bill Bigelow and Ursula Wolfe-Rocca with Rethinking Schools and the Zinn Education Project. Finally, thank you to Ashley Cordes (Coquille), Lydia Giomi, Jeanne Hall, Katie Jewel, Alex Pratt, Nellie Schmitke-Rosiek, Donovan Wilson, Randy Town, and Anna Tsoi.

Part I

INTRODUCTION

CHAPTER 1

Beyond Adventure

One and a half billion acres. This is the number calculated by Claudio Saunt (Onion & Saunt, 2014) when he developed an interactive map calculating the exact acreage the U.S. government has seized from the Indigenous peoples of North America since 1776. To be more precise, the exact number would be 1,510,677,343 acres. That is almost two million square miles. If you were to calculate the rate at which the U.S. government dispossessed Indigenous people of their lands, it would be "at a rate of two square miles per hour" (Spirling, 2011, p. 1).

These billions of acres of Indigenous land were seized by treaty and executive order, whittling away the vast stretch of Indian Country that encompassed all of North America to a mere 56.2 million acres (Bureau of Indian Affairs, 2017). Though millions of acres may appear a vast tract of land, it is less than 90,000 square miles, and hardly sufficient when considering it is divided among the 326 Indian land areas in the United States administered as federal Indian reservations. For example, Likely Rancheria, operated by the Pit River Tribe in California, is a 1.32 acre parcel that is just large enough for the cemetery. Further, the 326 land areas do not account for the nearly 600 federally recognized tribal nations in the United States, leaving many of those nations not with small patches of land, but landless. Moreover, those precious few acres of land must continually be defended by Indigenous people and nations who still face encroachment on their lands even today. The courage and resistance of the Bears Ears Inter-Tribal Coalition, Kanaka Maoli, Winnemem Wintu, Osage Nation, the Columbia River Inter-Tribal Fish Commission, Lummi Nation, and the Standing Rock Sioux, among other nations and intertribal organizations, demonstrate how the theft of Indigenous lands and resources creates present-day battlegrounds for Native nations. (For further reading and teaching ideas, refer to Teacher Resource 1: Native Lands Under Siege and Secondary Lesson Plan 5: Standing Rock and the "Larger Story.")

This story of dispossession—and resistance—has roots that are rarely examined. While most students have heard something about Manifest Destiny, very few have heard of the medieval white supremacist Doctrine of Discovery and the U.S. Supreme Court cases that enshrined that belief system into U.S. laws. Additionally, rarely do students learn that the instructions given to the Lewis and Clark Corps of Discovery to document and report their observations was part of a strategy to establish land claims justified by the Doctrine of Discovery. As Eastern Shawnee legal scholar Robert Miller (2008) states,

> When European and Americans planted their national flags and religious symbols in these "newly discovered" lands, they were not just thanking Providence for a safe voyage. Instead, they were undertaking the well-organized legal procedures and rituals of Discovery designed to demonstrate their country's legal claim over the "new discovered" lands and peoples. (p. 1)

Dominant narratives are reproduced as official knowledge in schools, particularly through the conventional ways the Corps of Discovery is framed in social studies textbooks. As we will discuss in Chapter 3, the conventional ways Lewis and Clark are framed are embedded with colonial logics and reproduce Indigenous erasure.

In textbooks, the Corps of Discovery is presented as a tidy narrative of exploration and science. For example, in *The United States: Making a New Nation (Harcourt Social Studies)* (Berson, Howard, & Salinas, 2012), an elementary textbook, students are presented the following excerpt:

> Little was known about the land in the Louisiana Purchase. President Jefferson wanted to learn what resources the area had. Jefferson chose a friend and army officer named Meriwether Lewis to plan and lead the expedition. Lewis asked his friend and fellow army officer William Clark to help. Clark was responsible for keeping records and making maps. . . . Lewis and Clark drew many maps showing mountain passes and major rivers. They brought back seeds, plants, and even animals. President Jefferson was proud of their success. (p. 430–431)

In *American History: Beginnings Through Reconstruction* (Davidson & Stoff, 2016), a secondary textbook, students are presented a similar passage:

> Jefferson asked Lewis and Clark to map a route to the Pacific Ocean. He also asked them to study the geography of the territory including: '. . . climate as characterized by the thermometer, by the proportion of rainy, cloudy, and clear days, by lightning, hails, snow, ice . . . the dates at which particular plants put forth or lose their flower, or leaf, times of appearance of particular birds, reptiles, or insects' (Thomas Jefferson, letter to Meriwether Lewis, 1803). Jefferson also instructed Lewis and Clark to learn about the Native American nations who lived in the Louisiana Purchase. (pp. 200–201)

In each of these passages (which reflect typical textbook portrayals of this era), little attention is given to multiple perspectives or historical thinking. Without tools and information to challenge these textbook portrayals, curriculum oversimplifies the Corps of Discovery, fueling "commonsensical ideas" that "makes it easy to continue teaching and learning in ways that allow the oppression already in play to continue to play out unchallenged in our schools and society" (Kumashiro, 2004, p. xxxvi). This book supports historical thinking and social science inquiry (Levstik & Barton, 2015; Monte-Sano, De La Paz & Felton, 2014; NCSS, 2013; Wineburg, Martin, & Monte-Sano, 2013) by encouraging active and critical engagement with history and the contemporary legacies and contexts we have inherited. In doing so, the lesson plans featured in *Teaching Critically About Lewis and Clark: Challenging Dominant Narratives in K–12 Curriculum* complicate narratives of "discovery" and "expansion," challenge Eurocentrism, decenter Eurocentric perspectives by incorporating Indigenous perspectives, and relate these histories to contemporary issues and events. *Teaching Critically About Lewis and Clark* resets the study of the Corps of Discovery through the context of the Doctrine of Discovery (Chapter 2). This results in understanding present-day conflicts over Indigenous lands as a legacy of the Doctrine of Discovery and its contemporary expression as it remains encoded in U.S. law (Miller, 2008). How might educators critically interrogate the assumptions that underlie the Doctrine of Discovery through their teaching? How might educators prepare their students to challenge these issues, to defend tribal sovereignty, and to stand in solidarity with Indigenous peoples? These questions lie at the heart of this book.

In mainstream accounts, Lewis and Clark are often framed as "trailblazers," as "ambassadors of peace, friendship, and trust," or as "innovators," "free thinkers," "risk-takers," or "mavericks" (contemporary descriptors drawn from an opening elementary lesson activity). Beyond oversimplifying the narrative, these accounts do not support multiple perspectives, historical thinking, or inquiry. However, when the Corps of Discovery is viewed through the Doctrine of Discovery, it is evident that Thomas Jefferson's intentions went beyond exploration and science. Read in light of anticolonial and Native perspectives, such as that of Roberta Conner, citizen of the Confederated Tribes of the Umatilla Indian Reservation and director of the Tamástslikt Cultural Institute, the expedition would be more accurately framed as "reconnaissance for an empire" rather than an "innocent journey" (Conner, 2006a, p. 105). Challenging popular belief by teaching about histories and legacies of conquest, Indigenous displacement, paternalism, and colonialism is necessary in order to teach a more complex, accurate, honest, and critical account of this shared history. This book challenges the innocence of nationalist narratives by making Eurocentrism explicit, insisting that Indigenous perspectives and various forms of resistance are included in curriculum, and inviting students to imagine alternatives to these histories and to work toward more responsible futures. As Bill Bigelow and Bob Peterson (1998) offer in their book *Rethinking Columbus: The Next 500 Years*, "Through critiquing traditional history and imagining alternatives, students can begin to discover the excitement that comes from asserting oneself morally and intellectually—refusing to be passive consumers of official histories" (p. 11).

Teaching Critically About Lewis and Clark provides K–12 teachers resources and teaching strategies to complicate existing elementary and secondary curriculum about the Corps of Discovery. This book has four key purposes: (1) to challenge the Eurocentric ways textbooks present the Corps of Discovery; (2) to examine the Corps of Discovery in the context of the Doctrine of Discovery; (3) to frame colonization and Indigenous dispossession as an ongoing legacy that Indigenous peoples continue to struggle with and resist today; (4) to embed Indigenous perspectives and contemporary issues within each lesson plan. To achieve these key purposes, we first lay out a framework to support educators in teaching social studies and Indigenous studies curriculum from an anticolonial stance.

FRAMEWORK: SIX ORIENTATIONS FOR ANTICOLONIAL CURRICULUM

In March 2018, the National Council for the Social Studies published a position statement titled "Toward

Responsibility: Social Studies Education that Respects and Affirms Indigenous Peoples and Nations." The recommendations presented in "Toward Responsibility" are intended to help teachers disrupt Eurocentric social studies curriculum that reproduces inaccuracies and erasure of Native peoples by offering educators guiding principles to responsibly design curriculum. These include committing to responsible representations, teaching current events and movements, teaching tribal governance and sovereignty as civics education, challenging Eurocentrism, and affirming Indigenous knowledge. In the statement, NCSS makes a call "for educators to look for more productive ways to disrupt . . . narrow stereotypes, and help their students develop more appropriate, accurate, and complex understandings of Indigenous Peoples and Nations" (NCSS, 2018). The framework organizing the curriculum in *Teaching Critically About Lewis and Clark* is directly informed by and reflective of the commitments outlined in the NCSS position statement. It is our hope that our six orientations—place, presence, perspectives, political nationhood, power, and partnerships—contribute to the efforts to extend and transform social studies curriculum that respects and affirms Indigenous peoples and nations.

The six orientations for anticolonial curriculum, referred to hereafter as the 6 Ps, are intended to interrupt tacit or taken-for-granted Eurocentric orientations within curriculum. These orientations support teaching that is responsive to and responsible for the colonial legacies of the present, and promote pedagogy that affirms Indigenous self-determination and sovereignty. These orientations explicitly support a context for more critical engagement with dominant narratives about Lewis and Clark, and we see them as broadly facilitating curriculum about Indigenous peoples and perspectives, laying a foundation for other critical social studies curriculum to challenge colonial ideologies and take seriously Indigenous perspectives and sovereignty. What follows is a description of each of the 6 Ps, adapted and compiled from previously published work (Sabzalian, 2019; Sabzalian, Miyamoto-Sundahl, & Fong, 2019).

Place

All education takes place on Indigenous lands, whether those lands were ceded through force or treaty and remain contested terrain today. Educators should recognize the Indigenous peoples and homelands of the place where they teach, including federally recognized tribal nations, unrecognized nations, and Indigenous spaces and presence in urban areas. Beyond acknowledgment, curriculum should be land-and place-based, centering local histories, presence, issues, and priorities. Educators should inquire into Indigenous place names when possible, inviting students to question colonial practices of naming.

Presence

The term *presence* orients educators to the contemporary presence of Indigenous peoples and nations as well as contemporary experiences and issues. In the United States, there are currently over 6 million people who are citizens or descendants of nearly 600 tribal nations. Recognizing the diverse and vibrant presence of Indigenous peoples challenges narratives of "progress" that assume Indigenous people vanished, a narrative compounded by curricular silences around Indigenous peoples today. Such a focus necessarily includes recognizing physical, cultural, geographic, linguistic, and political diversity, which disrupts static, stoic, and homogenous stereotypes of Indians that are pervasive in curricula, media, and society. As an effective social studies practice, lessons and units that foreground contemporary experiences or issues Native people face today can support curriculum that is interesting and relevant while affirming the continuance and survivance (Vizenor, 1999) of Native peoples and nations.

Perspectives

Critical approaches to curriculum invite students to evaluate the credibility, positionality, and various interests that underlie particular perspectives, as well as challenge dominant perspectives. This orientation calls on educators to explicitly foreground Indigenous perspectives as a way to challenge Eurocentrism and decenter dominant perspectives. Indigenous perspectives complicate mainstream approaches to curriculum that focus on "discovery." For example, the late Karenne Wood (2003), member of the Monacan Indian Nation, said that "Nothing was discovered. Everything was already loved" (p. 13). Similarly, Indigenous perspectives question and productively trouble the purportedly benign narratives of expansion, exploration, and progress that often permeate curriculum. The cover art for this book, *State Names* by Jaune Quick-to-See Smith (Confederated Salish and Kootenai Nation), which is also featured in Secondary Lesson Plan 1: "The Stories Maps Tell," exemplifies the ways Indigenous perspectives complicate dominant narratives. This orientation is important, not only to provide a fuller and more responsible understanding of history and the present, but also because it moves educators away from positioning Indigenous peoples as objects of study. Indigenous perspectives of history are important, but so too are Indigenous perspectives on land, environmentalism, science, literature, research, governance, and so on. Rather than learning *about* Indigenous peoples, this orientation invites educators to learn *from* Indigenous analyses, a positioning that reminds educators and students that Indigenous people are subjects, not objects, and have important experiences and knowledge that can inform a range of issues today, and enrich our understanding of the world more broadly.

Political Nationhood

Mainstream media, curricula, and discourse position Indigenous people as racial/ethnic minorities, typically focusing on the cultural aspects of Indigenous communities. However, Indigenous identities are political, rooted in the political relationship between Indigenous nations and the United States, and in Indigenous peoples' status as citizens and descendants of tribal nations. This orientation draws attention to the political status and rights of tribal nations and the political rights of tribal citizens affirmed in treaties, the U.S. Constitution, Congressional legislation, and Supreme Court decisions. Educators must be aware of and teach their students to recognize tribal sovereignty, which is both an inherent and a political right. Much as civics education is designed to cultivate students' understanding of local, state, and federal governments, this orientation affirms the sovereignty of tribal nations, including an emphasis on tribal governments, leadership, treaties, and laws. Lewis, Clark, and President Thomas Jefferson knew they were engaging in diplomatic relations with sovereign nations, as evidenced by their repeated reference to Indigenous peoples in such terms. For example, when writing about his concern in locating the Shoshone peoples to secure horses, Lewis writes, "if we do not find them or *some other nation* who have horses I fear the successful issue of our voyage will be very doubtful or at all events much more difficult in it's accomplishment" (emphasis added). Lewis, as was often the case, used the term *nation* to describe Indigenous peoples. This term is used repeatedly in the journals; however, this historic fact—that Indigenous peoples are *nations*—has been forgotten, unlearned, or reframed over the years.

Charles Mills (2007) suggests that such "forgetting" is part of a process of "collective amnesia" (p. 29) that

has facilitated colonization and nation building. Leech Lake scholar Scott Lyons (2000) argues that these shifts in language "[f]rom 'sovereign' to 'ward,' from 'nation' to 'tribe,' and from 'treaty' to 'agreement'" (p. 453) are part of a broader practice of rhetorical imperialism—the use of writing, words, and terms to facilitate colonization and undermine Indigenous sovereignty. Language that minimizes tribal nations' status as nations also functions to minimize the responsibility of the United States to redress historic wrongs and contemporary issues these nations continue to face today. It is imperative that educators counter rhetorical imperialism by emphasizing Indigenous sovereignty. Although characterized in federal law as "domestic, dependent nations," this orientation draws attention to the inherent sovereignty of Indigenous peoples, and complements cultural framings of Indigenous peoples by also teaching students about the political relationship between tribal nations and other governments, which includes teaching about tribal citizenship, nationhood, treaties, and sovereignty.

Power

Critical pedagogy draws specific attention to power relations within curriculum and society, and makes a point to incorporate counternarratives and standpoints of oppressed communities within curriculum (Au, 2012). Making relations of power visible requires asking questions, such as: Why is it that Indigenous peoples are continually framed as exotic objects of study, as Others, or as primitive in conventional textbooks and curriculum? Why doesn't curriculum focus more often on treaty rights, tribal nationhood, or sovereignty? Who benefits when curriculum focuses on the adventures of explorers rather than the experiences of those invaded? This orientation challenges the neutrality of curriculum, calling into question liberal approaches to inclusion that fail to draw attention to power dynamics. Educators have a responsibility to "explicitly name settler colonialism and empire and challenge the very foundations of democracy, freedom, and justice for which the United States claims to be built" (Sabzalian & Shear, 2018, p. 158).

Beyond critiquing relations of power such as colonialism or racism within curriculum, educators should also emphasize the ways Indigenous peoples have always engaged in organizing and activism to assert their collective power and enact change. Without this focus, curriculum that teaches about colonization risks reproducing narratives that Indigenous peoples are victims of colonial policies and practices. To counter these damage-based narratives (Tuck, 2009), students should learn about the various ways Indigenous peoples have been changemakers, in the past and today. Countless examples exist of Indigenous peoples seeking justice, embodying self-determination and sovereignty, and imagining and working toward a decolonial future that respects Indigenous rights.

Partnerships

An emphasis on partnerships recognizes the value of cultivating and sustaining meaningful and mutually beneficial partnerships with Indigenous peoples, organizations, and nations. This can take the form of organizing a site visit for students to an Indigenous organization or nation near school, or inviting local Indigenous people to visit the classroom as guest speakers (ensuring that the proper groundwork is laid so that students can learn from the speaker's expertise, rather than field stereotypical or unrelated questions). Partnerships can involve larger projects, such as a collaboration between a nation and a school or district to improve how that nation is represented in curriculum. Students can also learn of the ways that organizations, such as the U.S. Forest Service, or, in a case specific to Lewis and Clark, the National Park Service, seek to consult and collaborate with Native nations.

The six orientations informing the curriculum in *Teaching Critically About Lewis and Clark* support the College, Career, and Civic Life (C3) Framework from the National Council for the Social Studies (NCSS). Published in 2013, the C3 Framework "focuses on inquiry skills and key concepts, and guides—not prescribes—the choice of curricular content necessary for a rigorous social studies program" (NCSS, p. 6, 2013). Drawing from the C3 framework, the lessons in this book incorporate the four dimensions "which support a robust social studies program rooted in inquiry," which include (1) developing questions and planning inquiry, (2) applying disciplinary tools and concepts, (3) evaluating sources and using evidence, and (4) communicating conclusions and taking informed action (p. 12). In addition to identifying the relevant 6 Ps and C3 elements, applicable Common Core State Standards are identified and listed for the lessons in this book. We assume teachers using this curriculum are highly capable, smart, creative experts able to identify how this curriculum articulates with district and state standards used in their specific teaching context. We continue to be asked, "But will the students pass the tests?" Our first response is to question the validity of such measures, which are often embedded with racial and colonial biases. But a follow-up response is that yes,

this book is intended not only to equip students to "pass the tests," but also be empowered with the knowledge and skills to critique the tests. Students and teachers can be critical, active learners, *and* meet—even exceed—the content standards.

PEDAGOGICAL CONSIDERATIONS: WHAT TO CONSIDER BEFORE TEACHING

As should be clear from previous sections, this curriculum disrupts existing narratives about the Lewis and Clark Corps of Discovery. In addition, these lessons are meant to challenge conventional pedagogical approaches. Unfortunately, at times social studies teaching remains characterized by stubborn teaching routines: (1) it focuses on low-level facts, such as timelines, so that learning is seen as accumulating the necessary facts; (2) it implies that there is a single, objective, universally accepted story about the events being studied; (3) it sees students as passive receivers of knowledge that originates outside them; and (4) it sees these passive students as being without culture (Wineburg, 2001; Barton & Levstik, 2004; Lesh, 2011; Levstik & Barton, 2015; NCSS, 2018). Motivation for the development of the C3 Framework by the National Council for the Social Studies was derived from the aspiration to provide guidance "for states to update, revise, or reinvent their state social studies standards" and for educators "to strengthen their social studies programs by (1) enhancing the rigor of social studies disciplines, (2) building the critical thinking, problem solving, and participatory skills necessary for students to become engaged citizens . . ." (NCSS, 2013, p. viii). In addition to the efforts of the NCSS, we also know there is a long tradition of teaching social studies from critical, inquiry-oriented perspectives that challenge dominant narratives. The work of teacher-scholars illustrated in publications and projects like *Rethinking Schools*, *Teaching Tolerance*, Teaching for Change, and Zinn Education Project are examples of these efforts. So too are recent publications like *Race Lessons: Using Inquiry to Teach About Race in Social Studies* (Chandler, 2017), *It's Being Done in Social Studies: Race, Class, Gender and Sexuality in the Pre/K–12 Curriculum* (Willcox and Brant, 2018), or *(Re)Imagining Elementary Social Studies: A Controversial Issues Reader* (Shear, Tschida, Bellows, Buchanan, & Sayer, 2018).

The pedagogy of *Teaching Critically About Lewis and Clark* contributes to this tradition and the goals of the C3 Framework by: (1) supporting students' higher-order, disciplinary thinking, and social studies inquiry skills to critically examine historical events; (2) challenging students to investigate and evaluate multiple perspectives around any event, including consideration of how perspectives change over time; (3) recognizing students as active constructors of knowledge who bring their own experiences to learning; and (4) understanding that students' lived experiences, identities, cultures, communities, and histories deeply affect how they respond to the study of history and social studies broadly considered.

Inviting Students to Use Higher-Order Skills

Throughout the curriculum in *Teaching Critically About Lewis and Clark*, the teaching materials go well beyond fact-level learning. Rather than focusing on right answers, lessons ask students to analyze, predict, compare, evaluate, and support claims with evidence from a range of historical sources. In the process of inquiry, students are expected to practice articulating their own critical voice to push against dominant narratives. The scaffold of these lessons results in a layering of content to extend student understanding. Students draw upon their growing knowledge to communicate their ideas and arguments in the form of discussion (pairs, small groups, and larger groups), a variety of written responses, and independent or collaborative projects.

For example, Secondary Lesson Plans 2 and 3 are designed to complicate understanding of President Thomas Jefferson's goals for the Lewis and Clark Corps of Discovery by viewing his instructions through the Doctrine of Discovery. The first lesson in this sequence is a historical investigation using primary documents presenting President Jefferson's instructions and the second lesson extends the findings of this inquiry by focusing on the Doctrine of Discovery. Students are asked to make a judgment about who should prevail in the 1823 Supreme Court case *Johnson v. McIntosh*. Then, after providing information about the decision and reviewing the elements of the Doctrine of Discovery, students annotate an excerpt from Chief Justice John Marshall's ruling by identifying the principles of the Doctrine of Discovery underlying the case. Students are asked to evaluate the arguments used by the Supreme Court for justification of settling Native homelands and to challenge the assumption that U.S. government actions (and especially Supreme Court decisions) were based in justice and equity. Students then reexamine President Jefferson's instructions in the context of the Doctrine of the Discovery and in light of Haudenosaunee (Iroquois) perspectives today. Following the same technique of annotation in which

the principles of the Doctrine of Discovery were applied to an excerpt from the *Johnson v. McIntosh* (1823) decision, students identify the elements of the Doctrine of Discovery that are present within President Jefferson's instructions to Meriwether Lewis. The lesson closes with a summary of efforts directed at the Catholic Church demanding the rescission of the Doctrine of Discovery and an exploration of the variety of opportunities for student action, such as collaborative efforts to contribute to campaigns to rescind the Doctrine of Discovery or advocating for the Doctrine of Discovery to be included in social studies standards for teaching about Lewis and Clark.

Challenging Students to See Multiple Perspectives

Challenging dominant narratives of the Corps of Discovery requires incorporating sources that disrupt Eurocentric retellings of Lewis and Clark. It also requires addressing the ways in which the Corps of Discovery's legacy is still experienced and contested today. In this curriculum, we selected sources that reflect a range of Indigenous perspectives on the history and legacy of the Lewis and Clark military expedition. In drawing upon Indigenous poets and artists like Karenne Wood or Jaune Quick-to-See Smith, we invite students to understand the legacy from different perspectives. Students are invited to revisit their understanding in light of interviews, testimony, videos, and excerpts from articles and books written by Indigenous peoples. We also provide examples where non-Indigenous people, such as the descendants of William Clark, have sought to reconcile their family's participation in the Corps of Discovery. We include these sources and others as part of the curriculum featured in this book as a response to "the call for educators to address the hegemonic master narrative as it pertains to the stories of Indigenous Peoples in the United States . . . The power of a more complex narrative to liberate us from the grasp of hegemony is a worthy struggle that could lead to a more just society" (Shear, Knowles, Soden, & Castro, 2015, p. 91). It is our expectation that this curriculum results in students having a more complicated and responsible knowledge of the Corps of Discovery and be able to view the historical legacies and contemporary understandings of Lewis and Clark from new angles. One example of this approach is demonstrated in Elementary Lesson Plan 5, "'Everything was Already Loved:' Complicating Science and Discovery." In 2003, the opening ceremony for the bicentennial of the Lewis and Clark Corps of Discovery was held at Monticello, the home of President Jefferson. Karenne Wood (Monacan

Indian Nation) (2003) read her poem titled "Homeland." The ending lines of the poem are, "Nothing was discovered. Everything was already loved." Elementary Lesson Plan 5 begins with students discussing their interpretation of these lines and connecting them to their understanding of Sacagawea's knowledge of plants addressed in the prior lesson. Then a card game is introduced that features various plants with the names in Indigenous languages, examples of plant uses, and specific Native peoples who use the plant. The majority of plants used in this lesson are mentioned in the Corps of Discovery journals. Before playing, students use the information on the cards to research and draw pictures of some of the plants. Students learn that Indigenous communities possessed a wealth of scientific knowledge before the military expedition arrived, that these communities still carry scientific knowledge of plants, animals, and their homelands, and that European claims of scientific "discovery" have covered up these Indigenous ways of knowing.

Recognizing Students as Active Constructors of Knowledge

The curriculum offered in *Teaching Critically About Lewis and Clark* encourages students to actively question, problem-solve, entertain multiple perspectives, formulate and defend their opinions, and take action. One of the driving questions underlying the curriculum featured in *Teaching Critically About Lewis and Clark* is, "Now what?" Critically interrogating received histories as well as learning about the continuing legacy of colonialism often leaves students and teachers feeling overwhelmed, anxious, or upset. One way we anticipate and address these responses is by providing avenues for students to be agents of change. Through the lessons, students are presented with opportunities to apply, share, and carry forward their knowledge inside and outside the classroom. This goal is reflective of the C3 Framework's Dimension 4, "Communicating Conclusions & Taking Informed Action" in which students "represent their ideas in a variety of forms and communicate their conclusions to a range of audiences" and take action "grounded in and informed by the inquiries initiated and sustained" (NCSS, 2013, p. 61). Because this action is an outcome of student learning, it is "then purposeful, informed and reflective experience" (NCSS, 2013, p .62). Stories of resistance, perseverance, and determination surround the history and legacy of the Corps of Discovery. Throughout these lessons, we offer curriculum to inspire teachers and students to take action and to contribute, in ways

that directly reflect their experience of this curriculum and the history and legacy of the Corps of Discovery, in their own communities.

The elementary and secondary teaching resources and instructional ideas offered in Section 4 are demonstrative of this commitment. We encourage teachers to use their expertise to adapt these resources to the grade level of their students. One example of a teaching presented in Section 4 is built on the Confluence Project (www.confluenceproject.org/), a series of public art installations by famed artist Maya Lin in collaboration with Native nations, various government agencies, and the National Park Service. Among the goals of the sites, located throughout the Columbia River system, are to "connect people to a more inclusive and cultural environmental history of . . . place" and to "increase awareness of how we treat each other and the Earth." We recommend students and teachers use the resources from the Confluence Project to explore the installations and to see the legacy of the Corps of Discovery situated in the environmental, contemporary, and historical contexts. Then we encourage students and teachers to answer the same call Maya Lin accepted when she joined the Confluence Project by selecting a location and identifying partners to propose their own installation reflecting Native perspectives, environmental significance, and the present/past.

Another resource offered in Section 4 is a review and instructional ideas for the young adult novel *Piecing Me Together* by Renée Watson (2017). The book is about the experiences of Jade, a young Black girl attending an affluent, mostly white, private high school outside of her neighborhood. Primary themes include identity, intersectionality, and self-expression as Jade uses collage to explore the connections between the present/past, place, and her own identity. In the midst of events in her city that raise issues related to Black Lives Matter and Say Her Name, Jade finds connections to York and the Corps of Discovery. We encourage students and teachers to consider a variety of options for taking informed action inspired by *Piecing Me Together*. For example, students can create and publicly share their own collage projects reflecting their connections to the legacy of the Lewis and Clark Expedition.

Understanding Student Responses to Critical Curriculum

While critically challenging dominant narratives supports more responsible social studies teaching, it also brings up discomfort, vulnerability, and risk. This underscores the importance of creating a classroom learning community that allows students to take intellectual, social, and emotional risks. Students have different relationships to the curriculum. Some may find relief when teachers explicitly challenge dominant discourses, whereas other students may feel uncomfortable, perhaps even defensive, because their taken-for-granted worldviews have been disrupted. These relationships and reactions do not necessarily correspond with students' racial or cultural identities. For example, while some Native students' prior knowledge may emphasize critical and counternarratives of the Corps of Discovery, others' only exposure to Lewis and Clark may have come from traditional social studies curriculum in their schools. To create a supportive classroom community that facilitates discussion among students who bring different lived and learned experiences, teachers must emphasize the values of critical thinking and challenging dominant narratives. Doing so benefits all students.

Emphasizing the shared aims and benefits of critical thinking and challenging dominant narratives is one step in creating a classroom community to support this learning. However, doing so also requires intentionally setting up shared classroom norms and values that can support critical dialogues and inquiry. In our own teaching, we are influenced by the Courageous Conversations protocol and adopt agreements informed by the following:

- Stay engaged: Staying engaged means "remaining morally, emotionally, intellectually, and relationally involved in the dialogue" (Singleton, 2015, p. 71).
- Speak your truth: Speaking your truth "requires a willingness to take risks" by being "completely and audibly honest" in the dialogue (Singleton, 2015, p. 72).
- Experience discomfort: When engaged in authentic dialogue, discomfort (personally and collectively) is sometimes experienced. Awareness and reflection about this discomfort gives participants the opportunity to address "the reality of race and racism in an honest and forthright way" (Singleton, 2015, p. 74).
- Expect and accept non-closure: This means participating in dialogue with openness, willingness for unexpected outcomes, and acceptance of ambiguity. There is no "quick fix" and "participants must commit to an ongoing dialogue as an essential component of their action plan" (Singleton, 2015, p. 75).

Foregrounding shared student agreements like these recognizes that there is no suspending racism, classism, patriarchy, colonization, homophobia, ableism, heteronormativity, and so on. in the teaching context. The dynamics that our teaching seeks to challenge can surface within the very classroom communities inquiring into those dynamics. Instead of seeking "safe spaces" in our classrooms, we draw from Timothy San Pedro (2017) to foster what he refers to as sacred truth spaces:

Sacred truth spaces center students' ability to share their realities and experiences that counter/challenge/correct standard knowledge that leads to painful silencing experiences in schools. In sacred truth spaces, students are able to engage in the often vulnerable act of telling and hearing multiple truths. As such, safety is not necessarily the goal; the goal, rather, is creating a dialogic space to share our truths *and* to listen and learn the truths of others. (pp. 102–103)

San Pedro theorized sacred truth spaces as a way to make sense of the dynamics he witnessed within a multitribal and multiracial high school Native American Literature class. Students' "interactions with one another, helping each other make sense of the materials together, engaging in disputes respectfully, while revealing their truths in the face of discomfort" helped him understand other frameworks he knew, including Leigh Patel's (2016) "truth space" and Jeremy Garcia and Valerie Shirley's (2012) conception of "sacred space" (San Pedro, personal communication, December 16, 2019). Importantly, San Pedro recognized that

it was really the Native students allowing space for those troubling through difficult concepts like settler colonialism that made that space fertile and productive. They saw those struggling as in need and aided in their transformation by delaying frustration when racism crept in; they saw them as products of larger systems and were patient and nurturing during this time even when faced with microaggressions." (San Pedro, personal communication, December 16, 2019)

San Pedro's theory of sacred truth spaces offers us possibilities for classroom communities, while also recognizing that fostering those communities often requires labor from the very student communities that we are seeking to better understand and protect in our work.

There are a number of reasons why teachers gloss over creating community to focus on teaching learning objectives—standardized curriculum, standardized testing calendars, shortened school years, large class sizes, reduced planning time, professional development dedicated teaching standards, and so on. To do the teaching we describe in *Teaching Critically About Lewis and Clark* means investing in time to set up a classroom space in a way that San Pedro (2017) describes. It means giving attention to and encouraging authentic classroom relationships through which teaching occurs. It is our expectation that teachers will read this book and facilitate the lesson plans in ways that directly reflect knowledge of their unique teaching context. While we encourage this teaching variety, these unique expressions have in common a commitment to engaging, questioning, problem solving in a classroom setting in which difference is centered.

Centering difference, again, means that students will have differing relationships with language within primary source materials. For some students, reading in the primary documents the ways their communities are referred to as "savage," "red men," "children," "my servant," or "Negro" may be deeply hurtful. Such language may bring up historic or recent experiences with racism and colonialism that they or their families have endured. Teachers must explicitly prepare students for encountering derogatory terms in the curriculum by facilitating discussions about the multiple ways these words are experienced and setting expectations for how the words will be addressed in their specific learning communities.

CURRICULUM OVERVIEW

Teaching Critically About Lewis and Clark: Challenging the Dominant Narratives in K–12 Curriculum is organized in four sections. The first section presents a chapter offering background knowledge about the Doctrine of Discovery (Chapter 2). This is followed by a chapter supporting teachers to detect and interrupt colonial logics and ideologies within curriculum featuring Lewis and Clark (Chapter 3). In Section 2, we include lesson plans designed for upper elementary grades, as 4th grade is commonly the year to teach Corps of Discovery content (Elementary Lesson Plans 1–7). Section 3 presents lesson plans designed for middle/high school classrooms as "westward expansion" is typically taught in middle school social studies and high school U.S. history classes (Secondary Lesson Plans 1–7). Finally, Section 4 offers four resources teachers can use in a variety of ways to complement this curriculum or create culminating projects. Table 1.1 lists and describes the lesson plans included in this book.

The teaching strategies and resources featured in this book are directly informed by the framework described earlier (place, presence, perspectives, political nationhood, power, and partnerships), and we have made explicit the ways in which the lessons correspond to the C3 Framework and its emphasis on inquiry-based teaching and learning. Relevant Common Core State Standards are also identified for each lesson plan. While we have tried to create lessons that support elementary- and secondary-specific curriculum, we also encourage teachers to read across sections and imagine how to adapt instructional activities for their students' grade level.

A NOTE ON TERMINOLOGY

In this book, we use the terms Native and Indigenous peoples interchangeably. We do so while also recognizing that any such term glosses over difference and collapses the rich linguistic, cultural, spiritual, geographic, and political diversity of Indigenous peoples and nations. As Cherokee author Thomas King (2012) has noted, "there has never been a good collective noun because there never was a collective to begin with" (p. xiii). When appropriate, and as we have done throughout this introduction, we also refer to the specific tribal affiliations of Indigenous peoples we cite (e.g., Cherokee, Navajo), deferring to people's own preferences when relevant or appropriate (e.g., Tsalagai/Cherokee, Diné/Navajo). Per the Native American Journalists Association's (NAJA) "Reporting and Indigenous Terminology" guide, we capitalize Native and Indigenous, to demarcate these terms as "identities, not adjectives," and "to avoid confusion between indigenous plants and animals and Indigenous human beings" (najanewsroom.com/wp-content/uploads/2018/11/NAJA_Reporting_and_Indigenous_Terminology_Guide.pdf).

We also make a point to draw attention to Native nations *as* nations. *Indian* and *tribe* remain important terms, particularly because they reflect language used in treaties (as well as common terminology throughout Indian country); however, we use *nation* (i.e., Native, Indigenous, or tribal nation) to intervene into the common misconception that Indigenous peoples are racial/ethnic/cultural groups or communities, a discourse we believe undermines tribal sovereignty. Finally, in reference to Lewis and Clark, in lieu of the oft-used terms "journey" or "expedition," we specifically use the terms "reconnaissance mission," "Corps of Discovery," or "military expedition" interchangeably. *Reconnaissance mission* stems from

Table 1.1. List of Elementary and Secondary Lesson Plans and Teaching Resources

\u2003			
SECTION 2: ELEMENTARY LESSON PLANS			
Lesson Plan #	Title	Teaching Strategy	Purpose
1	"We're Still Here"	One-Pager	The purpose of this lesson is to provide context and introductory knowledge of contemporary Native peoples and their political status as nations today.
2	What were the goals of the Lewis and Clark Corps of Discovery?	Historical Investigation	Students often recount the Lewis and Clark Corps of Discovery as a journey of adventure, discovery, research, and peacekeeping. The purpose of this historical investigation is to complicate and extend students' prior knowledge to understand the intent of expansion in President Thomas Jefferson's instructions to the military expedition.
3	The Jefferson Peace Medals	Historical Investigation	As highlighted in Elementary Lesson Plan 2, the Jefferson Peace Medals were significant to the diplomatic goals of the Corps of Discovery. The historical and contemporary meanings of the Jefferson Peace Medals are the focal point for Lesson Plan 3.
4	Sacagawea: Beyond Interpreter and Guide	Historical Investigation	This lesson introduces students to all we do not know about Sacagawea and invites them into a conversation about how historians draw conclusions from limited evidence.
5	"Everything was Already Loved:" Complicating Discovery and Science	Card Game	Students are introduced to Indigenous knowledge about various plants from regions spanning the Lewis and Clark National Historic Trail. During the activities, students complicate the idea that Lewis and Clark "discovered" knowledge about plants along the trail.
6	A Stolen Canoe Returned	Caption Drawings	The Lewis and Clark Corps of Discovery stole a canoe from the Clatsop peoples on March 17, 1806. Two hundred years later, the Chinook Indian Nation held a ceremony to welcome the return of their canoe. This story is the focus of the lesson, and it introduces students to the importance of canoes to tribal cultures.
7	A Closer Look at York's Life	Close Reading and One-Pager	Drawing from the Teaching Tolerance project *Teaching Hard History: American Slavery*, this lesson foregrounds key essential knowledges about freedom, enslavement, resistance, and families that help students learn about York within the context of the institution of slavery he was born into and resisted.
SECTION 3: SECONDARY LESSON PLANS			
Lesson Plan #	Title	Teaching Strategy	Purpose
1	The Stories Maps Tell	Map Analysis	This lesson plan introduces students to the ongoing presence and political sovereignty of tribal nations today.
2	What were the goals of the Lewis and Clark Corps of Discovery?	Historical Investigation	The purpose of this lesson is to challenge textbook simplifications of the goals President Thomas Jefferson outlined for the Lewis and Clark Corps of Discovery. Students analyze primary source documents to answer the inquiry question.
3	*Johnson v. McIntosh* (1823) and the Doctrine of Discovery	Historical Investigation	The purpose of this lesson is to introduce students to the Doctrine of Discovery by examining Chief Justice John Marshall's ruling in *Johnson v. McIntosh* (1823). Then students revisit documents from the prior lesson to investigate President Thomas Jefferson's use of the principles of the Doctrine of Discovery.
4	Questioning *American Progress* (Gast, 1872)	Painting Analysis	Students apply their knowledge of the Doctrine of Discovery to critically examine paintings and make connections to the underlying purpose of the Corps of Discovery.

(continued)

Lesson Plan #	Title	Teaching Strategy	Purpose
5	Standing Rock and the "Larger Story"	Mystery	Using this student-centered teaching activity, students participate in a collaborative process examining the Corps of Discovery as part of the historical context for the events at Standing Rock.
6	Role Play: The Bicentennial of the Lewis and Clark Corps of Discovery	Role Play	The purpose of this lesson plan is for students to understand the different perspectives and concerns of stakeholders planning the bicentennial of the Corps of Discovery.
7	Revisiting What We Know About York	Historical Investigation and Mock Hearing	Students examine a timeline of York's life and letters authored by Clark describing York's desire for freedom by applying four themes from the Teaching Tolerance project *Teaching Hard History: American Slavery:* freedom, enslavement, resistance, and families. The purpose of this lesson is for students to learn about York within the context of the institution of slavery that he was born into and resisted. This lesson is an adaptation of Elementary Lesson Plan 7 for secondary students.

SECTION 4: TEACHING RESOURCES

Resource #	Title	Purpose
1	Native Lands Under Siege	A variety of historic and contemporary examples of Native Nations advocating for the protection, restoration, or repatriation of their homelands provide students a starting point for inquiry into contemporary issues of land dispossession and struggles for self-determination and sovereignty.
2	*Piecing Me Together* by Renée Watson (2017)	In *Piecing Me Together*, Renée Watson (2017) explores the contemporary meanings of learning about the Corps of Discovery through the experiences of a young African American girl named Jade. Jade finds connection between the story of York and her lived experiences. Teaching ideas for using *Piecing Me Together* to complement a unit about the Corps of Discovery are presented.
3	Partnerships Realized: The Confluence Project	The history, purpose, and description of the installations of the Confluence Project is presented. In addition, education and professional development programming is summarized. Teaching ideas inspired by the Confluence Project are offered.
4	Honoring Tribal Legacies: An Epic Journey of Healing	This ongoing project is funded by the National Park Service and the National Endowment for the Humanities. The curriculum guide, lesson plans, and resources featured in the digital collection are summarized.

Roberta Conner's observation, "If you look at the directives, whether you like the words [Jefferson] uses or not, it's clear that the Lewis and Clark Expedition was a reconnaissance mission" (as cited in Lang & Abbott, 2004, p. 120). The terms *Corps of Discovery* and *military expedition* are used to sustain attention on the militaristic content, character, and purpose of the mission.

We hope this discussion of terminology supports teachers' background knowledge and also provides context for teachers to explicitly lead discussions with students about the terms we use and why they matter.

CHAPTER 2

The Doctrine of Discovery

The "Age of Discovery" marked the age of colonialism, a time when our land suddenly came to be viewed as "your land." While military repression is not in North American vogue (at least with the exception of the Oka-Mohawk uprising of the summer of 1990), today legal doctrines uphold that our land is your land, based ostensibly on the so-called "doctrine of discovery." This justifies, in a so-called legal system, the same dispossession of people from their land that is caused by outright military conquest, but today, in a "kinder, gentler world," it all appears more legal.

—Winona LaDuke (Anishinaabe) (1992) from
"We Are Still Here: The 500 Years Celebration"

The original homelands of the Oneida Indian Nation, one of the Six Nations of the Haudenosaunee Confederation, were comprised of six million acres in what is now referred to as the state of New York. In 1788, multiple pressures resulted in the Oneida peoples ceding all but 300,000 acres of their homelands. The State of New York purchased more land from the Oneida Indian Nation in 1795 and received warning from the federal government the transactions were illegal because they were in violation of the Indian Trade and Intercourse Act of 1790. By 1920, the Oneida Indian Nation land holdings were reduced to 32 acres as a result of further transactions completed without federal government approval. Since this time the Oneida Indian Nation advocated for compensation for illegally purchased land and recouped some of the original homelands. An example of compensation occurred in 1985 with the Supreme Court ruling that land acquired in the 1790s by the State of New York was an illegal transaction, resulting in the Oneida Indian Nation receiving monetary damages (*County of Oneida v. Oneida Indian Nation of New York State*).

During the 1990s, the Oneida Indian Nation reacquired 17,000 acres of land within the original boundaries of the reservation established in 1788. The land was purchased through the open real estate market and presented the opportunity to expand economic development. For example, in the early 1990s the Oneida Indian Nation opened the first SavOn gas station and convenient store (it is now a chain with 12 locations). When billed for property taxes by the city of Sherrill, NY, the Oneida Indian Nation refused to pay and sued in federal court on the grounds that because the land purchased was located within the early reservation boundary, it was under tribal ownership, and thus tribal sovereignty applied. The case proceeded through the federal court structure and on January 11, 2005, Chief Justice William Rehnquist presided over the Supreme Court hearing of arguments in *City of Sherrill v. Oneida Indian Nation of New York*. On March 29, 2005, the court ruled 8–1 in favor of the city of Sherrill. The court determined that the Oneida Nation last possessed the two land parcels in 1805 and had failed to challenge the land transfers within a reasonable amount of time, thus "preclud[ing] the Tribe from rekindling embers of sovereignty that long ago grew cold" (p. 14). In the majority opinion, Justice Ruth Bader Ginsburg wrote,

> Given the longstanding, distinctly non-Indian character of the area and its inhabitants, the regulatory authority constantly exercised by New York State and its counties and towns, and the Oneidas' long delay in seeking judicial relief against parties other than the United States, we hold that the Tribe cannot unilaterally revive its ancient sovereignty, in whole or in part, over the parcels at issue. The Oneidas long ago relinquished the reins of government and cannot regain them through open-market purchases from current titleholders. (p. 2)

Later in the opinion, Ginsberg wrote that because the land had long been occupied by "non-Indians," who now comprised over 90% of the population, the Court was concerned that "a contrary conclusion would seriously disrupt the justifiable expectations of the people living in the area" (p. 15). Ginsberg concluded that "returning to Indian control land that generations earlier passed into numerous private hands" was impractical, if not impossible, and the Court did not want to disrupt the "settled expectations" of "innumerable innocent purchasers" (p. 18, 19). The Court's opinion is imbued with colonial logics, among them claims that: 1) the Oneida possess only an "ancient sovereignty" that is inapplicable today; 2) the Oneida waited too long, "belatedly" asserting their rights; 3) the Oneida's claim would disrupt the "settled expectations" of those living within Oneida territory; and 4) restoring Indigenous lands was too difficult or impractical an action (noted in Court's use of the "impracticability" doctrine). The Oneida Indian Nation asserted their inherent sovereignty, what they viewed as their irrevocable right. The Court, however, determined that the Oneida Indian Nation's sovereignty, and thus claims to their homelands, were ancient and had diminished over time.

This claim that Native nations have an inferior type of sovereignty than nation-states was expressed in the first footnote of the Court's opinion. In it, the Supreme Court references the Doctrine of Discovery, principles derived from a series of Papal Bulls issued in the 1400s, in support of the majority opinion. The footnote states, "Under the 'doctrine of discovery' . . . fee title (ownership) to the lands occupied by Indians when the colonists arrived became vested in the sovereign—first the discovering European nation and later the original States of the United States." The precedent of using the doctrine in deciding a Supreme Court case was set in 1823 when Chief Justice John Marshall wrote the opinion for the unanimous vote in *Johnson v. McIntosh*. Oren Lyons (2009), Faithkeeper of the Onondaga Nation (also one of the Six Nations of the Haudenosaunee), states, "This is not ancient history. . . . Whether 1823 or 2005, it's clear who is left out—the people who lived on the land for countless generations before Europeans arrived." The Supreme Court essentially ruled that the 2005 tribal sovereignty of the Oneida Indian Nation was checked by the 15th century Doctrine of Discovery, which declared European ownership of Indigenous land justified through discovery. The result is precisely what Winona LaDuke (1992) identifies in the opening quote for this chapter—a "kinder, gentler" means of denying sovereignty through the application of the Doctrine of Discovery, one that "appears more legal," but nevertheless continues to dispossess Indigenous peoples.

Recounting the ruling in *Johnson v. McIntosh* (1823) and *City of Sherrill v. Oneida Indian Nation of New York* (2005) is indicative of how understanding the doctrine is essential for a deeper understanding of the history of the United States and its relations with Native peoples. The process of transforming Indigenous homelands into the United States is not only historic, but one that continues to find voice in legal, political, and societal practices today. Settlement has become deeply naturalized in public discourse and policy. Some argue that that terms like "settlement" are too benign as they

do not adequately account for the active, brutal, and violent ways imperial powers dispossessed Indigenous peoples of their homelands (King, 2019). However, the aspect of the term "settlement" that has proved most difficult to dislodge, to unsettle, is the idea that colonization and settlement are finished business, that these matters are "settled" or "resolved." But these matters are not settled or resolved (Mackey, 2016). Indigenous studies scholars point to the endurance of Indigenous sovereignty, despite the historic and ongoing legacy of colonization (Wilkins & Stark, 2018). Further, they highlight the variety of structures and practices that actively work to maintain possession of Indigenous homelands. As Geonpul scholar Aileen Moreton-Robinson (2015) writes, "It takes a great deal of work to maintain Canada, the United States, Hawai'i, New Zealand, and Australia as white possessions" (p. xi).

The purpose of this chapter is to provide background knowledge for teachers about the Doctrine of Discovery, examine how it is encoded into law, consider the doctrine's role in the Lewis and Clark Corps of Discovery, and delve into its application today. This chapter is organized by the following questions:

- What is the Doctrine of Discovery?
- In what ways did the principles of the Doctrine of Discovery contribute to the establishment of the United States?
- How is the Doctrine of Discovery related to the Corps of Discovery?
- In what ways is the institution of slavery intertwined with the Corps of Discovery and the Doctrine of Discovery?
- What is the role of the Doctrine of Discovery in Manifest Destiny?
- How did the U.S. Supreme Court use discovery in *Johnson v. McIntosh (1823)*?
- How has the Doctrine of Discovery played out in federal policy toward Native nations?
- How has the Doctrine of Discovery been challenged?

In answering these questions, we hope to support teachers and students in their efforts to situate the Corps of Discovery within a broader context of global imperialism and colonialism. Examining the doctrine facilitates new ways to teach and learn about the Lewis and Clark military expedition along with enriching teacher and student understanding of other historical and present-day events that can be linked to the doctrine. Further, we hope to support teacher and students in finding ways to challenge the doctrine's application in present day policy.

WHAT IS THE DOCTRINE OF DISCOVERY?

The Doctrine of Discovery can be traced back to medieval Europe. As European Christian powers conquered and colonized lands outside their borders, they justified domination of the peoples in those lands in two key ways: (1) by asserting that Europeans were bringing the one true religion—Christianity—to the colonized people, and (2) by arguing that Europeans were inherently superior as a culture and as a race to the Indigenous peoples they were colonizing. But as various European powers eagerly embarked on these colonizing endeavors, they inevitably came into conflict. To navigate these conflicts, imperial powers developed a process for deciding who had the right to conquer, assume control of land resources, and exploit Indigenous peoples. This process was formalized through papal bulls, formal decrees issued by the Pope that granted Christian kingdoms the authority to "discover" non-Christian territories, conquer, convert, and enslave the inhabitants, and lay claim to those territories. By decreeing non-Christian peoples as "heathens," "pagans," or "infidels" among other terms, the Catholic Church declared its sovereignty over non-Christian lands throughout the world.

In 1452, for example, Pope Nicholas V issued the Papal Bull *Dum Diversas*, which granted King Alfonso V of Portugal

> full and free permission to invade, search out, capture, and subjugate the Saracens and pagans and any other unbelievers and enemies of Christ wherever they may be, as well as their kingdoms, duchies, counties, principalities, and other property [. . .] and to reduce their persons into perpetual servitude" (United Nations Economic and Social Council, 2010, p. 8).

In 1455, Pope Nicholas V issued *Romanus Pontifex*, which authorized King Alfonso V

> . . . to invade, search out, capture, vanquish, and subdue all Saracens and pagans whatsoever, and other enemies of Christ wheresoever placed, and the kingdoms, dukedoms, principalities, dominions, possessions, and all movable and immovable goods whatsoever held and possessed by them and to reduce their persons to perpetual slavery, and to apply and appropriate to himself and his successors the kingdoms, dukedoms, counties, principalities, dominions, possessions, and goods, and to convert them to his and their use and profit. (United Nations, 2010, p. 8)

These papal bulls established the framework used by Spain to justify exclusive rights to the lands "discovered" by Christopher Columbus in 1492. Columbus' claims were solidified in 1493 when Pope Alexander VI issued *Inter Caetera*, a papal bull, that divided "the undiscovered world between Spain and Portugal," and advocated for the spread of the Catholic faith and Christianity among "barbarous nations" who were to "be overthrown and brought to the faith itself" (Papal Encyclicals Online, 2017). Together, these early papal bulls came to be widely accepted as a doctrine of international law among European powers and provided a basis for determining which country had the "Discovery" right to colonize.

For a summary of the doctrine's principles, refer to Table 2.1 presenting the "Ten Elements of Discovery" from *Native America, Discovered and Conquered: Thomas Jefferson, Lewis and Clark, and Manifest Destiny* by Robert J. Miller (2008, p. 3–5).

Key conditions for a land claim included being the first to discover a land and then actually occupying and using the land (Table 2.1, elements 1 and 2). Once Europeans were there, they gained substantial property rights. While the doctrine acknowledged that the Native peoples retained title to the land while continuing to live there, it gave the Discovery country the exclusive right to buy the land from the Indigenous peoples—known as "preemption" (Table 2.1, element 3). But if only one buyer was available, then the Indigenous residents had little power to negotiate price. Similarly, the Discovery country had the right to control trade in the region, limiting the Indigenous peoples to trading with the conqueror (Table 2.1, element 5). The colonizing country had a variety of ways to acquire land under the doctrine beyond simply purchasing it. Under the principle of *terra nullius*, or "land belonging to no one," the colonizer could simply take land if it they decided it was empty or not being used "properly" (Table 2.1, element 7). Since the judgment of whether land was being used properly was entirely up to the Europeans who had a vested interest in seizing Indigenous lands, one can imagine how broadly the term was interpreted. Further, the doctrine allowed land to be taken in the event of a "just war." Again, the "justness" of a war was entirely decided by Europeans, and often meant "any time the Indigenous peoples resist exploitation" (Table 2.1, element 10).

IN WHAT WAYS DID THE PRINCIPLES OF THE DOCTRINE OF DISCOVERY CONTRIBUTE TO THE ESTABLISHMENT OF THE UNITED STATES?

The concept of the Doctrine of Discovery might be considered a relic of 15th-century history—however, it has been foundational to the development of the United

Table 2.1. "Ten Elements of Discovery"

1	First discovery	The first European country to "discover" new lands unknown to other Europeans gained property and sovereign rights over the lands. First discovery alone, without taking physical possession, was often considered to create a claim of title to the newly found lands, but it was usually considered to be only an incomplete title.
2	Actual occupancy and current possession	To fully establish a "first discovery" claim and turn it into a complete title, a European country had to actually occupy and possess newly found lands. This was usually done by actual physical possession with building of a fort or settlement, for example, and leaving soldiers or settlers on the land. This physical possession had to be accomplished within a reasonable amount of time after the first discovery to create a complete title to the land in the discovering country.
3	Preemption/ European title	The discovering European country gained the power of preemption, the sole right to buy the land from Native people. This is a valuable property right. The government that held the Discovery power of preemption prevented or preempted any other European or American government or individual from buying land from the discovered Native people.
4	Indian title	After first discovery, Indian Nations and the Indigenous peoples were considered by European and American legal systems to have lost the full property rights and ownership of their lands. They only retained rights to occupy and use their land. Nevertheless, the right could last forever if the Indigenous people never consented to sell their land. But if they ever did choose to sell, they could only sell to the government that held the power of preemption over their lands. Thus, Indian title was a limited ownership right.
5	Tribal limited sovereign and commercial rights	After first discovery, Indian Nations and Native peoples were also considered to have lost some of their inherent sovereign powers and the rights to free trade and diplomatic international relations. Thereafter, they could only deal with the Euro-American government that had first discovered them.
6	Contiguity	The dictionary definition of this word means the state of being contiguous to, to have proximity to, or to be near to. This element provided that Europeans had a Discovery claim to a reasonable and significant amount of land contiguous to and surrounding their settlements and the lands that they actually possessed in the New World. This element became very important when different European countries had settlements somewhat close together. In that situation, each country held rights over the unoccupied lands between their settlements to a point half way between their actual settlements. Most importantly, contiguity held that the discovery of the mouth of a river gave the discovery country claim over all the lands drained by that river, even if that was thousands of miles of territory.
7	*Terra nullius*	This phrase literally means a land or earth that is null or void. The term *vacuum domicilium* was sometimes used to describe this element, and this term literally means an empty, vacant, or unoccupied home or domicile. According to this idea, if lands were not possessed or occupied by any person or nation, or were occupied by non-Europeans but not being used in a fashion that European legal systems approved, the lands were considered to be empty and waste and available for Discovery claims. Europeans and Americans were very liberal in applying this definition to the lands of Native people. Euro-Americans often considered lands that were actually owned, occupied, and being actively utilized by Indigenous people to be "vacant" and available for Discovery claims if they were not being "properly used" according to European and American law and culture.
8	Christianity	Religion was a significant aspect of the Doctrine of Discovery and of Manifest Destiny. Under Discovery, non-Christian people were not deemed to have the same rights to land, sovereignty, and self-determination as Christians because their rights could be trumped upon their discovery by Christians.
9	Civilization	The European and later American definition of civilization was an important part of Discovery and the idea of Euro-American superiority. Euro-Americans thought that God had directed them to bring civilized ways and education and religion to Indigenous peoples and often to exercise paternalism and guardianship powers over them.
10	Conquest	We will encounter two different definitions for this element. It can mean military victory. We will see this definition reflected in Spanish, English, and American ideas that "just wars" allegedly justified invasion and conquest of Indian lands in certain circumstances. But that is not the only definition we will encounter. "Conquest" was also used as a "term of art," a word with special meaning, when it is used as an element of Discovery.

States. Under British colonial rule, for example, Maryland enacted a law in 1638 that gave the colony the right to regulate trade with the Native peoples, based on the "right of first discovery" (Miller, 2008, p. 27). Too, the colonies repeatedly exercised the principle of *terra nullius* to declare Native homelands as vacant and thus ripe for the taking. In particular, the Proclamation of 1763, issued by the Crown to reduce military costs by prohibiting American colonists from crossing the Appalachian Mountains, was firmly based on Discovery principles. The Proclamation stated that Native peoples were not to be "disturbed in the possession of such parts of our dominions and territories, as, not having been ceded to or purchased by us, are reserved to them." The claim that the land is "ours" pending cession or purchase is a clear statement of European title and of preemption—the discoverer's sole right to buy the land from the Native peoples.

The first constitution of the United States was the Articles of Confederation, ratified in 1781. Article IX, section 4, gave the Congress the "sole and exclusive right" of "regulating the trade and managing affairs with the Indians." After the Treaty of Paris in 1783, in which Britain ceded all sovereignty over all the "western" land to the Mississippi River, Congress wrestled with various states to enforce this claim. Eventually, the states all gave up their claims to the western land, and Congress passed the Northwest Ordinance, which contained specific language about Native rights in Article 3. This language is often seen as a goodhearted statement of intent to treat Native peoples fairly, but read with knowledge of the Doctrine of Discovery, its darker intent is revealed. It states:

> the utmost good faith shall always be observed toward the Indians; their lands and property shall never be taken from them without their consent; and, in their property, rights and liberty, they shall never be invaded and disturbed unless in just and lawful wars authorized by Congress.

While recognizing Native title to the land, an understanding of the dominating presence of Discovery principles points us to the implied principle of preemption—that only the U.S. government could purchase the land. In fact, under the Ordinance, numerous treaties were signed with the Native nations stating explicitly the principle of preemption. Further, the Ordinance explicitly states the "just war" concept for removal of Native title. The Articles of Confederation, though, as is well known, provided a very weak central government, and the Congress often had difficulty keeping individual states and rogue settlers and

squatters from creating conflicts with Native peoples. Along with other similar problems, this led to a push by elites for a new constitution that gave more power to the central government.

The Constitution continued the reliance on Discovery principles but provided far more enforcement power. Article I, section 8, gave Congress the sole right "to regulate commerce with foreign nations, and among the several states, and with the Indian tribes." As upheld by the U.S. Supreme Court, Miller (2008) notes that:

> This constitutional authority to be the only entity to control commercial affairs with the Indian nations, which obviously included the sole power of buying Indian land and trading with tribes, unambiguously granted the Doctrine of Discovery powers to Congress. (p. 44)

Under this authority, the first Congress passed a number of laws creating policy for Indian country. One such law, the first Indian Trade and Intercourse Act of 1790 (referenced in *City of Sherrill v. Oneida Indian Nation of New York*, 2005), explicitly stated that only the federal government, not states or individuals, could purchase land from the Indians—another clear use of the principle of preemption.

One may wonder why there was so much focus on preemption, as opposed to just taking the land. One clue lies in statements from founders indicating their assumption that Native peoples would eventually move off the land without the need for coercion. For example, in explaining why war against Native nations might not be necessary, George Washington wrote in 1783 that "the gradual extension of our settlements will as certainly cause the Savage as the Wolf to retire; both being beasts of prey tho' they differ in shape" (Washington to James Duane, September 7, 1783). The sense that the gradual takeover of Indigenous lands was inevitable, coupled with narratives that Indigenous peoples were "vanishing" (either physically, or culturally through assimilation and absorption into society), worked in tandem to justify the acquisition of Indigenous lands.

HOW IS THE DOCTRINE OF DISCOVERY RELATED TO THE CORPS OF DISCOVERY?

As the Doctrine of Discovery was deeply ingrained in early U.S. political and legal systems, it should not be a surprise that it was essential to President Thomas Jefferson's thinking as he carried out the Louisiana Purchase and sent Meriwether Lewis and William Clark on their military expedition. First, we must challenge what Miller (2008) calls the "common myth" about the 1803 Louisiana Purchase for $15 million: that the United States actually took ownership of the land for the incredible price of 3 cents an acre. Rather, as President Jefferson clearly understood,

> The Louisiana Purchase was not a real estate deal. The United States did not buy land in the Louisiana Territory because France did not own land in the territory. . . . Instead of real estate, the United States purchased what France and Spain did own in the region: their Discovery claims to a limited form of sovereign, political, and commercial power over the Indian Nations and the real-property right of preemption. (Miller, 2008, p. 71)

Said differently, Jefferson understood he was not purchasing the land from France; rather, "the United States had bought France's Discovery powers," which included the "right to be the only government Indian Nations could deal with politically or commercially" (Miller, 2008, p. 12).

The Louisiana Purchase altered the purpose of the Corps of Discovery, which had already been substantially planned. With this vast region now under U.S. sovereignty, it was now possible to imagine a country that spread across the continent, including the Pacific Northwest—the Oregon territory. Key evidence is in a second letter of instructions from President Jefferson to Meriwether Lewis on January 22, 1804. Under the new conditions of the Louisiana Purchase, President Jefferson instructed Lewis to make clear to Native peoples that the United States was now the sovereign, replacing the Spanish. Lewis and Clark were authorized to propose trade relations with Native nations, which would not have been permissible under Spanish/French sovereignty. The speeches and actions of Lewis and Clark reinforced the Discovery message that the United States was now the "great white father." The peace medals and American flags distributed by the military expedition now took on political significance—implying that by accepting the "gifts," Native nations were acknowledging U.S. sovereignty.

But President Jefferson had greater ambitions—he wanted the U.S. empire to extend all the way to the Pacific. The remaining region over which sovereignty had not been established was the Oregon territory of the Pacific Northwest. According to the Discovery principle of contiguity, control over the mouth of a river gained sovereignty over all the land drained by the river. The mighty Columbia River drained this large region, so it was critical to establish control over its mouth. Robert Gray had "discovered" the Columbia

in 1792, but that was not sufficient to establish sovereign control, which required permanent occupancy under the doctrine.

While the Corps of Discovery was not going to establish a permanent settlement at the mouth of the Columbia, it did carry out a number of actions that were internationally recognized as supporting a long-term claim under the doctrine. These included: (1) the building of Fort Clatsop, where the military expedition spent the winter of 1805–1806; (2) branding or carving names into numerous trees and stones in the area to signal U.S. presence; (3) extensive mapping of the area, which supported the claim to occupancy; (4) scientific explorations and the publishing of journals and accounts of the scientific knowledge obtained; and (5) finally, Lewis and Clark's deposition of an extensive document at Fort Clatsop, with copies distributed to local Native nations with the request that the documents be passed on to ships that came through the region—clearly meant to establish evidence of U.S. occupancy of the region.

As a direct result of the Corps of Discovery, and on the urging of President Jefferson, John Jacob Astor established a permanent fur trading post at the mouth of the Columbia in Astoria, OR, in 1811 (five years after the Corps of Discovery left Fort Clatsop). This further cemented U.S. claims to the region. The occupancy by Lewis and Clark as well as the trading post were used for the next several decades by U.S. diplomats to claim ownership over the entire Oregon territory. President Jefferson's understanding of the Doctrine of Discovery ultimately helped lead to a series of treaties with Great Britain, ending with the 1846 Treaty of Oregon that drew the boundary line between British Canada and the United States at the 49th parallel.

IN WHAT WAYS IS THE INSTITUTION OF SLAVERY INTERTWINED WITH THE CORPS OF DISCOVERY AND THE DOCTRINE OF DISCOVERY?

The role of slavery in the Corps of Discovery, though not a central focus of this book, is nevertheless crucial context to understanding the Lewis and Clark military expedition. As historian Hasan Kwame Jeffries (2018) writes, "It is often said that slavery was our country's original sin, but it is much more than that. Slavery is our country's origin" (p. 5). The Doctrine of Discovery not only justified European conquest and land theft, but also the enslavement of what Christian kingdoms deemed as "inferior" or "heathen" peoples. Premised on the deep-seated belief that some humans were inferior to others, the exploitation of enslaved peoples' labor to extract wealth from Indigenous homelands laid the foundation for the United States.

When the military expedition started in 1803, chattel slavery was a well-established institution, shaping the lives of those who envisioned the military expedition, as well as those who carried it out. By "institution," we mean that enslavement was built into the structure of the laws, culture, and daily life of much of the country. Enslavers such as Thomas Jefferson owned and enslaved over 600 people. William Clark also enslaved people, among them York. Some excuse the actions of enslavers by suggesting that they were "products of their time"; however slavery was an institution of power that was fiercely protected by those who profited from it. Further, abolitionists—those who deplored slavery and worked tirelessly and courageously to upend it—lived in that same era, but refused to sanction or participate in slavery (Sinha, 2017). Benjamin Rush, for example, a prominent physician in the 18th century who was asked by President Thomas Jefferson to provide medical training to Meriwether Lewis prior to the expedition, spoke out against slavery (though it should also be noted that his anti-slavery advocacy rested on assimilationist logic). Also, enslaved people having long known their worth, understood that the institution of slavery was abhorrent, and refused and resisted this system in various ways, big and small (Rodriguez, 2006).

The institution of slavery most directly contributed to the Corps of Discovery in the person of York, born into the third generation enslaved by William Clark. Clark inherited York, along with his parents Old York and Rose, from his father John Clark. York did not volunteer for the expedition, nor was he paid. But as a participant in a dangerous and difficult trip, he had to be relied on as any other member. There is evidence that, along with other members, he was allowed to carry firearms and vote on some decisions. In literature, and in children's books in particular, these details are often used to lift up some measure of "equality" that York experienced during the journey. However, Darrell Millner (2003) advocates for "a more complex analysis of York's position" in the historical record:

> It is naive to assert that York enjoyed some hypothetical "equality" with the other expedition members. He was black and a slave and they were white and free at a time in which such distinctions really did matter. Yet, York's status was also mediated by a confluence of unprecedented and unique circumstance. York could be, and was, both slave and significant. (p. 316)

York experienced some liberties that other enslaved people at the time did not, however, he was repeatedly referred to in the journals as "my Servant," "my Black servant," "my boy York," or "Capt. Clark's black man," among others. York was also not freed directly after the expedition, in contrast to a common myth. Unlike the other members, he did not receive double pay or hundreds of acres of land. Instead, he remained enslaved by William Clark until at least 1815. However, as recently discovered letters from Clark to his brother have shown, York was not passive about his enslavement. Clark's letters indicate that York wanted his freedom, and asked to rejoin his wife, hundreds of miles away. These requests infuriated Clark, who felt that York thought too much about his own freedom. Clark physically punished York, on one occasion put him in jail, threatened to send him to a more "severe Master," and eventually leased him to another enslaver, as was common at the time.

The expansion of the United States, partly enabled by the Corps of Discovery, was also intimately entwined with the expansion of slavery. The sectional differences over slavery that ultimately led to the Civil War centrally involved struggles over whether slavery would be allowed in the new territories and states that were formed out of the Louisiana Purchase, starting with the Missouri Compromise in 1820. Enslavers were constantly eager to get new land, because cotton, tobacco, and other crops cultivated through enslaved peoples' labor tended to deplete the land. Further, enslavers saw it as necessary to have one new "state that sanctioned slavery" for every new "free state," so as to ensure a continued balance of power in the Federal government.

WHAT IS THE ROLE OF THE DOCTRINE OF DISCOVERY IN MANIFEST DESTINY?

Many students learn the concept of "Manifest Destiny" as if Americans were destined by God to take over the whole continent of North America. In fact, it was a masterful example of propaganda and ideology—and was directly rooted in many of the previously noted aspects of the Doctrine of Discovery. As Miller (2008) summarizes: "The Doctrine of Discovery, in essence, became Manifest Destiny." (p. 118). The term was originally used by journalist John O'Sullivan, who wrote in 1845 of "our manifest destiny to overspread the continent allotted by Providence for the free development of our yearly multiplying millions." (Miller, 2008, p. 118). He repeated this language later in 1845 to justify the U.S. claim to the Oregon territory. Perhaps unsurprisingly, O'Sullivan explicitly uses Discovery terms in his essays.

He speaks of international law, right of discovery, civilization, and that (the Christian) God had "marked it for our own" (Miller, 2008, p. 119).

Thus, "Manifest Destiny" was not a concept suddenly invented in 1845 but was drawn from the history of the doctrine—and its particular manifestation in the United States as a combination of idealism and white Christian supremacism. While Manifest Destiny was never formally defined, it is generally accepted that it included: the unique virtue of America and Americans (often known as "American exceptionalism"); the mission to spread American ideals and practices; and that it was a God-given destiny to carry out this mission. These elements are exhibited continuously in the history of the United States from 1806 onwards. Almost immediately after the Corps of Discovery, politicians were speaking of "civilizing the savages" in the West and of making land available all the way out to Oregon. In 1811, John Quincy Adams, later to be the 6th President, famously said "The whole continent of North America appears to be destined by Divine Providence to be peopled by one nation . . ." (Miller, 2008, p. 130). Adams was instrumental in the negotiations with England and Russia regarding ownership of Oregon, which were based largely on Discovery principles. In 1825, the famous "moderate" Senator and Secretary of State Henry Clay voiced the opinion of many when he stated it was "impossible to civilize Indians . . . they were destined to extinction" (Miller, 2008, p. 144).

Members of Congress repeatedly urged the United States to take control of the Oregon territory. For example, in 1838 Caleb Cushing said "Here, then, we have the original title of the United States by discovery, fortified by the rights of France, continued by the exploration of Lewis and Clark, by the formal taking of possession, and by regular occupation, and completed by the recognition of Great Britain. . . . Oregon is a country ours by right, ours by necessity of geographic position; ours by every consideration of national safety" (Miller, 2008, p. 147). It is hard to imagine a clearer statement that ties together the Corps of Discovery, Discovery Doctrine, and Manifest Destiny.

Why does this understanding of Manifest Destiny matter? The politicians and people of the United States in the 19th century, for the most part, believed they were decent, law-abiding citizens, and thus needed a way to justify the mad land rush that swallowed up the land of Indigenous peoples. While Manifest Destiny provided a convenient theological justification, the principles of the Doctrine of Discovery provided a legal framework for conquest long before John O'Sullivan came up with his slogan.

HOW DID THE U.S. SUPREME COURT USE DISCOVERY IN *JOHNSON V. MCINTOSH* (1823)?

The Doctrine of Discovery has been accepted within the United States constitutional process, most notably in the 1823 Supreme Court decision in *Johnson v. McIntosh*. Prucha (2000) summarizes the case:

> The plaintiffs in this case claimed title to land in Illinois on the basis of purchase from the Indians; the defendant, on the basis of a grant from the United States. The Supreme Court decided in favor of the defendant and in doing so discussed the nature of the Indian land title under the United States. (p. 35).

In the decision on this case involving a property dispute between two settlers, Chief Justice John Marshall's opinion followed Discovery principles. He spelled out the history of the doctrine and explained how it was applied in this situation. A sampling of quotes illustrates how the Doctrine of Discovery justifies Chief Justice Marshall's opinion:

- The United States, then, have unequivocally acceded to that great and broad rule [Discovery] by which its civilized inhabitants now hold this country. They hold . . . the title by which it was acquired. They maintain, as all others have maintained, that discovery gave an exclusive right to extinguish the Indian title of occupancy, either by purchase or by conquest; and gave also a right to such a degree of sovereignty, as the circumstances of the people would allow them to exercise. . . . (Prucha, 2000, pp. 35–36)
- Conquest gives a title which the Courts of the conqueror cannot deny. . . . The British government, which was then our government, and whose rights have passed to the United States, asserted a title to all the lands occupied by Indians. . . . It asserted also a limited sovereignty over them, and the exclusive right of extinguishing the title which occupancy gave to them. (Prucha, 2000, p. 36)
- . . . the tribes of Indians inhabiting this country were fierce savages, whose occupation was war, and whose subsistence was drawn chiefly from the forest. To leave them in possession of their country was to leave them in wilderness. (Prucha, 2000, p. 36)
- However extravagant the pretension of converting the discovery of an inhabited

country into conquest may appear; if the principle has been asserted in the first instance, and afterward sustained; if a country has been acquired and held under it; if the property of the great mass of the community originates in it, it becomes the law of the land and cannot be questioned. (Prucha, 2000, p. 37)

Throughout the opinion, the superiority of the United States is asserted: framing U.S. citizens as "civilized inhabitants," giving the United States the power to "extinguish Indian title," claiming Indigenous peoples only had rights to "occupancy," and of course, calling Indigenous peoples "savages" who lived in the "wilderness" and needed Western civilized society. It was for these reasons that the decision favored McIntosh, who had bought the land from the United States, rather than the plaintiff, who had bought the same land from Indigenous peoples. Moreover, the decision affirms the recursive logic of discovery and conquest: even if justifying the sovereignty of the United States in conquest may appear "extravagant," it is now the law of the land, and "cannot be questioned." Such language provides justification for the superior legal title for discovering nations like the United States (Wilkins & Stark, 2018), a decision that set a precedent and remains encoded in U.S. law.

After *Johnson v. McIntosh* (1823), the Marshall court ruled on two other cases on Indigenous rights and sovereignty: *Cherokee Nation v. Georgia* (1831) and *Worcester v. Georgia* (1832). Together, these three cases are often referred to as the "Marshall trilogy." Prucha (2000) summarizes *Cherokee Nation v. Georgia* (1831)

When Georgia extended her laws over the Cherokee lands, the Indians brought suit against the state. The Supreme Court refused to accept jurisdiction because it declared the Cherokee Nation was not a "foreign nation" in the sense intended by the Constitution. John Marshall, who delivered the opinion, described the Indian tribes as "domestic dependent nations." (Prucha, 2000, p. 57)

Central to this case was the language characterizing Native nations as "'domestic dependent nations' whose citizens were nonetheless 'in a state of pupilage and subject to the guardianship protection of the federal government'" (as cited in Wilkins & Stark, 2018, p. 153). This affirmed Discovery principles by setting up a paternalistic relationship between the Native nations and the federal government of the United States, the latter having more sovereignty based on their status as a discovering power.

The following year, the Court ruled on *Worcester v. Georgia* (1832), again, summarized by Prucha (2000):

Samuel A. Worcester, a missionary among the Cherokees, was imprisoned because he refused to obey a Georgia law forbidding whites to reside in the Cherokee country without taking an oath of allegiance to the state and obtaining a permit. The Supreme Court decided in favor of Worcester, maintaining that the Cherokee were a nation free from the jurisdiction of the state. (p. 60)

In *Worcester*, "Chief Justice Marshall stated that tribes were 'distinct political communities, having territorial boundaries, within which their authority is exclusive'" (as cited in Wilkins & Stark, 2018, p. 153). While this was later seen as decision in favor of Indian country because it recognized some degree of tribal sovereignty against the states, the opinion still relied on Discovery principles and the *Johnson v. McIntosh* (1823) decision in emphasizing that the U.S. government held sovereignty and preemption rights over tribal homelands.

HOW HAS THE DOCTRINE OF DISCOVERY PLAYED OUT IN FEDERAL POLICY TOWARD NATIVE NATIONS?

The Doctrine of Discovery has been the foundation of federal Indian law to the present day. None of the Supreme Court decisions that relied on the doctrine have been overturned by the Court or revisited Congress. The doctrine underlay every moment of changing federal Indian policy. For example, the General Allotment Act (or Dawes Act) of 1887, which drastically reduced Indigenous homelands by dividing tribally held lands into individual plots of land, and opening up "surplus" lands to white settlement and eventual sale, was rooted in the doctrine's limitation of tribal sovereignty. This legislation stripped 90 million acres, or two-thirds of Indigenous lands, from Indigenous nations.

The Supreme Court even applied a version of the doctrine in the 1955 case *Tee-Hit-Ton Indians vs. United States*. After the United States had cut and sold trees on Native land in Alaska, a Tlingit Nation sued for compensation under the 5th Amendment. Using direct concepts from the doctrine, the Supreme Court said that the Tlingit did not have permanent rights and title to the land, and so deserved no compensation. A sampling of quotes from the Court's opinion illustrates the Doctrine of Discovery principles:

- "... after the coming of the white man," tribes held their lands "under what is sometimes termed original Indian title or permission from the whites to occupy. That description means mere possession not specifically recognized as ownership by Congress." (as cited in Miller, 2008, p. 57)
- After conquest they were permitted to occupy portions of territory. . . . This is not a property right but amounts to a right of occupancy which the sovereign grants and protects against intrusion by third parties but which right of occupancy may be terminated and such lands fully disposed of by the sovereign itself without any legally enforceable obligation to compensate the Indians. (p. 57)

Again, embedded throughout another Supreme Court legal decision are the Discovery principles. Miller (2008) argues that the decision misapplied *Johnson v. McIntosh* (1823) and other Supreme Court cases, which although they diminished Indigenous rights, nevertheless "had called the Indian real-property right a legal right of use, occupancy, and possession" (p. 57).

The Termination era of the 1950s and 1960s, under which the federal government ended its recognition of and trust relationship with over 100 Native nations and forcibly dissolved their reservations, was also based in the doctrine's supremacist thinking. Those advocating for termination policies claimed they would be beneficial for Indigenous peoples; however, Native nations were not consulted in the process. Though some Native nations avoided Termination, the policy devastated many others. "Between 1945 and 1960 the government processed 109 cases of termination 'affecting a minimum of 1,362,155 acres and 11,466 individuals'" (Wilkins & Stark, 2018, p. 158). As Wilkins and Stark continue:

> Tribal lands were usually concentrated into private ownership and, in most cases sold; the trust relationship was ended; federal taxes were imposed; the tribes and their members were subject to state law; programs and services designed for federally recognized tribes were stopped; and the tribes' legal sovereignty was effectively ended. (p. 158)

The Western Oregon Termination Act, 1954 (Public Law 588), for example, ended the trust relationship with more than sixty tribes and bands in Western Oregon, a direct assault on Indigenous sovereignty and nationhood. This law, along with Public Law 587 which affected the Klamath and Modoc tribes and the Yahooskin Band of Snake Indians, opened up thousands of acres of Indigenous homelands that were rich in timber to private and corporate interests.

As has always been the case, Indigenous peoples actively contested colonial policies and their own dispossession. Because of Indigenous resistance, organizing, and activism, and through strategic legal and political challenges, many termination policies were overturned. After decades of legal challenges, some Native nations successfully passed restoration policies in the 1970s and 1980s. However, Termination drastically changed the political landscape for Indigenous nations. In Oregon, for example, where 61 bands were terminated, there are currently nine federally recognized tribal nations. And although Restoration was successful in restoring the political status of these nations, their land bases have been greatly reduced. Tribal nations' struggles to regain recognition continue today. For example, the Chinook Indian Nation, whose homelands are the lower mouth of the Columbia River and whose ancestors helped the Corps of Discovery survive winters at Fort Clatsop, continues a campaign of over 150 years for restoration. In Kevin Gover's last act as Assistant Secretary for Indian Affairs, he signed federal recognition of the Chinook Indian Nation in January 2001. This was rescinded 18 months later by President George W. Bush's administration. As a tribal nation unrecognized by the federal government, the Chinook Indian Nation does not have access to federal funds or programs to help address the effects of colonization. The Chinook Indian Nation reached out to President Barack Obama with a letter-a-day campaign (www.chinooknation.org/justice/cejrp_index.html#) and filed a court case that remains active today. Though the Chinook Indian Nation lacks formal federal recognition from the federal government, it has long been recognized as a *nation*. For example, on February 20, 1806, Clark wrote in his journal "This forenoon we were visited by Tâh-cum, a principal Chief of the Chinnooks and 25 men of his *nation*" (emphasis added).

HOW HAS THE DOCTRINE OF DISCOVERY BEEN CHALLENGED?

Any history curriculum that addresses the Doctrine of Discovery also needs to include education about the way Native nations and peoples have resisted that doctrine. Anything less amounts to an erasure of the continuing presence and agency of Indigenous peoples. David Wilkins (2014), citizen of the Lumbee Nation and the McKnight Presidential Professor in American Indian Studies at the University of Minnesota, points to the importance of recognizing the long-standing efforts of Indigenous peoples to challenge the Doctrine of Discovery. He writes,

> To simplistically explain away loss of territory as the fault of the Doctrine of Discovery is to ignore our own retained land rights and forget that our ancestors were determined, intelligent, and politically astute people who defended their sovereign territories through strength and reason. To accept a dumbed-down version of history is to relegate our people to the role of victim.

However, Wilkins and his colleague Heidi Kiiwetinepinesiik Stark (2018) do advocate directly that Congress

> should disavow the doctrine of discovery (defined as vesting absolute or superior land title in the United States over the aboriginal land rights of Native peoples) and the use of the plenary power doctrine (defined as absolute and unlimited) as violating the limitations imposed by the U.S. Constitution and the bilateral treaty relationship. (p. 268)

Indigenous peoples have engaged in philosophical, legal, and political challenges to the foundational idea that settlers had preemptive rights to Indigenous homelands. Although such resistance is wide and varied, here we describe three basic forms: efforts to denounce and revoke the authority of the Doctrine of Discovery, efforts to overturn legal decisions that encoded the doctrine in U.S. law, and Indigenous peoples' efforts to maintain relationships with their homelands that are rooted in alternatives to notions of land as property. Examples follow for each form of resistance.

Denouncing and Revoking

Awareness of the Doctrine of Discovery, understanding its purpose, and analyzing its legacy is significant challenging its implementation. In *Pagans in the Promised Land: Decoding the Doctrine of Christian Discovery,* Steven Newcomb (Shawnee and Lenape) (2008) argues that learning about how the doctrine's principles are used to justify domination can "assist Indigenous nations and peoples on the path toward liberation and healing" (p. 130). This is reflected in the short film "The Doctrine of Discovery," part of the Digital Wampum Series (n.d.) made available by the Haudenosaunee

Confederation. Onondaga Tadadaho (tribal leader) Sidney Hill opens the segment by stating,

> We always, I think we always wondered why did they think it was right, or just, to do what they did. You know, to take our lands and push us off our lands and to try to eliminate us as a people. And then we discovered this Doctrine of Discovery. It just kind of made things understandable as to where they got their direction from.

This understanding results in action such as calling for the Doctrine of Discovery to be denounced and revoked. For example, in the Long March to Rome, a delegation representing Native nations whose homelands are in the United States and Canada traveled over 800 miles from Paris to Rome to deliver messages from Indigenous peoples around the world calling for the Vatican to revoke the doctrine. They arrived to meet with papal representatives on May 4, 2016—523 years to the day marking the issue of the Doctrine of Discovery. In the submitted testimonies, JoDe Goudy (n.d), Tribal Chairman of the Yakama Nation, stated,

> . . . Pope Francis ought to do the right thing by revoking the destructive edicts issued by his predecessors. By doing so, he will thereby be assisting in the work we are engaged to disestablish the Doctrine of Christian Discovery and Domination. He will relinquish the enabling documents that have allowed, and continue to allow nations to justify individual acts of destruction upon Indigenous (Original) nations and peoples throughout the globe.

Cardinal Silvano Tomasi, Chair of the Pontifical Council for Justice and Peace, met with the delegation and released a letter on August 1, 2016, condemning and declaring no legal value in the principles of the Papal Bulls, supporting the United Nations Declaration on the Rights of Indigenous Peoples (2007), and listing "constructive actions" related to the call of the Long March to Rome delegation. Cardinal Tomasi's letter is in the context of Pope Francis' statement on July 9, 2015, in Santa Cruz, Bolivia, when he apologized and asked for forgiveness "not only for the offense of the church herself, but also for the crimes committed against the native peoples during the so-called conquest of America" (Yardley & Neuman, 2015).

In 2018, a group of Native youth and their parents from Minnesota planned to travel to the Vatican to echo the same request as the Long March to Rome: Rescind the Doctrine of Discovery. Musician and educator Mitch

Walking Elk (Southern Cheyenne, Arapaho, Hopi and Choctaw) and Pastor Jim Bear Jacobs (member of the Stockbridge-Munsee Mohican Nation) led workshops and discussions for youth and adults in St. Paul, MN, to learn about the legacy of the Doctrine of Discovery and find ways of healing through education and action. In a local newspaper story about the students, Akili Day stated, "There's so many people who don't know about this. Even if we are a small group, we can shed light on it and what it has done to us" (Hopfensperger, 2018). Another student, Nina Berglund, added, "We live with historical trauma; it's in our DNA. It's from the taking of our land, the killing of our people. Every day we see it in suicides, drug and alcohol addiction, poverty. . . . We're still trying to deal with it" (Hopfensperger, 2018). The youth action in St. Paul is part of a wider movement of Native youth taking informed civic action to empower their nations.

Other faith communities have condemned the Doctrine of Discovery and called for it to be revoked through resolutions and statements. Examples include actions by the Community of Christ (in 2016), the Episcopal Church (in 2012), the Presbyterian Church USA (in 2016), the United Church of Christ (in 2013), and the United Methodist Church (in 2012). A recent example of interfaith efforts to revoke the doctrine occurred at the Standing Rock Sioux Reservation in North Dakota as Water Protectors gathered to defend Oceti Sakowin lands from a proposed pipeline slated to go through their traditional territory. On October 22, 2016, Chief Arvol Looking Horse, 19th Generation Keeper of the Sacred White Buffalo Calf Pipe Bundle, called religious leaders and people to support the struggles to protect the lands, waters, sacred sites, and nearby communities. On December 4, 2016, more than 500 clergy from twenty different faith communities answered the call to join the Water Protectors. The day of action included readings of the resolutions and statements from denominations formally renouncing the doctrine followed by a symbolic burning of the doctrine. Retired Reverend Marc Handley Àndrus, an Episcopal Bishop, stated to the Episcopal News Service, "By burning the copies of the Doctrine of Discovery, we were signaling an end to the past that has affected millions and millions of people. People who have been colonized and people who have been enslaved, but also the enslavers and the colonizers, it's affected us all" (Kuruvilla, 2016).

Overturning

Understanding how the Doctrine of Discovery is wielded as a legal principle has resulted in efforts to overturn its application through the court system. Since the 1970s, the Onondaga nation has submitted 30 legal actions related to land rights and all have been dismissed. This pattern was affirmed by Alex Tallchief Skibine (Osage) (2017), professor of law at the S.J. Quinney College of Law at the University of Utah, when reviewing 30 years (1987–2017) of Supreme Court cases directly related to Indian law. He analyzed a total of 66 cases and determined a 28% success rate. When Skibine (2017) evaluated the data in 15-year increments, he noted a success rate increase from 24.4% to 34.7% (p. 18). He writes this "may indicate that, for the tribes, the worst is behind them and there might indeed be a light at the end of this anti tribal sovereignty tunnel" (Skibine, 2017, p. 18).

An indication of the possible turn identified by Skibine (2017) is the recent Supreme Court ruling in *Washington State Department of Licensing v. Cougar Den* (2018). The court ruled that the Yakama nation–owned fuel distribution company, Cougar Den, was exempt from $3.6 million in taxes, fees, and penalties assessed by the state of Washington for transporting fuel on state highways. In a 5–4 decision, the court upheld provisions in the Yakama Treaty of 1855 establishing open commercial transportation for the Yakama nation. In a concurring opinion released on March 19, 2019, Supreme Court Justice Neil Gorsuch stated,

> Really, this case just tells an old and familiar story. The state of Washington includes millions of acres that the Yakamas ceded to the United States under significant pressure. In return, the government supplied a handful of modest promises. The state is now dissatisfied with the consequences of one of those promises. It is a new day, and now it wants more. But today and to its credit, the court holds the parties to the terms of their deal. It is the least we can do.

Included in the documents reviewed by the Supreme Court was an *amicus curiae* brief submitted by the Confederated Tribes and Bands of the Yakama nation in support of Cougar Den. Citing *Johnson v. McIntosh* (1823), the brief states,

> For nearly two centuries this Court has dehumanized original, free, and independent Nations and Peoples by issuing decisions and using language consistent with the doctrine's religious and racist foundations—e.g., red man, uncivilized, barbarous, ignorant, unlearned, non-Christians, heathens, savages, infidels—all in an effort to manufacture a legal basis for the physical and cultural genocide. . . . This doctrine of domination and dehumanization—Christian discovery—is not welcome

within Yakama Territory, and should no longer be tolerated in United States law. The Yakama Nation respectfully calls on this Court to repudiate the doctrine of Christian discovery and its racist foundations as the basis for federal Indian law, and instead acknowledge and rely upon the solemn Treaty negotiated between the Yakama Nation and the United States in this dispute and into the future. (*Washington State Department of Licensing vs. Cougar Den, Inc.*, 2018, p. 6)

When interviewed by the Spokane, WA, newspaper *The Spokesman Herald*, Margo Hill, a citizen of the Spokane nation and professor of tribal law and economic development at Eastern Washington University, stated, "In this one case, this one little case, the judges are reading the law the way they're supposed to. It's a small justice, but we'll take it" (Deshais, 2019). Perhaps an indication of justice, improved understanding of Indian law, and the possibility of change is that Justice Ruth Bader Ginsberg joined Justice Gorsuch in his concurring opinion in *Washington State Department of Licensing v. Cougar Den* (2018).

Challenging Notions of Land as Property

Another important way that Indigenous peoples challenge the Doctrine of Discovery is by maintaining relationships to land that are not based on Western notions of land as property, but rather on understandings of land as a relative and ancestor, as sacred, as a source of life, or as teacher, among others (Grande, 2015; Kimmerer, 2013; Tuck, 2013). As Quechua scholar Sandy Grande (2015) notes, the belief that land is property is rooted in other foundational beliefs, such as the secular (rather than sacred) nature of the universe:

> Unlike secular societies—where land signifies property, property signifies capital, and capital signifies wealth, status, and power—land in "sacred" societies signifies connection to family, tribe, and ancestors. Land is furthermore thought of in connection to sacred sites, burial grounds, and medicinal plants. (pp. 101–102)

When Indigenous peoples maintain these relationships with their homelands, they are inherently challenging the Doctrine of Discovery. These challenges come in a variety of forms, such as caring for and harvesting native plants and animals, conducting ceremonies and visiting sacred sites, using land-based pedagogies to teach Indigenous youth, or advocating for the personhood status of lands in an effort to protect them. A recent example is the White Earth Band

of Ojibwe's successful efforts to pass a law in 2018, legally recognizing the rights of Manoomin (wild rice). As stated by Frank Bibeau, Executive Director of the 1855 Treaty Authority and Minnesota Honor the Earth tribal attorney, "we understand WATER IS LIFE for all living creatures and protecting abundant, clean, fresh water is essential for our ecosystems and wild life habitats to sustain all of us and the Manoomin" (1855 Treaty Authority, 2019, n.p). Approaches to challenging the principles of the Doctrine of Discovery such as this are based, not only in the rights of land, but also in the responsibilities that humans have to lands, waters, and all forms of life they sustain. It is important that educators recognize the danger in stereotyping Indigenous peoples as "ecological Indians" or "noble savages" (a romanticized characterization of Indigenous peoples as close to or even one with nature). With care, however, educators can recognize and affirm Indigenous philosophies, perspectives, and relationships with land that reflect values such as respect, responsibility, and reciprocity.

HOW CAN I CHALLENGE THE DOCTRINE OF DISCOVERY AS A TEACHER?

This brief background on the Doctrine of Discovery makes clear how fundamental the papal bull has been to the justification of conquest and colonization of Indigenous people for hundreds of years. Embedded within the doctrine are deep-seated beliefs about the superiority of Western society and the inferiority of Indigenous societies, beliefs that permeate social studies curriculum. These colonial logics, which will be further discussed in Chapter 3, must be countered in curriculum. Teachers can challenge the Doctrine of Discovery directly by refusing to teach curriculum glorifying conquest or making the theft of Indigenous lands seem inevitable. Rather than teach the Corps of Discovery as an "adventure story," students can learn about the Doctrine of Discovery and the Corps of Discovery as a military endeavor. Further, we have pointed to a legacy of Indigenous resistance that we encourage teachers to use as curriculum. The specific examples we included, as well as the broad notion that Indigenous peoples have actively contested, and continue to contest, their own dispossession is an important lens through which students can learn about hope, agency, organizing, activism, and solidarity. In the next chapter, we unpack some of the ways colonial logics surface in curriculum about the Corps of Discovery, so that teachers can begin to make visible and counter these logics with students.

CHAPTER 3

Unpacking Colonial Logics in Lewis and Clark Curriculum

"Little was known about the land in the Louisiana Purchase."

> —*The United States: Making a New Nation*
> (Berson, Howard, & Salinas, 2012, p. 430)

"Nothing was discovered. Everything was already loved."

> —Karenne Wood (Monacan Indian Nation)
> (2003, p. 12–13)

"We were 'discovered' many times."

> —Roberta Conner (Cayuse, Umatilla, Nez Perce)
> (Lang & Abbott, 2004, p. 119)

As the previous chapter illustrated, colonial logics and policies have been foundational to the establishment of the United States. Colonial logics also permeate K–12 social studies curriculum. Sometimes colonial logics are explicit—referring to Indigenous peoples within texts as "hostile Indians," for example. Other times, colonial logics are subtler—framing curriculum through a lens of exploration, Westward expansion, or the growth of the nation, for example. This chapter supports teachers in recognizing how colonial logics and ideologies surface in educational curriculum, in part, by drawing attention to the biases embedded in language. To make this apparent, we unpack colonial logics that circulate in curriculum about Lewis and Clark. By providing examples focusing on the way language can legitimize or challenge dominant ideologies, this chapter extends teachers' critical anticolonial literacy skills so that they can support their students in detecting and interrupting bias and Eurocentrism in their own classrooms and communities.

CONTEXTUALIZING COLONIAL LOGICS

To understand how colonial logics surface in curriculum, educators must first understand the structure and practices of *settler colonialism*. Settler colonialism is a specific form of colonialism in which settlers invade Indigenous homelands with the intent of making those homelands their home. In contrast to other forms of colonialism in which settlers travel to distant lands in order to extract resources (e.g., minerals, spices, human beings who are enslaved and made into property/labor) and then bring those resources home to build the wealth of their empire, settler colonialism is unique in that "settler colonizers come to stay" (Wolfe, 2006, p. 388). When the Puritans traveled to America, for example, they had no intent of returning home; rather, their intent was to make America their new home, to stay. Similarly, when settlers traveled to lands acquired through the Louisiana Purchase and later through the Oregon Treaty, their intention was not to visit those lands, but to stay: to make Indigenous homelands their new home.

"Staying" on Indigenous homelands has required the erasure of Indigenous peoples. In early U.S. history, Indigenous erasure operated explicitly through violent means, such as warfare, treaties, or policies such as Indian Removal. Later, Indigenous erasure operated more subtly via policies of assimilation, termination, relocation, and adoption. Even subtler are the ways Indigenous erasures operate ideologically: through narratives that imply that Indigenous peoples have vanished or disappeared, through the use of colonial metrics like blood quantum, or via the absence of contemporary Indigenous peoples and issues in curriculum. Staying on Indigenous homelands has also required the creation and maintenance of a new society and institutions atop those lands, as well as narratives that frame this new society and these institutions as superior. Because the need to erase Indigenous peoples and assert settler superiority are both ongoing, it is important that teachers recognize that settler colonialism, as an ongoing practice of "elimination" and "invasion," is "a structure, not an event" (Wolfe, 2006, p. 388). In this light, settler colonialism is not history, but a contemporary feature of society that educators must challenge.

Challenging settler colonialism requires the ability to recognize the various ways colonial logics surface in curriculum. Indigenous studies scholars have worked meticulously to make these colonial logics visible. Social studies educators can learn a great deal from Indigenous studies analyses. What follows is a brief overview of three such concepts: settler grammars, firsting and lasting, and the civ/sav dichotomy. We offer these concepts as tools that teachers and students can use to make visible and challenge colonial logics and curriculum about the Corps of Discovery.

Settler Grammars

Mexican/Tigua scholar Dolores Calderôn (2014), for example, has demonstrated that colonial logics surface in *settler grammars*, subtle ideologies that naturalize colonialism within curriculum. The idea that Indigenous homelands were "empty," that the United States is a "nation of immigrants," or that settler society was "superior" to Indigenous societies, are examples of how settler grammars surface in social studies textbooks. Each of these grammars functions as a justification for domination and the dispossession of Indigenous peoples. The notion that lands west of the Mississippi were "uncharted," for example, is rooted in the idea that Indigenous homelands were empty wilderness, thus justifying the exploration of and eventual settlement within Indigenous homelands.

Firsting and Lasting

As another example, White Earth Nation scholar Jean O'Brien (2010) has documented "firsting" and "lasting" as explicit methods of Indigenous erasure. Firsting is a colonial tactic of erasing Indigenous peoples' presence, histories, and experiences by foregrounding various "firsts," such as the first explorer to visit an area, or the first settler home erected in a town. *Firsting* is a foundational principle of the ten elements of the Doctrine of Discovery addressed in Chapter 2 (Element 1). Closely coupled with firsting is *lasting*, which is evident in stories of the "last" remaining member of a tribal nation, or more broadly in the narratives of the disappearance of Indigenous peoples (i.e., the vanishing race).

Civ/Sav Dichotomy

Lastly, Plains Cree scholar Emma LaRocque (2010) has also argued that deep-seated ideas about Indigenous inferiority and Western superiority—often discussed in terms of Indian savagery and Western civilization—permeate settler societies.

LaRoque (2010) makes visible this "long-held belief that humankind evolved from the primitive to the most advanced, from the savage to the civilized" through what she calls the *civ/sav dichotomy* (p. 39). The idea that Indigenous peoples are an earlier form of humanity and Western society is the epitome of progress pervades social studies curriculum. On this linear continuum, Indigenous societies are designated as primitive and pre-historical while Western societies are framed as modern, sophisticated, and meant to be the future. The civ/sav dichotomy also surfaces in a "double standard" in how Indigenous and Western societies are discussed:

> In this war of words, Whites explore, Indians wander; Whites have battles or victories, Indians massacre and murder; Whites scout, Indians lurk; Whites go westward, Indians go bloodthirsty; Whites defend themselves, Indians "wreak revenge"; Whites appear as officials who simply assume authority, Indians are "haughty," "insolent," "saucy," or "impudent" (when they assume equality); Whites have "faiths" and so they pray; Indians have superstitions and so they conjure; Whites may be peasant, Indians are primitive; Whites may be "brutes," but Indians remain savage and barbaric in their "heathen" lands. (LaRocque, 2010, p. 50)

It is this civ/sav logic (Element 9 of the Doctrine of Discovery discussed in Chapter 2) that has enabled Western society to narrate Indigenous societies as primitive and inferior, justifying westward expansion and Indigenous dispossession. And even though Indigenous peoples have always had modern, advanced, and sophisticated societies and knowledge systems, they are rarely viewed in equal terms. Consider the following example from the text *Lewis and Clark for Kids: Their Journey of Discovery with 21 Activities* (Herbert, 2000) in a section titled, "Were They Really First?":

> Lewis and Clark are credited with discovering hundreds of plants and animals in the west, but the Native Americans had known of these plants and animals for centuries. When people refer to Lewis and Clark's "discoveries," they mean that though the captains might not have been the first people to see the plants and animals, they were the first to identify and describe them *in a scientific manner.* (p. 21, emphasis added)

Even though this excerpt acknowledges Indigenous presence and knowledges systems, it nevertheless frames Western scientific methods as superior to Indigenous knowledge systems, knowledge that despite being empirically accumulated over centuries, is not deemed worthy of the label "scientific."

These frameworks—*settler grammars, firsting and lasting, and the civ/sav dichotomy*—are important tools through which educators and students can interrogate and challenge social studies curriculum. We hope these analyses help teachers and students to complicate the colonial logics that permeate conventional curriculum about Lewis and Clark or even primary sources, such as the journals. When Lewis remarked of their historic departure on April 7, 1805, "we are now about to penetrate a country at least two thousand miles in width, on which the foot of civilized man had never trodden," we hope teachers will equip students to recognize and challenge the civ/sav logics within this entry. With these tools, for example, educators can ask critical questions of curriculum such as: In what ways do settler grammars, such as "empty lands," surface in curriculum? In what way does the curriculum foreground explorers or discovery, erasing Indigenous peoples' presence and perspectives? How do texts portray Indigenous peoples as vanishing? With whom does the curriculum seek to foster understanding or empathy? Or in what ways does this text portray Indigenous peoples and societies as primitive, uncivilized, or inferior to Western societies?

UNPACKING COLONIAL LOGICS

Although an exhaustive account of how colonial logics surface in curriculum is beyond the scope of this book project, this chapter will highlight four specific ways that colonialism surfaces in curriculum and pedagogy around Lewis and Clark: by framing the Corps of Discovery as uncontested and a neutral expedition, by framing the expedition as a contribution to society, by glorifying the expedition, and by inviting students to empathize with or imagine themselves as explorers. Each of these colonial logics rests on Eurocentric perspectives of the Corps of Discovery. Teaching about Indigenous peoples' histories and experiences prior to the Corps of Discovery, or teaching about the Corps of Discovery from Indigenous perspectives are both important anticolonial strategies to counter Eurocentrism. However, including Indigenous histories, experiences, or perspectives within curriculum that also glorifies discovery and exploration does little to disrupt the colonial momentum of dominant narratives. As such, this book incorporates Indigenous perspectives while *also* advocating for educators to critique dominant narratives of Lewis and Clark. The primary purpose of this chapter is to support educators in directly challenging narratives of discovery and adventure in Lewis and Clark curriculum.

The Guise of Neutrality

One of the subtle ways colonial logics operates is through the appearance of factuality, objectivity, or neutrality. Textbooks or websites, for example, typically describe the Lewis and Clark expedition in a neutral manner. This neutral narrative goes like something this:

> In 1804, the Lewis and Clark Expedition, led by Meriwether Lewis, William Clark, and a group of nearly 40 men, set out to explore lands recently purchased from the Louisiana Purchase. The purpose of the expedition was to document the plants and animals, learn about and establish trade with Native Americans along the way, and to find a waterway that led to the Pacific Ocean. Lewis and Clark met and were helped by a fur trapper named Toussaint Charbonneau, and his wife, Sacagawea, who helped the expedition as an interpreter and guide. The group faced many challenges along the way, but because of their bravery and the help of Sacagawea and other Native Americans, they were successful.

The language within this narrative—a neutral tale of adventure, discovery, and friendship—effectively transforms the Lewis and Clark expedition, a precursor to mass westward expansion (for Indigenous people read: encroachment and dispossession), into an "eat, pray, love" moment where two men bonded in friendship go on a cross-country journey, have exotic, friendly encounters with Indigenous peoples, are helped by Sacagawea, and eventually become American heroes. In *Two Centuries of Lewis and Clark: Reflections on the Voyage of Discovery* (Lang & Abbott, 2004), Lang summarizes the expedition as "a vignette that has been ripped out of historical context to become a universal, dramatic story of accomplishment" (p. 114).

Presenting historical narratives as uncontested, neutral, and as objective facts is problematic because, it portrays Eurocentric perspectives as objective truths sanitizing or glossing over problematic incidents that occurred, and typically ignoring the devastating consequences the Corps of Discovery had on Indigenous nations and their homelands. Moreover, such purportedly neutral narratives often include passive language to depict what were arguably active practices of colonization. For example, Core Lesson 2 in *United States History: The Early Years*, a 5th-grade social studies book by Houghton Mifflin, is titled "The Nation

Grows" (Viola et al., 2005). Not only does the term "grows" foreground Eurocentric perspectives (since Indigenous nations and homelands were simultaneously encroached upon and diminished), but the passive language and masked neutrality conceals the active processes, such as treaties that dispossessed Indigenous peoples or policies of removal and allotment, that allowed for such "growth." In the vocabulary section of this same text, the student preview for the term *corps* states, "More than 30 people explored the West with Lewis and Clark. This **corps** was a team of people who worked together" (p. 342). Although the teacher edition prompts educators to "Tell students that the word *corps* is commonly used to refer to divisions of the armed forces, such as the Marine Corps" (p. 342), the textbook definition gives the impression that the group of military men sent on a reconnaissance mission in the Northwest was little more than a "team" or group.

Neutrality can also limit students' understanding of and critical engagement with historical sources. *Lewis and Clark* (Sullivan, 2000), a widely used text, discusses the explorers' journals as "a national literary treasure" that "have enormous value" because "[t]hey give us the actual words of those involved in the event" (p. 8). Missing, however, is a critical discussion of *whose* words and perspectives are included in the journals. As Roberta Conner (2004) states, "the fact that the journals are littered with 'sq*w drudges' and 'heathens' and 'savages' and 'thieves' gives us a window into the worldview of the people who made the journey" (p. 131). Yet that worldview, latent with deep-seated assumptions of Western superiority and Indigenous inferiority, is rarely made visible and discussed. Moreover, what is *not* in the journals, including the histories of Indigenous peoples with whom the Corps of Discovery met but briefly, is also valuable. These oral narratives, however, are often considered less reliable sources than the journals; again, a Eurocentric framing of what constitutes "valuable," even "legitimate," historical evidence.

Even subtler is the practice of encoding Eurocentric perspectives into what appear to students as factual statements in textbooks. In the introduction to *Lewis and Clark* (Sullivan, 2000), the book states that Lewis and Clark "led the famous voyage of discovery into what is now the northwestern United States," which "was a vast wilderness at the time" (p. 5). Framing Indigenous homelands as wilderness functions to diminish Indigenous peoples' presence in the area, as well as their claims to land. Similarly, in the opening sentence to the lesson on Lewis and Clark in *The United States: Making a New Nation* (Berson, Howard, & Salinas,

2012) the text states "Little was known about the land in the Louisiana Purchase" (p. 430). Though this line masquerades as a neutral fact, this phrase more accurately refers to the idea that little was known *by white explorers*. As the epigraph to this chapter notes, "Nothing was discovered. Everything was already loved."

The Corps of Discovery set the stage for the dispossession of Indigenous peoples, a consequence that is rarely made visible in curriculum that purports neutrality. Moreover, when texts portray Eurocentric perspectives as objective truths, students miss the opportunity to critically interrogate how sources shape the ways history is told. As Lang (2004) writes,

> In the end, the significance of the Lewis and Clark Expedition and its personnel is an open and contested matter. Those who find it preeminently a story of adventure, achievement, and nationalistic accomplishment have plenty of drama to support their viewpoint. Those who see it as part of a long history of paternalistic and damaging engagements with Indian people in the Northwest can cite incident upon incident where the explorers appear arrogant and dismissive of Native people. (p. 56)

Unfortunately, the guise of neutrality that often frames textbook portrayals of the Corps of Discovery rarely supports students' understanding that its significance is an "open and contested matter."

The Expedition as a Contribution to Society

Another way colonial logics underpin the narrative of Lewis and Clark is by framing the Corps of Discovery as a "contribution" to the United States. Consider the following example from a 4th grade textbook:

> Lewis and Clark's exploration of the land west of the Mississippi River enabled other Americans to explore and eventually settle the land. Their journey was an important contribution to the development of our country. (Visla et al., 2005, p. 210)

Here, Lewis and Clark are credited with paving the way for settlement, an action that the text frames positively as an "important contribution" to the development of "our country." The term "our" centers settler perspectives, not Indigenous perspectives that likely did not view the Corps of Discovery as contributing to the development of Indigenous nations.

As another example, the *Oregon Studies Weekly* (StudiesWeekly, 2016) states that "The Lewis and

Clark expedition was a great success" and "paved the way for future travelers and strengthened America's claim on the western U.S. territory" (n.p.). Similarly, the high school text *The Americans* (Danzer, Klor de Alva, Krieger, Wilson, & Woloch, 2000) states that "The Lewis and Clark expedition took two years and four months and was a great success. It brought back invaluable information about the West and showed that transcontinental travel was possible. It also opened the way for settlement of the West and strengthened American claims to the Oregon Territory on the northwest coast" (p. 188). Again, framing the Corps of Discovery as a "success" erases perspectives that challenge the legitimacy and value of a reconnaissance mission that drastically altered the physical and political landscape that Indigenous nations had for millenia. This pattern of viewing the mission as a contribution stems from the broader idea that westward expansion and the acquisition of Indigenous homelands is beneficial. Discussing the value of the Louisiana Purchase, the 5th-grade textbook *United States History: Early Years v2* (Viola et al., 2005) invites students to answer the question: "Why was the Louisiana Purchase a good business deal for the United States?" (p. 355). The answer: "The United States doubled its size. It also now had control of the port of New Orleans" (p. 355). Despite the fact that the Louisiana Purchase represents the mass transfer of Indigenous homelands from the French to the United States *without Indigenous consent*, the curriculum frames this massive act of dispossession as "a good business deal." Such a view centers the desires of the nation-state, rather than considering how westward expansion came at the expense of Indigenous nations.

Glorification of the Expedition

An explicit way that colonial logics are reproduced is through curriculum that portrays the military expedition as an exciting adventure. As the aforementioned Scholastic publication *Lewis and Clark* (Sullivan, 2000) states, "The Lewis and Clark Expedition is one of the great adventure stories in American history" (pp. 7–8). Similarly, the *Oregon Studies Weekly* (StudiesWeekly, 2016) states, "One of the most exciting adventure stories in early America is the heroic trek of Meriwether Lewis and William Clark to the Pacific Northwest" (n.p.). The routine use of exclamation points to evoke enthusiasm about colonial processes is another example of such an approach. Consider an extension activity in Lesson 3, "Lewis and Clark," in the 4th-grade Houghton Mifflin textbook *Social Studies: States and Regions* (Viola et al., 2005) which begins with the heading "The Journey

Begins!" and ends with "The Pacific!" (p. 210). The exclamation points signal the excitement of the journey, framing what was arguably the beginning of a legacy of mass disenfranchisement as an adventure (!).

Textbooks also glorify the Corps of Discovery when they discuss the positive characteristics of the explorers. The 4th-grade Lewis and Clark lesson plan in *Social Studies: States and Regions* (Viola et al., 2005) encourages teachers to frame the tale of Lewis and Clark through the moral value of courage, and prompts teachers to invite students to make personal connections to Lewis and Clark and this value of courage: "Lewis and Clark showed **courage** by going on their journey. Talk about someone you know who has done something courageous" (p. 211). By framing Lewis and Clark as courageous, absent any discussion of other characteristics, the curriculum foregrounds Eurocentric perspectives. Though many may not contest that Lewis and Clark were, in fact, courageous, courage is only one of many descriptors that could be used. Audacious, irresponsible, ethnocentric, opportunistic, reckless, or unwise are other descriptors that, depending on perspective, may also accurately describe Lewis and Clark. The point is that courage is not a neutral term, even though it operates as such within the official curriculum. Rather, courage is one framing, a celebratory Eurocentric framing, that often comes to stand in as *the* framing of the explorers, a single story (Adichie, 2009) that narrates the Corps of Discovery as a virtuous adventure, eclipsing Indigenous and other critical perspectives that call into question its value. In planning discussions for the proposed bicentennial "celebration," for example, Allen Pinkham, a Nez Perce tribal leader, recalled "And we said no, if you want to have Indian involvement, don't call it a celebration because there's nothing that we have to celebrate" (historynewsnetwork.org/article/13473). Similarly, Pinkham questioned the narrative of heroism often attributed to Lewis and Clark. "All I read about is Lewis and Clark, the heroes of the day 200 years ago. Well, whose heroes? They're not my heroes." Teachers can learn to challenge narratives of adventure by incorporating Indigenous perspectives, as well as by asking critical questions about the perspectives that tacitly, as well as explicitly, shape curriculum.

Centering and Empathizing with Explorers

Closely coupled with the practice of framing exploration as an exciting adventure is the practice of inviting students to imagine themselves as Lewis and Clark, or as explorers or settlers more broadly. Such imaginative activities not only center the explorers, but also function to support students' empathy with them. There is a pattern in curriculum of inviting students to identify as and empathize with settlers. Examples of this approach abound.

For instance, in *The United States: Making a New Nation* (Berson, Howard, & Salinas, 2012), students are invited to "Imagine that you are looking for a route to the Pacific coast. As the expedition leader, you must make thoughtful decisions. Your decisions could mean life or death for your group" (p. 435). Students are then prompted to choose one of two decisions, and to think of the consequences of each choice. This prompt is located within the section on critical thinking skills, "Making a Thoughtful Decision." Students learn that "The Corps of Discovery had to make many thoughtful decisions while on their expedition" (p. 434) and are invited to practice that critical thinking skill.

Or consider the following framing of Lewis and Clark for kids (from an online course at the website Study.com):

> Think of a time when you visited a new museum, a new park, a new city or town, any place where you've never been before. Now imagine a world, a land, a continent full of rivers, lakes, mountains, plains, animals and native people that have never been discovered, and you and some friends are tasked with becoming explorers and discovering all of these new and wonderful things. (study.com/academy/lesson/lewis-clark-lesson-for-kids.html)

Another example is a prompt from a Lewis and Clark interactive tour:

Imagine this:

- Your arms are numb from fighting the raging current of the Missouri River for eight hours each day;
- Your life and the lives of every member of the expedition are threatened by hostile Native Americans;
- You've endured a winter in which soul-piercing temperatures regularly fell to –45 Fahrenheit, not including the wind;
- Vicious animals such as Grizzly Bears and rattlesnakes and thundering herds of Buffalo were constant threats;
- Finally, after you managed to survive and endure all of the hardships and physical and mental challenges, and at the climax of an epic journey, you spend an entire winter devoid of sunshine, soaked by an

unrelenting, cold rain in a 50 square foot, fetid cabin with at least 40 other people (mrnussbaum.com /lewis-and-clark-interactive-tour).

Consider, too, the following prompt from a Scholastic Teacher's Guide:

> Imagine that one morning you woke up and discovered your house had grown twice as big. How would you feel and what would you do? Well, in 1803, Americans faced a very similar situation on a much larger scale. President Thomas Jefferson had purchased 820,000 square miles from France (known as the Louisiana Purchase) and suddenly doubled the size of the United States. Americans were very excited about this new territory, but it was also a mystery. What did the land look like? How could you cross it? What kinds of animals and plants lived there? Would the Native Americans who lived there be welcoming? Very few white people had traveled to this western part of the country and the few maps that existed were patchy and unreliable. So President Jefferson decided to hire a group of men to explore this new America. (teacher.scholastic.com /activities/lewis_clark/prepare.htm)

Inviting students to imagine themselves as explorers is an explicit way of privileging Eurocentric perspectives. In each of these examples the West is framed as a place of excitement and curiosity. Further, these imaginative prompts are intended to figuratively put students in the explorers' shoes; to imagine what it feels like to explore, to discover, and to experience hardship, even danger.

What is dangerous about such activities is that they invite students to imagine themselves as, and thus empathize with, settlers. Students are not asked to imagine how they would feel if their homes or homelands shrunk in half. Instead, they are invited to identify with growth and expansion, not encroachment and loss. In this Eurocentric framing, Indigenous peoples are not afforded understanding or empathy. Rather, they are obstacles to progress, or worse, viewed as threatening and hostile. For Native students, particularly those whose families and nations have been impacted by the Corps of Discovery, this task could be dehumanizing. Imagine a Blackfoot student being asked to identify with the very men who shot one of their people. Imagine Nez Perce, Chinook, or Lemhi Shoshone students—students from communities that are still dispossessed from their homelands in the wake of the Corps of Discovery—to identify with those who dispossessed them.

The previous examples—of neutrality, contributions, glorification, and empathy—each demonstrate how curriculum, and the narratives upon which curriculum is built, can function to assert dominance. At issue are not only the ways Indigenous peoples are mis/represented in curriculum, but also the ways that dominant narratives permeate social studies curriculum, whether or not Indigenous peoples are present. Narratives of exploration, discovery, settlement, adventure, or contributions each function as national myths that justify the origins of the United States. For social studies teachers, this means it is important not only to *include* Indigenous perspectives, but also to *challenge* the ways texts reproduce colonial logics.

ANTICOLONIAL LITERACY

This book foregrounds and supports what we refer to as *anticolonial literacy,* the ability to detect and challenge colonial logics in curriculum, as well as in society more broadly (Sabzalian, 2019). As described in the introduction, a primary purpose of this book is to complicate narratives of discovery and adventure. Each lesson has been crafted to support this purpose. For example, the trading card game (Elementary Lesson Plan 5) directly challenges the narrative of discovery by highlighting Indigenous knowledge that has long existed, and continues to exist, in places "discovered" by explorers. Further, this lesson complicates Western notions of "science" by drawing attention to the value and legitimacy of Indigenous knowledge systems as scientific knowledge. As another example, the secondary lesson on *Johnson v. McIntosh* (1823) (Secondary Lesson Plan 3) provides students the opportunity to examine how colonial logics are embedded within the law and society more broadly. Within each lesson, we have also explicitly attended to various orientations—place, presence, perspectives, political nationhood, power, partnerships—which we believe complicate and enrich the ways Indigenous peoples are represented within curriculum.

Taken together, our hope is to support teachers and students in applying anticolonial literacy skills to complicate and question existing curriculum about the Corps of Discovery. Rather than a definitive account of what teaching the Corps of Discovery should look like, this book reflects our effort to wrestle with what an anticolonial stance could look like in classrooms. We encourage educators to carry forward this anticolonial approach and these ideas applied to the Corps of Discovery in their other social studies units. The concepts described in this chapter to unpack colonial logics in Lewis and Clark curriculum—firsting and lasting, settler grammars, and civ/sav dichotomy—can also be applied to other narratives of discovery and adventure within curriculum, such as the "glorification of Columbus," the "plight of the Pilgrims," or the "adventures along the Oregon Trail." We urge educators to carry forward these anticolonial analyses into their own contexts. We also encourage teachers to support students' anticolonial literacy by empowering them to do the kind of textbook and curriculum critiques that we have demonstrated in this chapter.

Part II

ELEMENTARY LESSON PLANS

"We're Still Here"

Teaching Strategy: One-Pager

Purpose: The purpose of this lesson is to provide context and introductory knowledge of contemporary Native peoples and their political status as nations today.

Connections to the Standards

6 Ps Framework	Place
	Presence
	Perspective
	Political Nationhood
	Power
	Partnership
C3 Framework	D2.His.10.3-5
	D3.1.3-5
	D4.2.3-5
	D4.6.3-5
Common Core State Standards	CCSS.ELA-Literacy.RI.4.1
	CCSS.ELA-Literacy.RI.4.2
	CCSS.ELA-Litearcy.RI.4.3
	CCSS.ELA-Literacy.RI.4.7
	CCSS.ELA-Literacy.W.4.8
	CCSS.ELA-Literacy.W.4.9
	CCSS.ELA-Literacy.SL.4.1
	CCSS.ELA-Literacy.SL.4.2
	CCSS.ELA-Literacy.SL.4.3

Introduction

People who wonder why we're involved need to understand that we are here today and at every other signature event in Lewis and Clark planning meetings, not because it's fun necessarily but because we're still here . . . because against incredible odds we have survived the last 200 years. Or, in the case of our friends from Monacan and other eastern tribes, the last 500 years. That's a story that's not told very often. We hope that the Bicentennial is that opportunity and most of you are in a position to help make that happen.

—Roberta Conner,'s (Cayuse, Umatilla, and Nez Perce) presentation titled "We Must Tell Our Story" (2006b).

During the bicentennial commemoration of the Lewis and Clark Expedition (2003–2006), the National Park Service presented *Corps of Discovery II: 200 Years to the Future*. This exhibit was a traveling education center that followed the route of the Lewis and Clark Corps of Discovery from Monticello to the Pacific Ocean and the return journey to St. Louis. The *Corps of Discovery II* stopped in 95 locations during the three-year commemoration, 14 of which were located within tribal communities. Over 500,000 people visited these sites. A feature of the traveling exhibit was the *Tent of Many Voices*. This was a performance space for Native presenters to share perspectives about the history and legacy of the military expedition along with contemporary experiences of Native peoples. The Tent of Many Voices was a result of programming guidance forwarded by the Circle of Tribal Advisors (COTA). Established in 2000, COTA was a delegation of representatives from Native nations ensuring the National Park Service recognized the following goals during the three-year commemoration: the accuracy and completeness of bicentennial programming, the promotion of respect and understanding of tribal sovereignty, and advocacy for the protection and restoration of Native homelands.

Inside the Tent of Many Voices, there were 5000 presentations from more than 400 Native storytellers, artists, musicians, historians, scholars, and leaders who shared about life before contact with the Corps of Discovery, what happened when the military expedition encountered Native nations, what has occurred during the 200 years between contact and the bicentennial, and what Native nations and people hope for the future. The stories people shared did not necessarily match the accounts in the journals of Lewis and Clark. Instead, their accounts often contrasted the official knowledge reflected within traditional American history textbooks. They revealed loss and tragedy, resilience, humor, resourcefulness, and sincere hope for the future generations. The presentations from the Tent of Many Voices were recorded, organized, and archived as the Tribal Legacy Project (lc-triballegacy.org /). In recording these stories, the National Park Service aimed to make the presentations from the Tent of Many Voices available to teachers and students to use in classrooms. The Honoring Tribal Legacies curriculum represents this commitment and readers are encouraged to explore the resources and lesson plans offered at the website (refer to Teaching Resource 4: Honoring Tribal Legacies, An Epic Journey of Healing).

The focus of this lesson is the Tribal Legacy Project website. The purpose of the lesson plan is to provide context and introductory knowledge about contemporary Native peoples, as well as about their political status as nations. Curriculum about Native communities is often confined to a chapter in history, perpetuating the false assumption that Native communities are absent today. As Roberta Conner states in her presentation "We Must Tell Our Story," the experiences of Native nations since contact with Lewis and Clark is a "a story that's not told very often" (Conner, 2006b). Roberta Conner (Cayuse, Umatilla, and Nez Perce) is the director of the Tamástslikt Cultural Institute located on the Confederated Tribes of the Umatilla Indian Reservation. She served as the Vice President of the National Council of the Lewis and Clark Bicentennial Board of Directors and was a member of the Circle of Tribal Advisors. This lesson intentionally opens a series of lesson plans about the Corps of Discovery from the perspective of Native nations who insist that "we're still here" as students are introduced to the Tribal Legacy Project website to learn about Native nations today.

Materials

- Copies of Student Handout A for all students
- Computers (with Adobe Flash Player) for all students

Duration

This lesson plan takes approximately 60 minutes.

Procedures

1. Project the homepage for the Tribal Legacy Project website (www.lc-triballegacy.org/), showing the map of the United States and the route of the Corps of Discovery (Adobe Flash Player is needed). Explain to students that during the journey, the Corps of Discovery traveled through the homelands of many Native nations. Say to students, "The Native peoples meeting with Lewis and Clark were organized by unique and complex forms of government. Today, Native nations and tribal governments are sovereign nations within the United States. This means they establish laws and government departments to serve their citizens. In today's lesson, our purpose will be to learn about different Native nations along the Lewis and Clark National Historic Trail."

2. Say to students, "The Corps of Discovery's trip took place from 1803 to 1806. Two hundred years later in 2003–2006 the National Park Service organized a three-year commemoration of the Corps of Discovery. Commemoration is a word that means remembering or recognizing." Tell students about the Tent of Many Voices touring exhibit and how the presentations were archived as the Tribal Legacy Project.

3. From the homepage of the Tribal Legacy Project website (www.lc-triballegacy.org/), play the Introduction. This brief video serves as a trailer to the website and includes a welcome message from Allen Pinkham (Nez Perce).

4. Enter the main page to the website (http://www.lc-triballegacy.org/main.php). Give students an overview of the website organization and features. Say to students, "We will be using this website to learn about Native nations along the Lewis and Clark National Historic Trail."

5. Distribute copies of Student Handout A. Review the instructions with students. Using the website, model how to find information for the one-pager categories. Emphasize how to find the tribal websites and what information is available about the Native nations. Consider sharing a completed example of the one-pager activity.

6. Next, give time for students to work independently to complete the one-pager activity. While students are doing the activity, circulate to check for understanding.

7. When students have finished, facilitate a class discussion of their findings and post the one-pagers on the walls of the classroom.

8. Say to students, "Now that we have completed our research, let's return to the word 'commemoration.' Why do you think the word commemoration was chosen for the bicentennial instead of the word celebration?"

9. After students share responses, tell students about Roberta Conner (and play the video of her presentation titled "We Must Tell Our Story" (1:55, www.lc-triballegacy.org/video.php?vid=744r; find it in the Contemporary Life section under "Educating Others"). Facilitate a discussion of students' responses to the video. Emphasize the significance of Conner's statement, "We're still here," and how it connects to the Native nations featured in the students' one-pager activity.

Student Handout A
Tribal Legacy Project One-Pager

Directions: Follow the steps to complete the one-pager activity.

1. Go to the main page for the Tribal Legacy Project website. The website address is: https://www.lc-triballegacy.org/main.php.
2. Select a geographic region by clicking one of the four areas on the map. (Mouseover to see them.)
3. Now you will see a list of Native nations for the geographic region you selected. Select one Native nation to be the focus of your one-pager. Click on the name of the Native nation.
4. Record the following information in the one-pager categories. Use the Tribal Legacy Project site for a, b, c, and g; click through to the website of your chosen Native nation for d, e, f, h, and i.
   a. Draw and color a picture of the Native nation's flag.
   b. Identify the geographic region where the Native nation is located.
   c. Write the name of the Native nation.
   d. Identify what languages are spoken by the citizens of the Native nation.
   e. Identify the name of the Native nation leader. Also, write down this person's title. Leadership titles might be words such as President, Tribal Chairman/Chairwoman, or Chief, among others.
   f. Write down three interesting facts about the Native nation.
   g. From the Tribal Legacy Project website, select a speaker from the Native nation. Record this person's name and the title of their presentation. Write down one thing you learned from the video.
   h. Write down two current events that are important to the Native nation.
   i. On the border of the one-pager, write down a sentence from the Native nation's mission or the section titled "About."

A

B

C

D

E

F

G

H

What Were the Goals of the Lewis and Clark Corps of Discovery?

Teaching Strategy: Historical Investigation

Purpose: Students often recount the Lewis and Clark Corps of Discovery as a journey of adventure, discovery, research, and peacekeeping. The purpose of this historical investigation is to complicate and extend students' prior knowledge to understand the intent of expansion in President Thomas Jefferson's instructions to the military expedition.

Connections to the Standards

6 Ps Framework	Presence
	Perspectives
	Power
C3 Framework	D2.His.16.3-5
	D3.3.3-5
	D3.4.3-5
	D4.6.3-5
Common Core State Standards	CCSSE.ELA- LITERACY.RI.4.1
	CCSSE.ELA- LITERACY.RI.4.2
	CCSSE.ELA- LITERACY.RI.4.3
	CCSSE.ELA- LITERACY.RI.4.9
	CCSSE.ELA-LITERACY.W.4.9
	CCSSE.ELA- LITERACY.SL.4.1

Introduction

On Monday, October 5, 2015, the University of Oregon and Nike announced that the university's football team, the Ducks, would wear uniquely designed "Pioneer" uniforms for the Saturday game against Washington State University. The uniforms were presented as a celebration of the Corps of Discovery. The description of the uniform called Oregonians "innovators, free thinkers, risk takers" and said that Lewis and Clark exemplified the same values. The new design thus honored the "maverick heritage" of Oregon. The uniforms were patterned in gray for the "achromatic look of a vintage map" with topographical markings of regions in the state including the Oregon Trail. The University of Oregon duck mascot along with Lewis and Clark were included in a black and gray decal image on the helmet "as a nod to the explorers." The front of the helmet was decorated with an image of a handshake referencing the Peace Medals that were given as diplomatic symbols of "peace, prosperity and trust." In the statement announcing the uniforms, Paul Sullivan, Nike NCAA football art director and lead designer for the uniform, stated, "The handshake signifies both what Nike was built upon . . . and what Thomas Jefferson wanted to advance as the Lewis and Clark Expedition traveled west" (Nike, 2015).

The announcement of the uniform was met with critique from Indigenous peoples in Oregon. Dr. David Lewis, member of the Confederated Tribes of Grand Ronde, published a response in *Indian Country Today* that came out on game day—October 10, 2015:

> The meanings behind the uniform, the symbolism of Lewis and Clark, their map and the other attributes, ignores and makes invisible the Native peoples of this region in favor of a whitewashed history of the beginnings of the state. The history of Native peoples during the colonization of Oregon deserves mentioning for their contributions and the well-documented effects of colonization. Without this history being told, only half of the history of the state is represented. . . . It's unconscionable to think that no one in the UO football program sought advice from the UO History or Anthropology departments, or from Native staff in the university administration. (Lewis, 2015, n.p.)

Others in the University of Oregon community—Indigenous faculty, staff, students, alumni, community members, and allies—also had critiques, which were conveyed to the University of Oregon administration through a tribal advisor. Nike and University of Oregon Athletics responded to those comments and critiques by adding nine stars to the back of the helmet to represent the nine federally recognized tribes of Oregon, and edited television copy along with the game announcer's introduction of the uniforms to include a statement about Indigenous peoples in Oregon. In an "Open Letter to University of Oregon Athletics and Nike: Pioneer Uniforms Celebrate Violence and Alienate Oregon Tribes," the Native Strategic Initiatives Coalition (2015) at the University of Oregon replied to these adjustments by writing,

> Such efforts . . . give the impression that the Nine Tribes endorse the pioneer theme, or that a simple acknowledgement of Native presence as an afterthought adequately addresses the more substantive issues of the public face of the flagship institution in the state celebrating the violent, at times genocidal, practices of conquest in the region.

On game day, the Ducks lost to Washington State in double overtime. The Pioneer uniforms were showcased to nearly 60,000 fans in the arena, and thousands more watching on the PAC-12 Network.

This story, building upon the knowledge of contemporary Indigenous peoples, nations, and issues explored in the first lesson, is the starting point for Lesson Plan 2 and foregrounds the contemporary complications of Lewis and Clark's legacy. Students will inquire into the following questions: Why do you think some Native community members were upset about the uniforms? What did the uniforms represent to Nike and the University of Oregon? What did the uniforms represent to some Native community members? What were the goals of the Corps of Discovery? To answer these questions, students will act as historical investigators, and look to primary source materials, each of which will contribute to a more nuanced and layered understanding of the purpose of the Corps of Discovery.

In teaching this lesson, it is important for students to recognize that different perspectives exist across as well as within communities. For this reason, we routinely utilize the term "some" when referencing Native perspectives (i.e., "Why do you think some Native community members were upset about the uniforms?").

Materials

- The lesson plan opens with the story about the University of Oregon Pioneer football uniform designed by Nike. For background information, it is recommended teachers read:

  - » "10 Things to Know About the New Oregon Duck Uniforms" news.nike.com /news/oregon-pioneers-football-uniform
  - » "Open Letter to University of Oregon Athletics and Nike: Pioneer Uniforms Celebrate Violence and Alienate Tribes" nativestudies.uoregon.edu/2015/10/13 /open-letter-to-university-of-oregon -athletics-and-nike-pioneer-uniforms -celebrate-violence-and-alienate-oregon -tribes/
- The following chart posted for class reference:

THE GOALS OF THE CORPS OF DISCOVERY				
Before: Our Ideas	**Activity 1:** Supply List	**Activity 2:** Jefferson's Instructions	**Activity 3:** Lewis' Speech	**After:** Revisiting Our Ideas

- Copies of Student Handouts A, B, and C for all students

Duration

Each activity takes approximately 45 minutes.

Procedures

Activity 1

1. Post the class chart titled "The Goals of the Corps of Discovery." Organize students into small groups.
2. Display images of the University of Oregon Pioneer football uniform designed by Nike. Tell students the story, point out the specific features of the uniform (i.e., the silhouette of the Oregon Duck with Lewis and Clark pointing west, the topographical maps and lines depicting the Oregon Trail, and the handshake), and summarize the concerns raised.
3. Explain to students that this current event is the entry point into the lesson. Say to students, "It is clear the uniforms have different meanings—they are worth celebrating to some and are deeply troubling to others. To understand these different perspectives, we are going to do what historians do and investigate."
4. Share the purpose of the lesson: 1) begin the study of the Corps of Discovery (the past) by

connecting to the football uniform story (the present); 2) examine the purpose of the Corps of Discovery; and 3) try to understand why some Native peoples challenged the football uniform.

5. Direct student attention to the class chart. Say to students, "Let's begin with what we know. What do we know about the goals of the Corps of Discovery? Let's take a few minutes (3–5) for you to discuss in your small group. Choose someone from your group who will report what you know." During the facilitation of the discussion, the teacher records information in the first column of the chart.

6. Say to students, "Now, let's see what we can learn about the goals of the Corps of Discovery by looking at the list of supplies they carried with them. There were a total of 34 members of the military expedition and one dog—there was a lot to prepare! We are going to see a list of some of these supplies." Distribute Student Handout A to students. Say to students, "In a secret memo sent to Congress on January 18, 1803, President Thomas Jefferson requested $2,500 to pay for the Corps of Discovery. Meriwether Lewis used some of these funds to purchase supplies for the journey. This handout lists a few of the items the Corps of Discovery used. For each of the supplies listed, finish the sentence, 'I think the Corps of Discovery used this item to . . .'" Encourage students to collaborate in their small groups.

7. While students are doing the activity, circulate among groups to check for understanding and group preparedness for sharing findings with the class.

8. Facilitate a class discussion in which groups share their observations and answers to the sentence prompts. Using the class chart, record student answers to the sentence prompt "We think the goals were to . . .'" under the column "Activity 1: Supply List." Compare and contrast the column "Before: Our Ideas" with the new information under "Activity 1: Supply List."

9. If students are not completing Activity 2 on this day, conclude with the goal for the next lesson (i.e., "Next class, we will look closely at the instructions President Thomas Jefferson gave to Meriwether Lewis to investigate further the goals of the expedition.").

Activity 2

1. Organize students into small groups.
2. Explain to students the next step in the historical investigation is to examine additional sources to see what can be learned about the purpose of the Corps of Discovery. Distribute Student Handout B to all students. Say to students, "Now let's look at the instructions President Thomas Jefferson gave to Meriwether Lewis." Read the instructions for Student Handout B.
3. While students are working in small groups, circulate among the groups to check for understanding and group preparedness for sharing their findings to the class.
4. After students have discussed the documents in small groups, facilitate a class discussion in which groups share their observations and evidence. Record student findings for the goals outlined by President Thomas Jefferson in 1803 and 1804 under the chart paper column "Activity 2: Jefferson's Instructions." Explore the ways the supply list items have new meaning after reading the instructions from 1803 and 1804. During the discussion, highlight the ways in which new knowledge is complicating student understanding across the columns of the chart paper.

Activity 3

1. Organize students into small groups.
2. Say to students, "We are beginning to have a more complicated understanding of the purpose of the Corps of Discovery. The meaning of the supply list is starting to change as we understand President Jefferson's intentions about expansion. We have one more source to investigate."
3. Distribute Student Handout C to all students. Tell students you will read a speech that Meriwether Lewis gave to the Yankton Sioux on August 30,1804. Say to students, "Each time Lewis and Clark met with a Native nation during their journey, they organized an assembly. All members of the Corps of Discovery wore their Army-issued dress uniforms. They would shoot their air rifle to try and impress those who watched. Gifts were exchanged including the flag, Jefferson peace medals, and other items we saw on the supply list. Student Handout C contains excerpts of

the speech Meriwether Lewis delivered at these assemblies."

4. Read with emphasis, in particular, on the words *children, Great Father, Old Fathers, obey, your only father, only friend, Cities as numerous as the Stars in the heavens.* Encourage students to follow along as you read and circle or underline any words that stand out to them. As the excerpt is read, you may want to stop and ask questions about what the students find significant. For example, ask students about why they think the word "children" was used. If needed, clarify that it was a way to reinforce U.S. power and authority over Native peoples and lands.

5. Record a summary/paraphrasing of students' comments under the column "Activity 3: Lewis' Speech." Compare and contrast as a class the understandings and interpretations between the columns.

6. Tell students to see the reverse side of Student Handout C. Say to students, "If someone asked you now, 'What were the goals of the Lewis and Clark Corps of Discovery?' what would you say now that we have completed this historical investigation?" Provide a few minutes for students to confer with a partner. Then, complete the handout by individually responding to the sentence prompts. Facilitate a discussion in which students share their responses in small groups or as a class. Record a summary/paraphrase of students' comments under the column "After: Revisiting Our Ideas." Compare and contrast as a class the understandings and interpretations between the columns with emphasis on "Before" and "After."

8. Return to the image of the Pioneer football uniforms that was shown at the beginning of the lesson. Facilitate a discussion by asking the following question, "Now that we have examined the purpose of the Corps of Discovery, why do you think some Native people were upset by the uniforms? In what way has your understanding of the images on the uniforms changed?"

Student Handout A

Directions: This is a list of some of the supplies the Corps of Discovery took with them on the journey. For each of the supplies listed, finish the sentence, "I think the Corps of Discovery used this item to . . ." (last column of the chart).

What did Lewis and Clark take with them on the journey?	I think the Corps of Discovery used this item to . . .
1 Keeled Boat: A large boat. A small gun was mounted on the bow (front) and a gun on the stern (back).	
2 Pirogues: A boat with a flat bottom.	
193 pounds of portable soup stored in 32 canisters: Dried soup that becomes broth when hot water is added.	
Army Dress Uniforms: Lewis and Clark were captains in the Army. Other members of the military expedition were soldiers in the Army. Their clothing was issued by the Army.	
Medical supplies: Lewis and Clark carried a variety of medicine and instruments for surgery.	

What did Lewis and Clark take with them on the journey?	*I think the Corps of Discovery used this item to . . .*
176 pounds of gun powder packed in 52 lead canisters: Explosive black powder was carried in protective canisters.	
Weapons: Members of the military expedition carried guns issued by the Army. In addition, the military expedition brought 15 rifles and 15 muskets.	
1 air gun: Long-barreled air-pump gun that fired 20–40 shots at a time.	
Branding iron: When the branding iron was heated and pressed against an object, it left a mark with Captain Lewis' name.	
1 Hadley's quadrant and 2 sextants: Instruments that calculate longitude and latitude.	
Quill, pens, small notebook, and ink powder	

(*continued*)

What did Lewis and Clark take with them on the journey?	I think the Corps of Discovery used this item to . . .
89 Jefferson Peace Medals: The medals were ordered in five different sizes.	
20 pounds of assorted beads (mostly blue) and 5 pounds of small, white glass beads	
U.S. flags: Fifteen-star flag representing the number of states at the time of the Lewis and Clark Expedition.	

Based on the supplies, what do you think were the goals of the Corps of Discovery?

I think the goals of the Corps of Discovery were to . . .

I think this because . . .

Student Handout B

Directions: President Thomas Jefferson gave two sets of instructions to the Corps of Discovery. As a small group, read the (edited) documents and identify the goals listed by President Jefferson. Record your findings under "Our Notes." Choose a member of your group to share your findings with the class.

June 20, 1803	Our Notes
The object of your mission is to explore the Missouri River to see if its river system meets the Pacific Ocean. You will also explore other rivers to see if there is a direct route across the continent.	*President Jefferson instructs Lewis and Clark to. . . . .*
You will likely meet and trade with native people along the way. Record the names of the native nations and their population. Describe how they live, what they eat, what they wear, and how they care of the sick.	
Because all nations want to grow bigger and stronger, it will be useful to find out what you can about their religion, laws, and beliefs. This information will help those who try to civilize and teach them.	
Also pay attention to the land and soil, the growth of vegetables, especially those not of the United States. Pay attention to the animals, especially those not known in the United States. Also, the mineral productions of every kind, but more particularly metals. Finally, pay attention to the climate and record the weather.	

Excerpt adapted from www.loc.gov/exhibits/lewisandclark/transcript57.html

January 22, 1804	Our Notes
We gained control of New Orleans on the 20th of December and we established our troops and government there. Your instructions were given to you prior to this development.	*President Jefferson instructs Lewis and Clark to. . . . .*
The United States now has authority over the land from the Louisiana Purchase. The United States now is the country allowed to set up trade with natives living on this land. You should inform the various people you meet on your journey the Spaniards have agreed to withdraw all their troops from all the waters and country of the Mississippi and Missouri. Now all the Spaniards and French people who settled there will be under the government of the United States. From now on, we are their fathers and friends and they should embrace this change.	
Tell the people you meet that we have sent you to find out about the country and the nations living there. We want to find out where, when, and how we should trade with them and what to trade for their furs. Tell them as soon as you return with this information, we shall send our supplies and people to meet with them.	
We shall get to know them as soon as possible. They will find us faithful friends and protectors.	

Excerpt adapted from cdn.loc.gov/service/mss/mtj//mtj1/029/029_0957_0958.pdf

Student Handout C

Directions: Each time Lewis and Clark met with a Native nation, they organized an assembly. This was the speech Captain Lewis delivered at the gatherings. As you listen to the speech, read along circle and/or underline words and phrases that are meaningful to you.

Children.—It gives us much pleasure to have met you in council. We salute you as the children of your Great Father the great Chief of the United States of America. . . . Now open your ears so that you may hear his words and clear your minds to understand them.

Children.—We have come to inform you, and all other native nations, that a great Council was held between this great Chief of the United States of America, and your Old fathers the French and Spaniards. In this council, it was agreed that the white men on the waters of the Missouri and Mississippi will obey the commands of the Great Chief of America. He has adopted them as his children and they are now one family with us. You were trading with the French and Spaniards. Now you are trading only with the United States. They are bound to obey the commands of President Thomas Jefferson, who is now your only Great father.

Children.—The Great Chief of the United States of America has become your only father. He is the only friend you can look to for protection. He will take care of you, serve you, and not deceive you.

Children.—Know the great chief who has offered you the hand of friendship, is the Great Chief of the United States of America, whose Cities are as numerous as the Stars of the heavens.

Children.—Follow the Councils of your great father, and the great spirit will smile upon your nation, and in future years will make you outnumber the trees.

Excerpt adapted from https://www.nps.gov/mnrr/planyourvisit/upload/L&CSpeech.pdf.

Directions: Now that we have completed our investigation, reflect on what you think were the goals of the Corps of Discovery. Finish the sentences.

1. After our historical investigation, I think the goals of the Corps of Discovery were . . .

2. The evidence that supports what I think is . . .

    A.

    B.

    C.

The Jefferson Peace Medals

Teaching Strategy: Historical Investigation

Purpose: As highlighted in Elementary Lesson Plan 2, the Jefferson Peace Medals were significant to the diplomatic goals of the Corps of Discovery. The historical and contemporary meanings of the Jefferson Peace Medals are the focal point for Lesson Plan 3.

Connections to the Standards

6 Ps Framework	Presence
	Perspectives
	Power
	Partnership
C3 Framework	D2.His.5.3-5
	D2.His.10.3-5
	D2.His.16.3-5
	D3.3.3-5
	D3.4.3-5
	D4.6.3-5
	D4.7.3-5
Common Core State Standards	CCSS.ELA-Literacy.RI.4.1
	CCSS.ELA-Literacy.RI.4.2
	CCSS.ELA-Literacy.RI.4.3
	CCSS.ELA-Literacy.RI.4.7
	CCSS.ELA-Literacy.RI.4.9
	CCSS.ELA-Literacy.W.4.9
	CCSS.ELA-LITERACY.SL.4.1
	CCSS.ELA.LITERACY.SL.4.2

Introduction

The supply list for the Corps of Discovery included 89 peace medals in five different sizes. The peace medals were significant to the assemblies organized with each of the Native nations Lewis and Clark met during the military expedition. Dressed in Army dress uniforms and ready with gifts, the protocol included the "Great Father" speech delivered by Meriwether Lewis and a demonstration of military strength by firing the air gun. Based on their judgment of tribal leader status and organization, Jefferson Peace Medals were distributed by size as Lewis and Clark selected a "Great Chief" to get a large medal and secondary chiefs to receive medium or small medals. Gerard Baker (Mandan-Hidatsa), former Superintendent of the Lewis and Clark National Historic Trail, observes in an interview included in this lesson that members of Native nations meeting with Lewis and Clark "had been visited by quite a few people. I think by then they realized it was a routine that they had to go through." Gift-giving and chief-making with medals were strategies used by the British, French, and Spanish to assert authority in the context of the Doctrine of Discovery.

"Peace and friendship" are the words inscribed on one side of the Jefferson Peace Medals. The words and actions accompanying the delivery of the medals suggest different intentions of President Thomas Jefferson. The "Great Father" speech included instructions to remove

> all the flags and medals which you may have received from your old fathers the French and the Spaniards, or from any other nation whatever, your father will give you new flags and new medals of his own in exchange. . . . It is not proper since you have become the children of the great chief . . . of America, that you should wear or keep those emblems of attachments to any other great father but himself, nor will it be pleasing to him if you continue to do so. (August 30, 1804; Retrieved from https://www.nps.gov/mnrr/planyourvisit/upload/L&CSpeech.pdf)

Included with receiving the medals was the "Certificate of Loyalty." Signed by the selected chief and Meriwether Lewis, the standardized form declared this leader "to be the friend and ally of the said States: the government of which will at all times be extended for their protection, so long as they do acknowledge the authority of the same" (1803; Retrieved from www.loc.gov/exhibits/lewisandclark/lewis-landc.html#43). The function of the assemblies, speech, medals, and certificates is further made clear with the historical record of a meeting taking place in the fall of 1804 between

François Larocque, a French-Canadian fur trader working for the British Northwest Company, and Lewis and Clark at Fort Mandan. The journals authored by military expedition member Patrick Gass note Larocque and those traveling with him were met with suspicion by Lewis and Clark. In Larocque's journal, he recounts that

> Just as I arrived, they were dispatching a man for me, having heard that I intended giving flags and medals to the Indians, which they forbid me from giving in the name of the United States, saying that the Government looked upon those things as the sacred emblems of the attachment of the Indians to their country. As I had neither flags nor medals, I ran no risk of disobeying those orders, of which I assured them. (November 29, 1804;Mussulman, n.d.)

In the context of the Doctrine of Discovery, it becomes clear that Lewis and Clark were leaving tangible evidence to establish claim through the principles of the Doctrine of Discovery. Robert Miller (2008) refers to Lewis and Clark's actions as "accepted practices and rituals of Discovery" (p. 110). The assemblies, speeches, medals, gifts, and certificates—along with mapping, naming places, branding trees, constructing forts, recording enormous amount of information—were "designed to have legal significance under the Doctrine" (Miller, 2008, p. 111). The military mission left an abundance of evidence the United States occupied and claimed the land.

This lesson plan centers the narratives held by Native peoples about contact with the Corps of Discovery. Students rotate through six stations (one reading and five videos). The videos are from the Tribal Legacy Project website (www.lc-triballegacy.org/) used in the first lesson plan. The selected material for this lesson plan focuses on Native perspectives related to first impressions of the Corps of Discovery along with experience at the assemblies in which the Jefferson Peace Medals were received. Students compare and contrast the multiple meanings of the Jefferson Peace Medals held by Native peoples and the Corps of Discovery.

Materials

The following chart is posted for class reference:

The Jefferson Peace Medals	
Native Peoples' Perspectives	Lewis and Clark's Perspectives

- Copies of Student Handout A and B for all students
- One copy of the station description for each station site
- Computers for showing videos at Stations 2–6

Duration

Activity 1 will take approximately 80 minutes. Activity 2 will take approximately 30 minutes.

Procedure

Activity 1

1. Post the class chart titled "The Jefferson Peace Medals." Organize students into six small groups.
2. Project visuals of the Jefferson Peace Medals. Explain to students that today's lesson plan will focus on the Jefferson Peace Medals. Ask students to share what they learned about the Jefferson Peace Medals from the prior lesson plan. During discussion, review with students the significance of the assemblies Lewis and Clark organized with tribal nations. Reference the content of Meriwether Lewis' speech delivered at these assemblies and the use of the Jefferson Peace Medals. Ask students, "What did the Jefferson Peace Medals mean to Lewis and Clark?" Record student comments under the column "Lewis and Clark's Perspective."
3. Next, ask students what they think Native peoples might have felt or experienced during the assemblies and receiving the Jefferson Peace Medals. Say to students, "We are going to explore these perspectives by visiting six stations featuring stories about contact with the Corps of Discovery from Native perspectives." Distribute Student Handout A and review instructions for the activity.
4. In small groups, students rotate through the six stations (approximately 8 minutes at each station). For Stations 2–6, video transcripts are available at each website. Each station description includes information about the author and speakers. Students record three things they learn about contact with the Corps of Discovery from Native perspectives.
5. After students have visited each station, facilitate a discussion in which students discuss their findings. Ask students, "What

were the meanings of the Jefferson Peace Medals to Native nations?" Record student comments under the column, "Native Peoples' Perspectives." It is important to observe with students how the meanings and stories are unique. When recording student observations, model how to cite evidence. For example, "The Arikara were confused by Lewis and Clark naming a 'Great Chief' because they had three equal leaders" (Greta White Calf and Yvonne Fox).

Activity 2

1. Distribute copies of Student Handout B to all students.
2. Say to students, "The National Park Service recognized the 200th anniversary of Lewis and Clark in 2003–2006. The 'Corps of Discovery II Logo' was designed in 1999 and the 'Inclusion Logo' was designed in 2004." Project images of the logos and read the descriptive text on Student Handout B for each logo. Ask students, "What is the message of each logo?" Invite students to also reflect on how different choices for symbols and words impact the message and significance of the Corps of Discovery 200 years later. Consider providing further context by showing one or both of the following videos from the Tribal Legacy Project: "Not Reconciling but Healing" (Otis Halfmoon, Nez Perce) (1:50, www.lc-triballegacy.org/video.php?vid=289&query=otis%20halfmoon) and "Hope for the Future" (Gerard Baker, Mandan Hidatsa) (4:54, www.lc-triballegacy.org/video.php?vid=1044&query=Gerard%20Baker). (Adobe Flash Player is required for the Tribal Legacy Project website.)

3. Next, project the image of the logo designed by the Circle of Tribal Advisors and read the descriptive text. Ask students to share their observations and consider how this logo relates to the stations.
4. Tell students to turn over Student Handout B. Explain to students that they are going to use their knowledge of perspectives of the Jefferson Peace Medal to imagine a redesign of the logo for the 300th anniversary of the Corps of Discovery in the year 2106. Before students begin the activity, share the recommendations published by the Circle of Tribal Advisors in *Enough Good People: Reflections on Tribal Involvement and Inter-Cultural Collaboration 2003–2006*. Use the following link to access the publication: cms.lc-triballegacy.org/book. Click on "Recommendations."
5. After students have completed the activity, facilitate time for students to share the symbols and meanings of their logos. Post the logos in the classroom.

Extension Activities

- As a class or individually, students write a letter to the Superintendent of the Lewis and Clark National Historic Trail with recommendations and suggested logo designs for the tricentennial of the Corps of Discovery.
- The "Recommendations" page from *Enough Good People: Reflections on Tribal Involvement and Inter-Cultural Collaboration 2003–2006* lists several commemoration events for tribal involvement. Students select an event and make recommendations for programming with tribal partnership.

Student Handout A

Directions: During this activity, you will visit six stations. Each station provides Native peoples' perspectives of contact with the Corps of Discovery. First, read the description of the content. Second, read the document (Station 1) or watch the video (Stations 2–6). Third, write three things you learn from the speaker. Be prepared to share what you learn with our class.

Station	Speaker	Write three things you learned from the speaker.
1	Gerard Baker (Mandan-Hidatsa)	1. 2. 3.
2	Angel Sobotta (Nez Perce)	1. 2. 3.
3	Germaine White (Salish & Pend d'Oreille)	1. 2. 3.
4	Robert Miller (Shawnee)	1. 2. 3.
5	Greta White Calf and Yvonne Fox (Arikara)	1. 2. 3.
6	Roberta "Bobbie" Conner (Cayuse, Umatilla, Nez Perce)	1. 2. 3.

STATION 1: GERARD BAKER (MANDAN HIDATSA)

Title	"Interview with Gerard Baker" (Reading)
Description	This interview is posted on the Public Broadcasting Service (PBS) website featuring the Corps of Discovery. Gerard Baker, Mandan-Hidatsa, worked for the National Park Service for 34 years and retired in 2010. He held important positions such as Assistant Director for American Indian Relations and Superintendent of the Lewis and Clark National Historic Trail. During the Winter of 1804–1805, the Corps of Discovery built and lived in Fort Mandan in what is now referred to as central North Dakota. There were five Native towns in the area (two Mandan and three Hidatsa) that were farming and trading communities. Today, the Mandan and Hidatsa are joined by the Arikara Nation and referred to as the Three Affiliated Tribes (www.mhanation.com/). The Mandan, Hidatsa, and Arikara Nation is located on the Fort Berthold Indian Reservation consisting of 988,000 acres in central North Dakota.
Source	www.pbs.org/lewisandclark/living/idx6.html (The excerpts presented in this handout are edited from the original.)
	When Lewis and Clark talked about a new "Great Father" in Washington, how did the Indians react? **Gerard Baker:** I do not think they would think about it a whole lot. The French and the British told them the same thing. I think by the time Lewis and Clark travelled through, they had been visited by quite a few people. I think by then they realized it was a routine that they had to go through. They would list to the speeches, accept the medals and gifts. In fact, the tribe at the time expected gifts. *What was the meaning of the peace medals?* **Gerard Baker:** Peace medals symbolized two different things to Native people and Lewis and Clark. For Thomas Jefferson's captains, the peace medal meant a recognition of United States authority. For Native people, accepting a peace medal might simply mean recognition that we are equals. We are not fathers and children, but we are all one.

STATION 2: ANGEL SOBOTTA (NEZ PERCE)

Title	"Lewis and Clark Smelled"
Description	In this video recorded in 2006 and posted on the Tribal Legacy Project website, Angel Sobotta, Nez Perce, shares a story about the Nez Perce's first impressions of the Corps of Discovery. The Corps of Discovery traveled through Nez Perce homelands in the fall of 1805 and on their return journey in the spring of 1806. At that time, the Nez Perce lived and moved seasonally across 17 million acres of land that is now known as Idaho, Oregon, Washington, and Montana. Today, the Nez Perce Indian Reservation is 750,000 acres and located in north-central Idaho (www.nezperce.org/).
Source and Video Link	www.lc-triballegacy.org/video.php?vid=420&query=sobotta (Find on the Tribal Legacy website under Contact/Lewis and Clark.)

STATION 3: GERMAINE WHITE (SALISH & PEND D'OREILLE)

Title	"Salish Meet Lewis and Clark"
Description	In this video recorded in 2005 and posted on the Tribal Legacy Project website, Germaine White, Salish & Pend d'Oreille, shares a story passed down from generations and told by elders about the Salish meeting members of the Lewis & Clark Expedition. Oral history and archeological studies report the Salish living in what is now known as Montana for over 12,000 years. Today, the Salish, Pend d'Oreille, and Kootenai together inhabit Flathead Indian Reservation located on 1,317,500 acres of land in northwestern Montana (www.cskt.org/).
Source and Video Link	www.lc-triballegacy.org/video.php?vid=514&query=germaine%20 white. Find on the Tribal Legacy website under Contact/Lewis & Clark.

STATION 4: ROBERT MILLER (SHAWNEE)

Title	"The Peace Medals" (3 minutes and 45 seconds)
Description	In this video recorded in 2006 and posted on the Tribal Legacy website, Robert Miller shares Indigenous perspectives about the meaning of the Jefferson Peace Medals. Robert Miller is a citizen of the Eastern Shawnee in Oklahoma (www.estoo-nsn.gov/). He is a professor of law at the Sandra Day O'Connor College of Law at Arizona State University.
Source and Video Link	www.lc-triballegacy.org/video.php?vid=1417&query=robert%20 miller (Find on the Tribal Legacy website at Contact/Lewis and Clark.)

STATION 5: GRETA WHITE CALF AND YVONNE FOX (ARIKARA)

Title	"Lewis & Clark and the Idea of a 'Grand Chief'" (4 minutes and 40 seconds)
Description	In this video recorded in 2004 and posted on the Tribal Legacy Project website, Greta White Calf and Yvonne Fox share the story of the Arikara meeting Lewis and Clark on October 8, 1804. At this time, the farming communities of the Arikara consisted of three large settlements on what is now known as northern South Dakota along the Missouri River. The Arikara grew crops of corn, beans, squash, tobacco, watermelon, and pumpkins. They traded with the Teton Sioux. The political and trading life of the Arikara was longstanding and complicated. Lewis and Clark did not understand the government structure of the three leaders of the Arikara towns. They selected one of the leaders to be a "Grand Chief" and gave many gifts to this leader. This caused confusion because the three leaders were viewed as equals by the Arikara. Today, the Arikara are joined by the Mandan and Hidatsa and referred to as the Three Affiliated Tribes (www.mhanation.com/). The Mandan, Hidatsa, and Arikara Nation is located on the Fort Berthold Indian Reservation consisting of 988,000 acres in central North Dakota.
Source and Video Link	www.lc-triballegacy.org/video.php?vid=900&query=greta%20white%20calf (Find on the Tribal Legacy website at Contact/Lewis and Clark.)

STATION 6: ROBERTA CONNER (CAYUSE, UMATILLA, NEZ PERCE)

Title	"Prophecy for Difficult Times" (3 minutes and 15 seconds)
Description	In this video recorded in 2006 and posted on the Tribal Legacy Project website, Roberta (Bobbie) Conner shares the story of events occurring on April 27 and 28, 1806. The Corps of Discovery was returning east and camped for two nights with Chief Yel-lep-pit and the Walla Walla tribal nation. At that time, the Walla Walla, along with the Cayuse and Umatilla, moved with the seasons in the Columbia River region that is now known as northern Oregon and southern Washington. Today, the Walla Walla are part of the Confederated Tribes of the Umatilla Indian Reservation (ctuir.org/) consisting of 172,000 acres in northeast Oregon.
Source and Video Link	www.lc-triballegacy.org/video.php?vid=737&query=conner (Find on the Tribal Legacy website at Contact/Lewis and Clark.)

Directions: Compare and contrast the bicentennial logos with the Jefferson Peace Medals. Record and share your observations.

National Park Service (1999) **Corps of Discovery II Logo** The National Park Service used the image from the original Jefferson Peace Medal as inspiration for the logo.	
National Park Service (2004) **Inclusion Logo** This logo was released as an update to the 1999 emblem. It represents how the National Park Service was changed by the listening sessions conducted with Native nations about the plans for the bicentennial.	
Circle of Tribal Advisors (1999) The Circle of Tribal Advisors was created to give guidance to the National Park Service and organize tribal participation during the bicentennial commemoration. The committee released this logo in response to the National Park Service 1999 emblem of "celebration."	

Design a Logo for the National Park Service

Directions: The year is 2106 and it is 300 years after the Lewis and Clark Corps of Discovery. The National Park Service is honoring the tricentennial (three hundredth anniversary) of the Corps of Discovery with events planned across the nation. You have been asked to design a logo for the National Park Service. The National Park Service would like the logo to be an update of what was used for the 200th anniversary. The goal of the National Park Service is to provide the perspective of Native peoples to understand the history and legacy of the Corps of Discovery.

Tricentennial of the Corps of Discovery, 2106

Sacagawea: Beyond Interpreter and Guide

Teaching Strategy: Historical Investigation

Purpose: This lesson introduces students to all we do not know about Sacagawea and invites them into a conversation about how historians draw conclusions from limited evidence.

Connection to the Standards

6 Ps Framework	Perspectives
	Power
C3 Framework	D1.5.3-5
	D2.His.1.3-5
	D2.His.3.3-5
	D2.His.9.3-5
	D2.His.10.3-5
	D2.His.12.3-5
	D2.His.17.3-5
	D3.3.3.5
	D4.2.3-5
Common Core State Standards	CCSS.ELA-Literacy.RI.4.2
	CCSE.ELA-Literacy.RI.4.3
	CCSE.ELA-Literacy.RI.4.6
	CCSS.ELA-Literacy.RI.4.9
	CCSS.ELA-Literacy.W.4.9
	CCSS.ELA-Literacy.SL.4.1
	CCSS.ELA-Litearcy.SL.4.4

Introduction

There are hundreds of monuments to Sacagawea across the country. She is depicted in paintings installed in museums and government buildings. There are peaks, lakes, rivers, roads, schools, parks, and interpretative centers named after Sacagawea. The Sacagawea dollar was introduced in 2000 and in circulation starting in 2002. There are hundreds of children's books about Sacagawea. Many of these books have been reviewed negatively by Indigenous scholars like Debbie Reese (Nambé Owingeh), founder of the blog American Indians in Children's Literature (AICL) (americanindiansinchildrensliterature.blogspot.com).

There were two ships in the U.S. Navy named the USS Sacagawea during World War II and in 2006, descendants of Sacagawea participated in the sponsorship and launching of the USNS Sacagawea. Underlying all the commemoration, the only historical records of her life are the oral histories shared by her descendants and the journals from the Corps of Discovery. Between November 4, 1804, and August 17, 1806, she is mentioned 73 times in the journals (Thomasma, 1997, pp. 93–95) and there are 23 different spellings of her name (Saindon, 1988, p. 7). We do not know exactly when she was born or when she died. We do not know much about her childhood or her life after the expedition. We have no historical record authored by Sacagawea herself and there is no consensus on how her name is spelled or pronounced. Rather than seek certainty about these questions, this lesson introduces students to all we do not know about Sacagawea and invites them into a conversation about how historians draw conclusions from limited evidence.

The lesson plan begins with a Visual Thinking Strategies (VTS) exercise to elicit students' prior knowledge about Sacagawea by viewing images of the mural painting *Lewis and Clark at Three Forks* (Edgar S. Paxson, 1912) and adapting the VTS protocol for social studies to examine a timeline of Sacagawea's life derived from three sources (*Sacagawea,* Lise Erdrich, 2003; *Fort Clatsop: A Charbonneau Family Portrait,* Irving Anderson, 2002; and "Lewis and Clark: Inside the Corps" [www.pbs.org/lewisandclark/inside/index.html]). As described by Philip Yenawine (2014) in *Visual Thinking Strategies: Using Art to Deepen Learning Across School Disciplines,* VTS involves selecting an image and allowing students to view the image silently, then asking three questions: What is happening in this picture or document? What do you see that makes you say that? What more can we find? During the discussion, the teacher signals listening by providing a "visual paraphrase" (Yenawine, 2014, p. 28–29), pointing to elements in the painting and document. In addition, the teacher offers a verbal paraphrase after a student's observation. As the discussion unfolds, the teacher links comments from students to emphasize agreement, disagreement, and connections "to indicate that individual contributions matter" (Yenawine, 2014, p. 29). The teacher does not contribute interpretation and remains a neutral facilitator throughout the process. Yenawine argues that "by letting the students go through their own process, they learn how knowledge is created: that is not simply 'delivered' by the teacher, a parent, or media" (p. 30). In this way, VTS is similar to the inquiry process as outlined by the C3 Framework for Social Studies and the Common Core State Standards. The final step of the process is for the teacher to extend a thank you to students, such as, "I am grateful for and excited about your observations and ideas." This affirms that the process "isn't about right or wrong but about thinking, and indicates, through paraphrasing and linking, that the students singly and together are capable of wonderful, grounded ideas" (Yenawine, 2014, p. 31).

When viewing *Lewis and Clark at Three Forks* during the VTS activity, students often first identify Sacagawea and frequently observe she is "pointing the way" and carrying a baby. Sometimes they share learning that she was an interpreter for the expedition. Commonly they identify York (a Black man enslaved by William Clark who accompanied the military expedition; refer to Elementary Lesson Plan 7), the captains, and speculate about who is depicted on the left and right. Occasionally, they wonder why the artist did not include Seaman, the dog. Next, students view the timeline of Sacagawea's life. Teachers using this lesson frequently share that some students are surprised by Sacagawea's age and then others point out her exact age is unknown. Students are interested in the entries about her capture, the multiple entries about her death, and the different spellings of her name (Sacagawea, Sacajawea, and Sakakawea are listed). One teacher shared that students wanted to revisit the painting to try and identify Charbonneau after discussing the entries about Sacagawea's marriage. The result of using VTS as an opening activity is that students arrive at the purpose of the lesson through their own observations.

The jigsaw activity that follows the opening VTS exercise is inspired by a lesson plan titled "Seeking Sacagawea's Role" presented by the Missouri Historical Society for the Lewis and Clark Bicentennial Exhibition (1999–2003) in which students are introduced to Sacagawea's contributions beyond interpreter and guide (www.lewisandclarkexhibit.org/4 _0_0/page_4_1_7_1_3_4.html). In the jigsaw activity for this lesson plan, students explore the limited historical record about Sacagawea and how this presents challenges for historians in representing her story. Topics include: the multiple spellings of Sacagawea's name, the perspectives of Lemhi Shoshone as well as Mandan and Hidatsa peoples, and excerpts from the Corps of Discovery journals. After conferring with classmates assigned the same topic, students return to base groups to share their knowledge about their topic. Teachers using this jigsaw activity report students begin to create a fuller understanding of Sacagawea as a result of their collaboration. This carries forward into the final activity of the lesson plan.

While Secondary Lesson Plan 2 is an example of using a textbook section to begin a teaching activity, this lesson plan is an example of how to end with a textbook excerpt. Textbooks often represent Sacagawea as a guide and interpreter to the Corps of Discovery. After students have participated in the VTS and jigsaw lesson plan sequence, they can add to this story of Sacagawea. Examples of words students come up with to describe Sacagawea (handout G) are: brave, teenager, strong, scientist, peacemaker, resourceful, friend, sister, Lemhi Shoshone, Mandan and Hidatsa, voter, patient, calm, provider, curious, and focused. Such a list indicates that students understand Sacagawea beyond interpreter and guide.

Materials

- Copies of Student Handout A for all students and one copy for the teacher to project
- Copies of Student Handout B for all students
- One copy of Student Handouts C (blue paper), D (green paper), E (yellow paper), F (purple paper), and G for each group. For organizing the jigsaw activity, Student Handouts C, D, E, and F are copied on the color paper listed.
- Teacher Handout A

Duration

Activity 1 takes approximately 30 minutes. Activity 2 takes approximately 45 minutes. Activity 3 takes approximately 5–8 minutes.

Procedures

Activity 1

1. Arrange students in small groups of four.
2. Say to students, "Today we are going to begin by looking at a painting. After I project the first image, we will look at it silently before discussion." Project the image of *Lewis and Clark at Three Forks* (Edgar S. Paxson, 1912) (mhs.mt.gov/education/Capitol/Art/House -Lobby).

3. Once students have viewed the image silently, begin the protocol for Visual Thinking Strategies by asking: What is happening in this picture? What do you see that makes you say that? What more can we find? Facilitate the discussion by using visual paraphrase, verbal paraphrase, and linking student comments. Close the discussion with a thank you by saying, "Your observations about the painting were excellent. In particular, you made important observations about Sacagawea. Today our focus is going to be learning about Sacagawea."

4. Distribute copies of Student Handout A to all students and project the handout. Say to students, "Just like we did with the painting, look at this document silently before discussion."

5. Once students have viewed the document silently, begin the protocol for VTS adapted for social studies by asking: What is happening in this document? What do you see that makes you say that? What more can we find? As students begin sharing their observations of the document, use the following questions to set the foundation for the lesson plan purpose: Why do you think some dates are listed as "about" while others are listed as a date? What evidence do you think historians use to determine the timeline listings? There is no direct record of the date of Sacagawea's birth and there are different accounts about her death. How do you think historians make decisions on what to say about Sacagawea? Close the VTS discussion with a "thank you."

6. Say to students, "Sacagawea is one of the most famous women in U.S. history. There are hundreds of children's books about her, there are places named after her, there are many statues of her, she is on a U.S. gold coin, and Navy ships have been named after her. However, there are no historical records written by Sacagawea about her life and experiences. The only written record about her is from the military expedition journals. What do you think is helpful about the journals? What do you think are the limits of the journals? The purpose of today's investigation is to explore how Sacagawea is represented in the historical record."

Activity 2

1. Distribute copies of Student Handout B to all students. Distribute one copy of Student

Handout C (blue paper), D (green paper), E (yellow paper), and F (purple paper) to each group. Explain to students they will work as a team to learn about Sacagawea. Say to students, "Each member of your group will investigate one topic about Sacagawea. You will do this by meeting with classmates who are investigating the same topic. Then, you will return to your base group to share what you learned."

2. Say to students, "Each base group member is assigned one topic: Sacagawea's Name (Student Handout C, blue paper), Lemhi Shoshone Perspective (Student Handout D, green paper), Mandan and Hidatsa Perspective (Student Handout E, yellow paper), or the Lewis and Clark Journals (Student Handout F, purple paper)."

3. After each base group member is assigned a topic to investigate, say to students, "Now, find classmates with the same color paper as you. Work together to answer the questions on Student Handout B. Your goal is to become an expert on this topic so you can teach your base group about what you learned." Assist students in reorganizing into topic groups.

4. While students are doing the activity, circulate among groups to check for understanding and preparedness for sharing findings with base groups.

5. Say to students, "Now that you have completed the investigation on your topic, return to your base groups. When you are ready, begin sharing information with each other and complete the chart."

6. While students are doing the activity, circulate among groups to check for understanding and preparedness for sharing findings with the class.

7. After students complete Student Handout B, facilitate a discussion using the following questions: What is something new you learned about Sacagawea? What do you think is important to remember about her story?

Activity 3

1. Direct students to the section in their textbook about Sacagawea or project Teacher Handout A for examples. Say to students, "Sacagawea's story is often simplified when she is described in textbooks. What does our textbook say about her?" (Or, if using Teacher Handout A, "What do these examples say about her?") As a class, read the short excerpts and note the words

used to describe Sacagawea and the spellings given for her name. Emphasize the recurring description as "interpreter" and "guide."

2. Say to students, "Now that we have completed our investigation, we can add to this version of her story." Distribute one copy of Student Handout G to each group. Review the instructions.

3. When students are finished, collect the handouts. Say to students, "Tomorrow I will show you Word Art based on our lists."

4. Using the Word Art website (wordart.com), generate an image presenting the words students listed.

5. The next day, share the Word Art image with students. Say to students, "If someone asks you about Sacagawea, what will you say? What makes you say that?"

6. Project the original painting *Lewis and Clark at Three Forks* again and ask students: "How does this new knowledge of Sacagawea impact your interpretation of this painting?" Follow-up questions might prompt students to consider when the painting was created (over 100 years after the Corps of Discovery), what information the artist likely used to create the painting, what message the students thought the artist was trying communicate, and so on.

Student Handout A
Sacagawea: Timeline

The following timeline of Sacagawea's life was adapted from three sources: *Sacagawea* by Lise Erdrich (2003), *Fort Clatsop: A Charbonneau Family Portrait* by Irving Anderson (2002), and "Lewis and Clark: Inside the Corps" (www.pbs.org/lewisandclark/inside/index.html).

About 1788	Sacagawea is born in present-day Idaho into the Lemhi Shoshone Tribe.
About 1800	At about 12 years of age, Sacagawea is captured by the Hidatsa people in present-day Montana and brought to a Hidatsa village in present-day North Dakota.
About 1803	At about 15 years old, Sacagawea is given in marriage to Toussaint Charbonneau. He is a French-Canadian fur trader.
October 26, 1804	The Corps of Discovery arrives at the Mandan and Hidatsa villages where Sacagawea lives along the Knife River in present-day North Dakota.
February 11, 1805	At about 17 years old, Sacagawea gives birth to a son named Jean Baptiste Charbonneau at Fort Mandan near present-day Washburn, ND.
April 7, 1805	The Corps of Discovery, including Sacagawea, Jean Baptiste, and Charbonneau, leave Fort Mandan.
May 14, 1805	Sacagawea rescues the expedition's supplies after the boat she was traveling in nearly capsizes in high wind. Lewis and Clark name a river after her.
July 28, 1805	The military expedition reaches the Three Forks of the Missouri River, the site where the Hidatsa captured Sacagawea from the Lemhi Shoshone Tribe.
August 17, 1805	Sacagawea is reunited with the Lemhi Shoshone people and recognizes her brother, Cameahwait. Cameahwait is now a chief.
November 24, 1805	Members of the military expedition vote to determine where they will spend the winter. Sacagawea's vote is recorded. Fort Clatsop is constructed inland from the Pacific Ocean.
March 23, 1806	The Corps of Discovery begins the return journey.
August 14, 1806	The military expedition returns to the Mandan and Hidatsa villages at Knife River. Sacagawea, Jean Baptiste, and Charbonneau stay while Lewis and Clark continue east. Charbonneau is paid $500.33 for his service with the expedition.
About 1809	Sacagawea and Charbonneau leave Jean Baptiste (about 4 years old) with William Clark in St. Louis.
Summer 1812	Sacagawea gives birth to a daughter named Lizette.
December 20, 1812	A clerk at Fort Manuel records the death of "the wife of Charbonneau." The clerk does not write her name and Charbonneau had several wives.
August 11, 1813	William Clark adopts Jean Baptiste and Lizette.
1825–1828	On the cover of his cash book, William Clark writes, "Se car ja we au Dead."
1869	According to the oral tradition of the Three Affiliated Tribes of North Dakota (Mandan, Hidatsa, and Arikara), an elderly Hidatsa woman named Sakakawea is killed by an enemy war party in Montana.
1884	Some say a woman named Sacagawea dies on the Wind River Reservation in Wyoming.

Student Handout B

Directions

1. You are assigned one of the topics about Sacagawea to investigate and become the expert for your base group. Meet with classmates investigating the same topic as you to fill in the chart for your topic.
2. Return to your base group and share the information.
3. Complete the chart by recording what you learn about the other topics from the experts in your base group.

Student Handout C (Blue) **Sacagawea's Name**	What sources typically confirm the spelling of a name? How many spellings are listed for Sacagawea? With so many different spellings, historians had to choose one. If you were a historian, which would you choose and why?
Student Handout D (Green) **Lemhi Shoshone Perspective**	Why are some Native people critical of Sacajawea? What does Rod Ariwite want people to know and remember about Sacajawea? What does Rose Ann Abrahamson value about Sacajawea's story?
Student Handout E (Yellow) **Mandan and Hidatsa Perspective**	According to Amy Mossett, what did Sakakawea learn from the Mandan and Hidatsa? As described by Keith Bear, what are the ways Sakakawea used science to help her people and members of the expedition?
Student Handout F (Purple) **The Journals of the Corps of Discovery**	What is Sacagawea doing in each of the journal entries? List words that describe her actions.

Student Handout C
Sacagawea's Name

There are no historical records of how Sacagawea spelled or pronounced her name. This table lists various spellings of her name, the dates listed in the journal, and the author of the spelling. The information presented in this table was adapted from Robert A. Saindon (1988), "Sacajawea, Boat Launcher: The Origin and Meaning of Name . . . Maybe," in *We Proceeded On, 14*(3), pp. 4–10 (available at www.lewisandclark.org/wpo/pdf/vol14no3.pdf#page=4).

Sah-kah gar we a	April 7, 1805 (William Clark)
Sah-ca-gah Mea-ah	May 20, 1805 (Meriwether Lewis)
Sar-kah gah-We-a	May 20, 1805 (William Clark)
Sah-cah-gah we a	June 10, 1805 (Meriwether Lewis)
Sahcahgagwea	June 10, 1805 (William Clark)
Sah-cah-gah	June 10, 1805 (John Ordway)
Sar-car-gah-we-a	June 22, 1805 (William Clark)
Sar kar-gah We a	July 10, 1805 (William Clark)
Sah-cah-gar-we-ah	July 28, 1805 (Meriwether Lewis)
Sah-cah-gar-weah	August 17, 1805 Meriwether (Lewis)
Sah-cah-gar-we-ah	August 17, 1805 (Meriwether Lewis)
Sah-car-gar we-ah	August 19, 1805 (Meriwether Lewis)
Sah-cah-gar Wea	August 22, 1805 (Meriwether Lewis)
Janey	November 24, 1805 (William Clark)
	August 20, 1806 (William Clark)
Sahcargarweah	April 28, 1806 (Meriwether Lewis)
Sah-cah-gah-weah	April 28, 1806 (William Clark)
Sahcargarweah	May 16, 1806 (Meriwether Lewis)
Sacajawea	Shoshone (meaning "boat puller or boat launcher")
Sakakawea	Hidatsa (meaning "bird woman"); official spelling of the Three Affiliated Tribes of North Dakota (Mandan, Hidatsa, and Arikara); official spelling in the state of North Dakota
Sacagawea	Widely used spelling based on the historical record of the Corps of Discovery journals; used by the National Park Service, U.S. Board of Geographic Names, and the U.S. Mint

Student Handout D
Sacajawea: Lemhi Shoshone Perspectives

Sacajawea was born into the Lemhi Shoshone Tribe. The following excerpts provide Lemhi Shoshone perspectives about Sacajawea from today.

Rod Ariwite	Like all of us, Sacajawea was molded by her family, her tribal members, and her experiences. To us she represents all that is good about our people, the Lemhi Shoshoni. Some Native people criticize Sacajawea for helping the majority culture travel through our lands and eventually dominate us completely. However, we realize Sacajawea was only eleven years old when she was captured. . . . She was a teenager when Lewis and Clark enlisted her and her husband to help them travel to and from the Pacific Ocean.
	The explorers came to Sacajawea first and eventually to our people with glowing promises of peace and prosperity. How could sixteen-year-old Sacajawea or our people foresee what the future actually held for them and all native people? We know Sacajawea did what she thought was correct. We know from all the words written about her that she was an outstanding human being.
	. . . . We honor Sacajawea for who she was—not for what she did to help Lewis and Clark. We know she was a good woman and a fine mother. For these things we proudly want the world to know Sacajawea is Lemhi Shoshoni.
	(From *The Truth about Sacajawea* by Kenneth Thomasma, 1997, p. 9)
Rose Ann Abrahamson	The challenges she was willing to face will show young women of today that we are capable of facing hardships. We've come a long way from that time period but in many ways we are faced with similar challenges. The men of the Corps of Discovery spoke highly of Sacagawea's characteristics. Her most important value to me as a woman, as a Native American teacher, is that she stayed true to her traditions.
	(Retrieved from *The Journey of Sacagawea*, idahoptv.org/lc/sacagawea /index.cfm)

Student Handout E
Sakakawea: Mandan and Hidatsa Perspectives

When Sakakawea was approximately 12 years old (in about 1800), the Hidatsa captured her from the Lemhi Shoshone Tribe in an area now referred to as Three Forks, MT. She was taken to a Hidatsa village on the Knife River in an area now referred to as Bismarck, ND. The following excerpts provide the Mandan and Hidatsa perspectives about Sakakawea from today.

Amy Mossett	She grew into womanhood in the Hidatsa culture. She came here as a young Shoshoni girl and when she lived among the Shoshoni. I am sure she learned all the things that young Shoshoni girls learned. And when she came here and lived among the Mandan/Hidatsa she would have learned all the things that young women would learn. I believe that is what she took with her, that nurturing, that care giving, that calm, quiet ability to cope with crisis. Those are the things that she learned as she grew into womanhood. (Retrieved from *The Journey of Sacagawea*, idahoptv.org/lc /sacagawea/index.cfm)
Keith Bear **ingenious:** clever, resourceful **serendipitous:** fortunate, lucky	While she was here, she learned a lot of medicine from the earth, from the ground. And I'm sure she did from her people up there in the mountains too so as they traveled along wherever they went, if they needed medicine for the cramps or the boils and the things that they had, this young woman would find those things. When they were hungry, very, very hungry, she would find nuts, and she would find roots, and she would find berries, and she would set traps and fish things and get those things and feed those men. She made a lot of clothing for them and showed them how to make their own clothing. This was a very **ingenious** young woman and it was **serendipitous**, I guess, for them to take her along. She ended up being so valuable by the contributions she made along the way. (Retrieved from *The Journey of Sacagawea*, idahoptv.org/lc /sacagawea/index.cfm)

Student Handout F
Sacagawea: The Corps of Discovery Journals

The following excerpts about Sacagawea are adapted from the Corps of Discovery journals. For the purpose of this handout, "Sacagawea" is used as the spelling of her name. The excerpts were adapted from two sources: *The Truth about Sacajawea* by Kenneth Thomasma (1997) and *The Journals of the Corps of Discovery*, edited by Gary E. Moulton for the University of Nebraska Press (available at lewisandclark-journals.unl.edu/).

Date	Journal Entry
Monday, February 11, 1805	At about five o'clock this evening, Sacagawea delivered a fine boy.
Tuesday, April 9, 1805	When we stopped for dinner, Sacagawea began searching for wild artichokes. She did this by using a sharp stick to dig in the ground. She found a good quantity of these roots.
Thursday, May 16, 1805 On Tuesday, May 14, 1805, a boat Sacagawea was traveling in nearly capsized in high wind. In this entry, Lewis describes Sacagawea's actions **fortitude:** courage **resolution:** focus	By 4:00 in the evening our instruments, medicine, gifts, and food were perfectly dried, repacked, and put on board the pirogue. The loss we sustained was not so great as we had at first thought. We lost medicine, garden seeds, some gunpowder, and some food. Sacagawea, with **fortitude** and **resolution,** equal to anyone on the boat at the time of the accident, caught and saved most of the light supplies which were washed overboard.
July 22, 1805	Sacagawea recognizes the country and assures us that this is the river on which her people live, and that the Three Forks are near distance. This information has cheered the spirits of our expedition.
August 17, 1805	After this conference was to be opened, Sacagawea was sent for. She came into the tent, sat down, and was beginning to interpret when she recognized Chief Cameahwait as her brother. She instantly jumped up and ran to embrace him.
October 19, 1805	The sight of Sacagawea, wife to one of our interpreters, confirmed to these people of our friendly intentions, as no woman ever accompanies a war party of Indians.
November 24, 1805 Members of the military expedition voted to winter on the south side of the Columbia River. Sacagawea's vote was counted and recorded. Potas are roots used for food.	Janey in favor of a place where there is plenty of Potas.
Monday, January 6, 1806	Captain Clark set out after an early breakfast with the party in two canoes. Charbonneau and Sacagawea were also in the party. Sacagawea was eager to be permitted to go and was given permission. She said that she had traveled a long way with us to see the great waters and she had yet to see the ocean. She wanted to see the large blue whale that was washed ashore on the beach.

Student Handout G
Our Words to Describe Sacagawea

Directions: As a small group, list 10 words you would use to describe Sacagawea.

1.

2.

3.

4.

5.

6.

7.

8.

9.

10.

Teacher Handout A
Sacagawea: The Textbook Story

Example 1

Oregon Studies Weekly

Week 11: Lewis and Clark (Vol. 16, Issue 2, Second Quarter, StudiesWeekly, 2016, p. 1)

The party of 33 departed in May 1804 from St. Louis. By late fall, they reached North Dakota, where they wintered. Their French guide had brought with him his wife, an American Indian woman named Sacagawea. She was Shoshone and knew much about the country. She also helped negotiate with American Indians as an interpreter.

Example 2

The United States: Making a New Nation (Harcourt Social Studies) (Berson, Howard, & Salinas, 2012, p. 433)

When Lewis and Clark hired Charbonneau for their expedition, they asked Sacagawea to come along as a translator. Sacagawea helped find routes for the explorers to follow.

Example 3

United States: Adventures in Time and Place (McGraw Hill) (Banks et al., 1999, p. 382)

There they met a French fur trapper named Toussaint Charbonneau. He and his Shoshone wife, Sacajawea, were asked to join the expedition. Lewis and Clark needed Sacajawea to translate for them when they reached Shoshone lands.

Example 4

Social Studies: Building a Nation (Scott Foresman) (Boyd et al., 2005, p. 374–375)

During their first winter, they hired French Canadian fur trapper and his Shoshone wife, Sacagawea, to act as interpreters and guides. Sacagawea helped Lewis and Clark establish good relations with Native Americans along the way. She helped translate Indian languages for the expedition. The baby she carried on her back signaled the peaceful purposes of the expedition.

"Everything Was Already Loved": Complicating Science and Discovery

Teaching Strategy: Card Game

Purpose: Students are introduced to Indigenous knowledge about various plants from regions spanning the Lewis and Clark National Historic Trail. During the activities, students complicate the idea that the Corps of Discovery "discovered" knowledge about plants along the trail.

Connections to the Standards

6 Ps Framework	Place
	Presence
	Perspectives
	Power
	Partnership
C3 Framework	D2.His.4.3-5
	D3.1.3-5
Common Core State Standards	CCSS.ELA-Literacy.RI.4.7
	CCSS.ELA-Literacy.W.4.8
	CCSS.ELA-Literacy.SL.4.1
	CCSS.ELA-Literacy.SL.4.4

Introduction

As discussed in Chapter 3, "Unpacking Colonial Logics in Curriculum," one of the ways colonial logics surface in curriculum is by framing the Corps of Discovery as a neutral expedition that weaves and emphasizes themes of adventure, discovery, and friendship. Textbooks often present a neutral summary of President Thomas Jefferson's instructions to the Corps of Discovery that typically include mention of the responsibility to record and report their observations. A noted in Chapter 2, "The Doctrine of Discovery," the meticulous documentation evident in the Corp of Discovery journals was a means to apply the principles of Discovery. Roberta Conner (Cayuse, Umatilla, and Nez Perce) (2006a) states,

The idea that an official government-ordered expedition of discovery conducted by a military unit is or was altruistic, innocent, virtuous, and heroic must come from the discoverer's vantage point. Such a notion is naive, or disingenuous and reckless. (p. 107)

In this lesson, students learn that a wealth of knowledge already existed about indigenous plants before Lewis, Clark, and other settlers arrived. For example, Indigenous peoples living in the Pacific Northwest have long known western red cedar's many uses, such as using roots to make cooking baskets, old-growth tree trunks to make canoes, and bark for clothing. In Chinuk Wawa, the western red cedar is known as the *ɬuš stik* due to its many uses. Similarly, most Indigenous peoples of the Pacific Northwest gather one or more varieties of huckleberry as a primary food source and celebrations and ceremonies. The versatile huckleberry is eaten fresh, stored, frozen, dried, canned, and made into jam. Red Huckleberry sticks are gathered and used for roasting eels (and other types of meat) on the fire. The sticks are stored away until needed again.

By learning about into Indigenous knowledge of various plants during the lesson plan activities, students are complicating the idea that the Corps of Discovery "discovered" knowledge about plants along the trail. At a broader level, they are also complicating the idea that "science" is a Western concept. Indigenous peoples have always been scientists. As the collective of Indigenous scientists wrote in their declaration of support for the March for Science in 2017:

As original peoples, we have long memories, centuries old wisdom and deep knowledge of this land and the importance of empirical, scientific inquiry as fundamental to the well-being of people and planet. Let us remember that long before Western science came to these shores, there were Indigenous scientists here. Native astronomers, agronomists, geneticists, ecologists, engineers, botanists, zoologists, watershed hydrologists, pharmacologists, physicians and more—all engaged in the creation and application of knowledge which promoted the flourishing of both human societies and the beings with whom we share the planet. We give gratitude for all their contributions to knowledge. Native science supported indigenous culture, governance and decision making for a sustainable future—the same needs which bring us together today. As we endorse and support the March for Science, let us acknowledge that there are multiple ways of knowing that play an essential role in advancing knowledge for the health of all life. Science, as concept and process, is translatable into over 500 different Indigenous languages in the U.S. and thousands world-wide. Western science is a powerful approach, but it is not the only one. (SUNY ESF, 2017)

Through the game, students will learn the properties and uses of various plants. More importantly, however, they also learn that Indigenous communities have extensive knowledge about their homelands and the plants within them. This knowledge is important: Indigenous peoples consistently advocate that their knowledge systems and relationships with their lands and the various forms of life those lands sustain are crucial to protecting the planet. Grand Ronde artist and educator Greg Archuleta teaches the public about the ethnobotany of tribal nations in Western Oregon by facilitating guided walks at the Vancouver Land Bridge and the Sandy River Delta with the Confluence Project (refer to Teaching Resource 3: Partnerships Realized, the Confluence Project). In addition to sharing stories about cultural and historic connections between Western Oregon tribal nations and the Columbia River, Archuleta emphasizes contemporary connections and the ongoing conservation efforts of Native peoples. For example, he teaches about the return of the wapato to the Sandy River Delta after the U.S. Forest Service answered the call to remove dams built for flood control. The wapato is growing again, but is threatened by pollution and the heavy impact of visitors hiking with dogs off leash. In describing a tour of the Sandy River Delta led by Archuleta (2019), he states,

> . . . we go down there and tie the old stories—pieces of the old stories—to the river. . . . And then, you know, ask them and talk about what's missing, what's not there that should be there. . . . And wapato was one of those, . . . Then they can see through the restoration process . . . how the wapato came back. (www.confluenceproject.org/library-post/greg-archuleta-wapato-returns-to-the-sandy-river-delta)

Connecting students to knowledge of the land, plants, and ecosystems can support them in understanding that our future is tied to the future of the land. When students recognize this relationship, they are more likely to feel a sense of responsibility to care and protect the land.

This lesson begins with students discussing the meaning of the concluding lines from "Homeland" by Karenne Wood (2003), "Nothing was discovered. / Everything was already loved" (pp. 12–13). To reflect on the meaning of these words, students are asked to recall what they learned in the previous lesson about how Sacagawea's scientific knowledge contributed to the expedition. Following this discussion, the card game, played in groups of four, is introduced. There are 24 plant cards and all but three of the plants were recorded in the Corps of Discovery journals (Indian carrot, bear root, and cutleaf coneflower were not listed in the plant species described by Clark; related species were described). Greg Archuleta and Chris Remple, both members of the Confederated Tribes of the Grand Ronde, provided all information for the plant cards: plant names in Native languages, description of plant uses, and examples of Native peoples who use the plants. Some of the cards do not have pictures. Before playing, students research and draw the pictures of these plants. The card game is similar to Uno or Crazy Eights with a unique rule that playing a card requires sharing a fact about the plant on the card.

Materials

- Copies of Student Handout A and Student Handout B for each group of four students
- Teacher Handout A

Duration

Activity 1 and Activity 2 will take approximately 40 minutes.

Procedures

Activity 1

1. Organize students into groups of four.
2. Say to students, "From our earlier historical investigations, we learned the instructions to the Corps of Discovery from President Thomas Jefferson included recording observations about plants. Before leaving on the military expedition, Meriwether Lewis prepared for this responsibility by studying the science of plants. He and others on the

military expedition recorded observations and collected samples of over 60 plants."

3. Write on the dry erase board or project the concluding lines from "Homeland" by Karenne Wood (Monacan) (2003), "Nothing was discovered. Everything was already loved." Explain to students that Karenne Wood shared this poem at an opening ceremony for the 200th anniversary commemoration of the Corps of Discovery. After reading the lines out loud, ask students, "What do you think this means?" Facilitate a discussion of student responses and interpretations.

4. Extending student comments, say to students, "The Corps of Discovery passed through the homelands of Native peoples who use their scientific knowledge of plants for purposes such as, food, medicine, and ceremony. As Karenne Wood says in her poem, 'Everything was already loved.' What examples can you recall from our previous lesson about Sacagawea's knowledge about plants?" Add to students' knowledge about Sacagawea by sharing that she taught members of the Corps of Discovery how to boil elk bones into grease and how to use mud or crushed bulbs of wild onions to spread on their skin to prevent bites from bugs such as mosquitoes. Say to students, "The purpose of our lesson today is to challenge the assumption that Lewis and Clark 'discovered' these plants."

5. Distribute one copy of Student Handout A to each group of students. Say to students, "Today we are going to play a card game that features examples of plants Native peoples 'already loved' before the Corps of Discovery's arrival on Native homelands. Many of the plants we learn about today were described in the journals."

6. Project Teacher Handout A to show students the features of the game cards and action cards: number (1, 2, 3, 4), geographic region (Pacific Forest, Columbia Plateau, Rocky Mountains, High Plains, Tallgrass Prairie, and Eastern Deciduous Forest); name of the plant; picture (not all game cards include a picture); description of the plant's significance to Native peoples and examples of Native peoples who use the plant.

7. Instruct students to use their scissors to cut out the game cards. Students need to sort the

game cards by number (1, 2, 3, 4) and set aside the action cards.

8. Then, each member of the small group chooses a number. Four of the plants in their shape pile will need pictures to complete the game cards. Explain to students they will research what the plant looks like and draw a picture. Using the computer, model how to find a picture and what to draw.

9. While students are doing the activity, circulate among groups to check for understanding and group preparedness.

10. Once students have finished the drawings, the card game is ready for playing.

Activity 2

1. Project Student Handout B and distribute copies to each group of students. Review the instructions and explain how to play the game. Tell students they will have 15–20 minutes to play as many rounds as they can.

2. While students are doing the activity, circulate among groups to check for understanding.

3. After the playing session ends, ask students, "What is something new that you learned today? How does this extend your understanding of what it means when Karenne Wood says in her poem, 'Nothing was discovered. Everything was already loved'?"

4. As an exit ticket, direct students to the section in the textbook about Lewis and Clark collecting plant specimens. Read the section aloud. Facilitate a discussion in which students compare the textbook section with their new knowledge. Then, using one sheet of paper per group, students collaborate to rewrite the information adding sentences that accounts for their deepened understanding.

Extension Activities

• (Optional hook if time): What does a scientist look like? Invite students to "Draw a scientist doing science." Then, compare/contrast student images and use the discussion to introduce the themes and purpose of this lesson plan. For more information about this idea, refer to the California Academy of Sciences website: www.calacademy.org /educators/lesson-plans/draw-a-scientist.

- Create a handout presenting a two-column table. Column one lists a selection of plants featured on the cards (e.g., wapato, dogbane, prickly pear cactus, willow, wild rice, and squash). For column two, students search for the plants using the online expedition journals (lewisandclarkjournals.unl.edu/journals), record a date the plant is described, and write a quotation from the journals. For example, "prickly pear cactus" is referenced, described, and complained about many times in the journals. One example occurs on July 20, 1805, when Lewis writes, "the prickly pears are so abundant that we could scarcely find room to lye."

- In partnership with Indigenous experts about plants specific to your area, students can create additional cards to add to the game. Also, consider adding cards about animals and places!

Number	Geographic Region
Number	**Geographic Region**
1, 2, 3, 4	Pacific Forest, Columbia Plateau, Rocky Mountains, High Plains, Tall Grass Prairie, Eastern Deciduous Forest

Names of Plant

Examples of plant name in Indigenous languages
and the English name.

Plant Drawing

Plant Description

Examples of plant uses and Indigenous peoples who use the plant.

Student Handout A

1 Pacific Forest	**2 Pacific Forest**

1 Pacific Forest

wapᴴtu (Chinuk Wawa)

wáqᴴat (Clackamas Chinook)

mámpᴴtu (Tualatin-Yamhill Kalapuya)

wapato (English)

Wapato is an aquatic plant that grows in wetlands. A method of gathering the wapato is wading into shallow water in bare feet to feel for the tubers. The tubers are loosened with the feet and float to the top for collecting. They are placed on hot coals and baked like a potato, so wapato is also known as Indian potato. Examples of Native peoples who use wapato: Lower Chinook, Clatsop, Kathlamet, Multnomah, Clackamas Chinook, Watlala (Cascade Chinook), Tualatin Kalapuya, and British Columbia First Peoples.

2 Pacific Forest

k'anawi (Chinuk Wawa)

acorns (English)

Several varieties of acorns come for different oak trees, such as the White Oak, Black Oak, Live Oak and Tan Oak. The acorns are bitter tasting when raw. Native peoples have different ways of removing tannin that creates the bitter taste. For example, some people store acorns in baskets by springs and others grind the acorns and then run water through the flour. Examples of Native peoples who use acorns: Tualatin Kalapuya, Multnomah Chinook, Clackamas Chinook, Santiam Kalapuya, Mary's River Kalapuya, Takelma (Rogue River), and Shasta.

3 Pacific Forest

kʰalakwati-stik, ɬush-stik, or kənim-stik (Chinuk Wawa)

íshkan (Clackamus Chinook)

amálli (Tualatin-Yamhill Kalapuya)

aláa (Santiam-Mary's River Kalapuya)

western red cedar (English)

The western red cedar tree has many uses. The roots are used to make cooking baskets. The old-growth tree trunks are used for making canoes, building plank and longhouses, and for carving a wide range of items. The cedar bark is used for basketry, rope making, mats, and pounded for clothing. Examples of Native peoples who use western red cedar: Clackamas Chinook, Tualatin Kalapuya, Puget Sound Tribes (Coast Salish Peoples), Tillamook.

4 Pacific Forest

ulali (Chinuk Wawa)

huckleberries (English)

Huckleberries are a primary food source for tribes in the Pacific Northwest. Tribal families are often in the mountains gathering berries during harvest time. They are eaten fresh, stored, and frozen. They are dried, canned, and/or made into jam. Also, huckleberries are important for trading, gifts, and ceremony. All tribes of the Pacific Northwest use one or more varieties of huckleberries. The Tillamooks gather red huckleberries and wild blueberries. The Clackamas, Molalla, Wasco, Yakama, Warm Springs, and Nez Perce gather mountain huckleberries.

1 Columbia Plateau

sawítk (Umatilla, Walla Walla)

cawíitx (Cayuse, Nez Perce)

Indian carrot (English)

The Indian carrot can be eaten raw, baked or steamed. The roots have a good flavor and are nutritional. In addition to being an important food, it is used in celebrations and ceremonies. The raw root can be used as a laxative for medicine. Examples of Native peoples who use the Indian Carrot are: Yakama, Wishram, Tenino, Cayuse, Umatilla, Walla Walla, Northern Paiute, Spokane.

2 Columbia Plateau

taxús (Umatilla, Rock Creek Sahaptin)

dogbane or Indian hemp (English)

Dogbane is used to make string, cordage, and basketry. The beautiful baskets and hats of the Columbia Plateau are traditionally made of dogbane. It is an important trade item to other tribes outside the Columbia Plains region. Also, women use a ball of dogbane to create knots recording important life events. Examples of Native peoples who use dogbane are: Wasco, Yakama, Clackamas Chinook, Umatilla.

3 Columbia Plateau

pyaxi (Umatilla, Walla Walla)

łitáan (Cayuse, Nez Perce)

bitterroot (English)

Bitterroot is an important food of the Columbia Plateau region that is available in late spring and early summer. It is one of the first foods in the gathering cycle for many tribes. The roots are harvested with diggers made of hardwood or antlers. The taste is bitter and the roots are cooked in a mix with meat or berries. Bitterroot is gathered for celebrations and ceremony. Examples of Native peoples who use bitterroot are: Umatilla, Walla Walla, Cayuse, and Nez Perce.

4 Columbia Plateau

xawš (Sahaptin)

xaush (Wasco)

qáamsit (fresh) (Cayuse, Nez Perce)

biscuitroot (cous) (English)

Biscuitroot is found in rocky, dry areas on the high plateaus. The plant has yellow flowers and when they seed it is time to dig the roots. It is one of the first foods in the gathering cycle for many tribes. The roots are used for seasoning salmon. Biscuitroot is high in calories and is important for ceremonies. Also, the seeds can be used for a love potion. Examples of Native peoples who use biscuitroot are: Wasco, Warm Springs, Paiute, Yakama, Umatilla, Walla Walla, and Cayuse.

1 Rocky Mountains

ha'ich'idéé (Jicarilla Apache)

kwiyag'atʉ tʉkapi (Ute)

osha or bear root (English)

Osha is a medicinal plant known to be used by the bears of the Rocky Mountains. Depending on the tribe, it is used as a medicine for colds, flu, and indigestion. It is also known to be used as a snake or insect repellent. A person gathering osha needs to be careful because it looks similar to poisonous plants. Today, the root is threatened and the plant has not been successfully grown outside its natural area. Examples of Native peoples who use osha are: Nez Perce, Couer d'Alene, Shoshone-Bannock, Salish Kootenai, Ktunaxa, Apache, Ute, Cheyenne.

2 Rocky Mountains

xapi (Kutenai)

sχʷeʔelí (Flathead)

miss-issa (Blackfeet)

camas (English)

Camas is an important food for tribes of the Rocky Mountain region. The gathering of camas begins in the late spring and into the late summer. Usually, tribal families have their own digging area. The camas bulbs are baked and dried for several days. They can be made into camas cakes, bread, or ground into flour. A person gathering camas for food needs to be careful because a related species, the Death Camas, is poisonous. But, the Death Camas is sometimes gathered for medicinal purposes. Examples of Native peoples who use camas are: Nez Perce, Couer d'alene, Shoshone-Bannock, Salish Kootenai, Ktunax.

3 Rocky Mountains

istis (Nez Perce)

prickly pear cactus (English)

The prickly pear cactus is used for food and medicine. It may be eaten fresh or dried. The stems and fruit can be used to make a dye. Some tribes use a poultice to put on sores and infections. Examples of Native peoples who use prickly pear cactus are: Nez Perce.

4 Rocky Mountains

Veʔeve-shestotoʔe (Cheyenne)

six-in-oko (Blackfeet)

Rocky mountain juniper (English)

The juniper berries are eaten raw, boiled, or grounded for berry cakes. Many tribes of the Rocky Mountain region use juniper berries for medicinal purposes. For example, teas are made to stop vomiting, relieve arthritis, and to treat colds, fevers, and pneumonia. The durable wood is used to make bows. The Cheyenne use juniper to make flutes. Also, juniper is an important incense for ceremonial purposes. Examples of Native peoples who use rocky mountain juniper are: Cheyenne, Blackfeet, Flathead, Nez Perce, Kutenai.

1 High Plains

čhaŋpȟá (Lakota/Dakota/Nakota)

Nopa-zhinga (Ponca/Omaha)

Puckkeep (Blackfeet)

Monotse (Cheyenne)

chokecherry (English)

Chokecherry is an important plant food source in the high plains. Tribal people gather the berries when they turn dark red in late summer. Chokecherries can be used to make jam. One method of preparation used by the Lakota/Nakota/ Dakota is to mash chokecherries and mix with thin strips of buffalo meat and tallow to make *wasna*. Chokecherry is known to have many health benefits. Also, chokecherry branches are used to make drumsticks and arrows. Examples of Native peoples who use chokecherry are: Lakota/Dakota/ Nakota, Blackfeet, Ponca, Cheyenne.

2 High Plains

Mirahací (Mandan/Hidatsa/Crow)

čȟoȟáŋ waŋžíča (Lakota/Nakota/Dakota)

méno'ke (Cheyenne)

willow (English)

Willow can be found growing near water. Native peoples in the high plains use willow poles to make their sweat lodges. Willow poles and their bark are strong and flexible when wet and can be used to make a variety of durable items. The inner bark of willow has pain-relieving properties and can either be chewed or applied as a poultice to wounds. The name Hidatsa comes from Hiraacá, which roughly translates to "people of the willow." Examples of Native peoples who use willow are: Mandan, Crow, Cheyenne.

3 High Plains

wazí čháŋ (Lakota/Dakota/Nakota)

hooxe'e (Cheyenne)

manistami (Blackfeet)

lodgepole pine (English)

Lodgepole pine trees grow to about 50 feet tall and have a gentle, tapering trunk that makes them ideal for tipi poles. The sticky pitch can be used with animal tendons (sinew) to create permanent bindings for items such as arrows and spearheads. Examples of Native peoples who use lodgepole pine are: Lakota/Dakota/Nakota, Blackfeet, Cheyenne.

4 High Plains

pȟeží hóta (Lakota/Dakota/Nakota)

kaximí (Blackfeet)

hetanévánó'ėstse (Cheyenne)

prairie sage (English)

Prairie sage is used by Native peoples for smudging. Plant leaves and stems are burned. Then, the smoke is breathed in and fanned around the body for purification. Prairie sage leaves can also be crushed and applied as a poultice to wounds. Today, many different species of sage, especially California White Sage, are at risk of becoming endangered. Examples of Native peoples who use sage are: Lakota/ Dakota/Nakota, Blackfeet, Cheyenne.

1 Tallgrass Prairie **pakâni** (Sac and Fox) **pacane** (Illinois) **fạla** (Choctaw) **Sohi aninvhida** (Cherokee) **pecans** (English) Pecan trees on average grow to over 100 feet tall and are found in grasslands throughout the Midwest. The nuts ripen in mid-fall and store easily, making them an ideal winter food source. Many tribes also have various medicinal uses for the bark and leaves of the pecan tree. The name pecan is from the Illinois-Algonquin word pacane, which translates to "needs a stone to crack." Examples of Native peoples who use pecans are: Illinois, Cherokee, Choctaw.	**2 Tallgrass Prairie** **Manoomin** (Anishinaabe) **manômini** (Sac and Fox) **Omāēqnomenew** (Menominee) **wild rice** (English) Wild rice is the only grain native to this continent. It grows in lakes and ponds in the Great Lakes region. It is traditionally harvested by a pair of people via canoe. A poler will sit in front and guide the canoe through the water while the knocker collects manoomin by knocking it into the boat with a pole. The Menominee people refer to themselves as Mamaceqtaw, but other local tribes would refer to them as the Menomini, "wild-rice people," which is the origin of the Menominee name. Examples of Native peoples who use wild rice are: Mamaceqtaw, Sac and Fox, Anishinaabe.
3 Tallgrass Prairie **wiingashk** (Anishinaabe) **motsé'eonȯtse** (Cheyenne) **wishkbemishkos** (Potawatomi) **sweet grass** (English)  Sweetgrass grows in cool wetlands and shady grasslands and is adapted to withstand cold weather. Its scent is drawn out by rain, burning, or cutting. Sweetgrass is considered one of the four sacred herbs by many tribes and is most commonly used for smudging. The Anishinaabe and Potawatomi teach that sweetgrass is the hair of the earth and is best respected by braiding it. Examples of Native peoples who use sweet grass are: Anishinaabe, Cheyenne, Potawatomi.	**4 Tallgrass Prairie** **Tse'-wa-the** (Osage) **čeráp** (Ho-chunk) **poohkhšikwalia** (Miami) **lotus flower** (English) The American lotus flower grows in shallow water and high on the banks of slow-moving streams. The roots are usually gathered early fall and are eaten raw or baked or are dried for winter. Immature lotus seeds are also eaten raw. The Osage harvest lotus roots by wading in the shallow water or mud and feeling for tubers with their feet or digging them up with a willow pole. Examples of Native peoples who use lotus flower are: Osage, Ho-chunk, Miami.

1 Eastern Deciduous Forest

Ohósera (Mohawk)

ohó:sela' (Oneida)

i'deha (Cherokee)

basswood (English)

The basswood is a softwood deciduous tree that grows throughout the eastern half of the country. Its close-grained wood makes it ideal for carving tools and figures such as masks. Numerous tribes prize its fibrous inner bark, fine enough to be used as string and tough enough to be made into rope. Sheets of the bark along with cattail mats are also used as wigwam coverings. The Cherokee have teachings that the basswood tree is never struck by lightning and are advised to shelter under one if caught in a storm. Examples of Native peoples who use basswood are: Mohawk, Oneida, Cherokee.

2 Eastern Deciduous Forest

se'lu, tuya, squa'si (Cherokee)

Ewáchimineash, manusqussêdash, askutasquash (Narragansett)

three sisters or corn, beans, squash (English)

Corn, beans, and squash are referred to as the three sisters by many tribes. Each one provides support for the other, causing them to grow better together than by themselves. In addition to their important role as food, squash gourds are also used as rattles or drinking containers. The Haundenosaunee creation story speaks of how the three sisters grew from the grave of Sky Woman's daughter to feed the people. Examples of Native peoples who use three sisters are: Cherokee, Haundenosaunee, Narragansett.

3 Eastern Deciduous Forest

Sochan (Cherokee)

cutleaf coneflower (English)

Cutleaf coneflower grows near creeks, rivers, and other cool and shady areas. Its early spring leaves are tasty and highly nutritious. They are eaten by tribes throughout the eastern part of the country, but are especially prized by the Cherokee People. Examples of Native peoples who use cutleaf coneflower are: Cherokee.

4 Eastern Deciduous Forest

oyë'kwa'öweh (Seneca)

tsalu agayvli (Cherokee)

La'thema (Shawnee)

Indian tobacco (English)

The tobacco plant traditionally used by Native peoples is a different species from the commercial tobacco plants grown today. When smoked, it is not inhaled into the lungs because it is meant to carry prayers from the person's mouth to the creator above. It is also given by numerous tribes as an offering when asking for help from a plant, human, or spirit. The Seneca teach that the best time to harvest tobacco is when a thunderstorm is approaching. Examples of native peoples who use Indian tobacco are: Seneca, Cherokee, Shawnee.

ACTION CARD	ACTION CARD
SKIP	REVERSE
ACTION CARD	ACTION CARD
DRAW 2	WILD 1, 2, 3, 4

Student Handout B

Instructions

- Select one person to be the dealer. This person will shuffle the cards and give each person 5 cards. The remaining cards are placed in a draw pile (face down). The top card on the draw pile is flipped over (face up) and set next to the draw pile to create a new stack of cards called the discard pile.
- The person to the left of the dealer goes first.
- The goal is to match one of your cards to the card in the discard pile. If you have a match, place the card on the top of the discard pile and share one fact about the plant with the other players. There are two ways to make a match: NUMBER (1, 2, 3, 4) or GEOGRAPHIC REGION (Pacific Forest, Columbia Plateau, Rocky Mountains, High Plains, Tallgrass Prairie, and Eastern Deciduous Forest). You can only play one card at a time.
- If you do not have a card to match or an Action Card, you will take one card from the draw pile and the game continues to the next player.
- If you do not have a card to match and you do have an Action Card, you can play an Action Card.
    a. SKIP: The next player skips a turn.
    b. REVERSE: The direction of play switches.
    c. DRAW 2: The next player picks up two cards from the draw pile and loses their turn.
    d. WILD: This card represents all four numbers (1, 2, 3, 4). The player decides what number they want to play to make a match. The game continues with the number selected by this player.
- The first player to run out of cards is the winner! The winner shuffles and deals the cards for the next round.

A Stolen Canoe Returned

Teaching Strategy: Caption Drawings

Purpose: The Corps of Discovery stole a canoe from the Clatsop peoples on March 17, 1806. Two hundred years later, the Chinook Nation held a ceremony to welcome the return of their canoe. This story is the focus of the lesson, and it introduces students to the importance of canoes to tribal cultures.

Connections to the Standards

6 Ps Framework	Presence
	Perspectives
	Political Nationhood
	Power
C3 Framework	D2.His.2.3-5
	D2.His.4.3-5
	D.2.His.14.3-5
	D4.2.3-5
	D4.6.3-5
Common Core State Standards	CSSE.ELA-Literacy.RI.4.1
	CCSS.ELA-Literacy.RI.4.2
	CCSS.ELA-Literacy.RI.4.3
	CCSS.ELA-Literacy.W.4.0
	CCSS.ELA-Literacy.SL.4.1
	CCSS.ELA-Literacy.SL.4.2

Introduction

When working with teachers, one of the first questions we ask is, "What do your students care about?" Teachers often tell us about how their students care about fairness, respecting each other, being listened to, belonging, friendship, and teamwork. These are the themes present in the story of "A Stolen Canoe Returned." The story of the Corps of Discovery stealing a canoe from the Clatsop peoples on March 17, 1806, provides entry into a larger context that includes the return of the canoe over two hundred years later, the importance of canoe culture to the Chinookan speaking peoples on the lower Columbia River, including the Clatsop tribe of the Chinook Indian Nation, and the significance of tribal sovereignty. This lesson is intended to emphasize Indigenous peoples' resilience in maintaining their cultural traditions. Further, by highlighting the way the Clark family worked to right a historic wrong, the lesson provides an example of healing and justice.

Each year, over 100 Native nations from the West Coast of the United States and Canada participate in *Canoe Journey* (also called Tribal Journey) to affirm and honor the importance of canoes to tribal cultures. Paddle to Seattle was the first Canoe Journey in 1989 and it became an annual event starting in 1993. The final destination for Canoe Journey changes each year, and some canoes will travel for a month over hundreds of miles with several stops along their routes. Thousands of people participate as canoe families (those paddling the canoe), as communities hosting canoe families as they travel to the final destination, as the destination hosts who coordinate and welcome the canoes, or as spectators waiting to celebrate the exciting arrival of the canoe families. This lesson plan focuses on two elements of Canoe Journey: "Ten Rules of the Canoe" and the protocols for canoe landings and launchings.

First, the Ten Rules of the Canoe were developed soon after the Paddle to Seattle by the Qyuileute People to help canoe families "pull with pride and purpose" (ASFC & ITC, 2011, p. 4). They are now used by many of the Native nations participating. This lesson plan introduces students to the ten rules followed by a discussion exploring themes such as teamwork and trust. Second, *protocols* are an important way of creating and sustaining relationships between Native nations. These protocols are rooted in values of respect and reciprocity. Landing and cultural protocols for coming ashore are a way for canoe families to recognize they are visiting another nation's homelands. In describing protocols, Chinook Tribal Council Member Rachel Cushman states,

One of the central protocols in Tribal Journeys is the request to come ashore. As the canoes and the travelers they carry come to the shores of the host community they must get permission from that community before landing. While there is no exact formula for this protocol of permission, it usually includes the following: a statement of identity by a canoe family representative, a declaration that they have arrived peacefully, an account of the day's travel noting that the members of the canoe are tired and hungry, and that they are there to share songs and dances, and then finally the request to come ashore. A representative of the host community then welcomes and recognizes the canoe family and gives them permission to come ashore. In many cases this protocol is done in the traditional languages of the participants and often notes family and community ties. In the case of the final landing, where there are dozens of canoes waiting to come ashore, this protocol can last for many hours. (Cushman, Daehnke, & Johnson, in press)

This lesson plan emphasizes the presence of Indigenous peoples and cultural practices, and the importance of Indigenous sovereignty and reciprocity that is enacted through the protocols of Canoe Journey. This builds upon students' understanding of tribal sovereignty that was introduced in Elementary Lesson Plan 1: We're Still Here.

Materials

- This lesson plan opens with a description of Canoe Journey and focuses on two elements of the event (Ten Rules of the Canoe and protocols for coming ashore). For background and more information about Canoe Journey, it is recommended teachers refer to *Tribal Journeys Handbook and Study Guide* (2011) (http://canoeway.com/Tribal_Journeys _Handbook.pdf).
- Copies of Student Handout A and B for all students

Duration

This lesson plan takes approximately 40 minutes.

Procedures

1. Before describing Canoe Journey to students, do an Internet search for the most recent Canoe Journey website for location and itineraries. As you tell students about Canoe Journey, show the website features that include images and maps. Show the video "Canoe Journey 2018—Lummi Landing"
(6:13, www.youtube.com/watch?v=H06y2QE -j0M) as an example of the sights and sounds from Canoe Journey.

2. Say to students, "We will focus on two elements of Canoe Journey today. The first is learning about the Ten Rules of the Canoe. Soon after the first Tribal Journey, Ten Rules of the Canoe were developed by the Qyuileute People to help canoe families 'pull with pride and purpose.' These rules support canoe families working together to prepare for and during the journey. They are now used by many of the Native nations participating. Let's look at these ten rules." Show the video "Ten Rules of the Canoe" (2:01, www.youtube.com /watch?v=3EFgr406Kvs). After watching the video, consider showing students the expanded version of the Ten Rules of the Canoe on pages 4–5 of the *Tribal Journeys Handbook and Study Guide*. Facilitate a discussion with the following questions: In what way are the 10 rules of the canoe similar to the rules of group activities you participate in? In what ways are the 10 rules of the canoe different?

3. Say to students, "In addition to the Ten Rules of the Canoe, there are also protocols that guide the canoe families in how to behave when they arrive. Protocols are a set of rules or procedures." Read the description of the protocols by Chinook Tribal Council Member Rachel Cushman presented in the introduction to this lesson plan. As you read the description, consider showing the picture of the canoes waiting together as they ask permission to come ashore on page 10 from the *Tribal Journeys Handbook and Study Guide*. Say to students, "Protocols are an important way of creating and sustaining relationships between Native nations. These protocols are rooted in values of respect and reciprocity (or giving back). They are also an important aspect of Indigenous sovereignty." Show the video "Canoe Journey: Following Traditional Protocol" (2:30, www.youtube.com/watch?v =hzA0eSaLDyE).

4. Next, say to students, "When the Corps of Discovery arrived on the lower Columbia River, they were impressed by the canoe construction and navigation expertise of the Chinookan speaking peoples, including the Clatsop and Lower Chinook tribes. Today, we are going to read about a canoe that members of the military expedition stole from the

Clatsop peoples in 1806 and the returning of a canoe 205 years later." Distribute copies of Student Handout A and Student Handout B.

5. Before reading the article (Student Handout A), review the instructions (Student Handout B: Side one). Then, read aloud the first part of the story, "The Stolen Canoe," modeling and encouraging students to underline phrases to help them identify the 5 Ws.

6. Next, give time for students to work independently and/or work in small groups to complete the 5 Ws reading activity (Student Handout B: Side one) for "The Stolen Canoe." While students are doing the activity, circulate among groups to check for understanding and group preparedness for sharing findings with the class.

7. Repeat this process for the second part of the story, "The Canoe Is Returned."

8. After the discussion of the 5 Ws reading activity for "The Canoe Is Returned," tell students turn to Student Handout B: Side two. Say to students, "We have learned about how the Corps of Discovery stole a canoe. We have learned about how the canoe was returned. We have also learned about the importance of canoe cultural traditions to Native nations and how these traditions are actively practiced today. What is one thing you have taken away from today's lesson?" Facilitate a discussion of student responses to this question. Then

overview the instructions for the caption drawing activity.

9. When students have finished the caption drawing activity, post the drawings on the wall for a gallery walk or use the document camera for students to share their work with each other.

Extension Activities

- Show the documentary *Canoe Way: The Sacred Journey* (2008) (31:29, www.youtube.com /watch?v=QJOC92S98C4).

- To explore canoe carving, show students the video "Introduction—NW Coast Indian Canoe Project" (6:04, www.youtube.com/watch?v =R_HOla2FjFE). Also available from the same project, a time lapse video showing a three-month carving process in ten minutes (10:11, www.youtube.com/watch?v=NZ1po-YKngY). (JayHawk Institute)

- Examine the importance of tribal sovereignty by showing the film *Promised Land* (2016). This film tells the story of the Duwamish and the Chinook Nations' efforts to restore federal recognition and treaty rights. After viewing the film, facilitate a discussion for students to consider what actions they can to take to educate others and support the Duwamish and Chinook Nations. Educational copies can be purchased at the following website: www .promisedlanddoc.com/about.

Student Handout A
A Stolen Canoe Returned

The Stolen Canoe

After traveling over 4,000 miles and arriving at the Pacific Ocean on November 7, 1805, the Corps of Discovery stayed in the area where the Columbia River meets the Pacific Ocean for five months. During their stay on the lower Columbia River, the Corps of Discovery traded with the Clatsop and Lower Chinook tribes. The Lower Chinook lived on the north side of the river and the Clatsop lived on the south side. The Corps of Discovery built Fort Clatsop on the south side and lived there from December 23, 1805, to March 23, 1806.

The tribes were experienced and experts at trading. Before Lewis and Clark arrived by land and river, the Clatsop and Chinook peoples traded with tribes in the region and with **merchants** who arrived by sea. The Lower Chinook and Clatsop peoples expected a variety of **goods** for trade. By the time the Corps of Discovery reached the Pacific Coast, the military expedition had limited supplies for trading. They had few items of interest to the Clatsop and Lower Chinook peoples. Lewis and Clark did not understand the **expectations** of the tribes and prices were higher than what Lewis and Clark wanted to pay. The Clatsop and Lower Chinook did not visit Fort Clatsop often because they knew trading with the Corps of Discovery was limited. In the journals, Lewis and Clark sometimes wrote about their **frustration** and **mistrust** of the tribes.

The **strained relations** increased during a series of events that took place in February and March of 1806. On February 6, 1806, members of the military expedition went hunting for **elk**. After the hunt, they hid the elk they shot and returned to Fort Clatsop. They planned on coming back for the meat and **hides** in a few days. Members of the Clatsop thought the meat was **abandoned** and took six of the elk. Lewis and Clark informed Clatsop Chief Coboway about the elk being taken. On February 12, 1806, he sent three dogs to Fort Clatsop as payment for the meat and believed the situation was settled. This event added to Lewis and Clark's **mistrust**. On February 20, 1806, Meriwether Lewis wrote in his journal that he thought the Clatsop peoples were trying to deceive or trick them and his men must remember to not trust the Clatsop peoples.

By the month of March, the Corps of Discovery was preparing to leave Fort Clatsop and return east. Lewis and Clark wanted to trade with the Clatsop for a canoe to take on the return journey. They admired the canoe carving and paddling skills of the Clatsop and Lower Chinook. Purchasing a canoe was an expensive trade because the Clatsop and Lower Chinook considered canoes to be living beings and members of the tribes. When Lewis and Clark tried to trade with the Clatsop for a canoe, they refused because the items offered for trade were not valuable. On March 17, 1806, Lewis wrote, "We yet want another canoe, and as the Clatsop will not sell us one at a price we can afford to give, we will take one from them **in lieu of** the six elk which they stole for [from] us in winter." The next day, while Chief Coboway was visiting Fort Clatsop, members of the military expedition secretly went to his village and stole a canoe. Chief Coboway returned to Fort Clatsop to recover the stolen canoe. Lewis and Clark stated the it was payment for the six elk. James Ronda,[1] a Lewis and Clark **historian**, said, "The captains were abandoning a two-year tradition of never stealing from the Indians. It was **theft**, and a **malicious** thing to do."

On March 23, 1806, the Corps of Discovery left Fort Clatsop for the return journey. They traveled in five canoes, including the canoe stolen from the Clatsop.

The Canoe Is Returned

Two-hundred-five years after the canoe was stolen, relatives of William Clark raised money to pay for a canoe to be carved and given to the Chinook Indian Nation. The ceremony and **potlach** to welcome the canoe took place in 2011. Guests and Chinook peoples gathered together to receive the canoe from the Clark family members. Lotsie Holton,[2] a **descendant** of Clark, said, "We are here to right a wrong. It is never too late to apologize." Chinook Chairman Ray Gardner[3] said, "They took one of our people, as far as we're concerned. It's a great start to the healing. This is a day for the history books." The Chinook named the canoe *Kɬmin* (KuthMEEN). This means "moon," and it is also the name of a Chinookan speaking chief living around the time of the Corps of Discovery. With the welcoming of *Kɬmin*, the people of Chinook Indian Nation have an additional canoe for Tribal Journeys to celebrate the **restoration** of canoe culture, pride, community, and healing.

Chinook Justice Today

The Chinook Indian Nation, which today has approximately 3,000 **citizens**, has always been viewed by others as a nation. Clark knew this when he wrote in his journal on February 20, 1806, "This forenoon we were visited by Tâh-cum, a principal Chief of the Chinnooks and 25 men of his *nation*." The federal government understood the tribes of Chinook Indian Nation were nations when they signed **treaties** at Tansy Point in 1851—because governments only make treaties with other nations. Chinook Indian Nation is made up of the five western-most Chinookan speaking tribes—the Clatsop, Calthlamet (Kathlamet), Lower Chinook, Wahkiakum, and Willapa. The U.S. **Congress** and **Supreme Court** have also agreed in the past that the Chinook Indian Nation is a nation and represents those tribes. However today, the Chinook Indian Nation is still fighting for this right.

Being recognized as a nation is important so that the Chinook Indian Nation can set up its own **reservation**, protect its fishing rights, and offer health, education, and cultural services to its **citizens**. For Tribal Council Member Rachel Cushman, this struggle is about justice: "We know who we are. Our neighbors know who we are. We are seeking justice. What the Chinook Indian Nation needs is for the U.S. government to also confirm Chinook Indian Nation's status as a nation. Everything Chinook Indian Nation's leadership does, every decision we make, is with our peoples' best interest in mind. It is our job to protect the rights of our nation's citizens." Returning the canoe was an important first step toward healing and restoration. Now the Chinook Indian Nation wants the federal government to treat them as a nation.

NOTES

1. Duara. N. (2011, September 21). "Uh, Sorry About that Canoe . . .". *Portland Press Herald:* https://www.pressherald.com/2011/09/23/capt-clarks-descendants-makebramends-for-stolen-canoe/.

2. Mapes, L. (2011, September 24). "William Clark's Descendants 'Right a Wrong' with Chinook Tribe. *Seattle Times:* https://www.seattletimes.com/seattle-news/william-clarks-descendants-right-a-wrong-with-chinook-tribe/.

3. Mapes, L. (2011, September 24). "William Clark's Descendants 'Right a Wrong' with Chinook Tribe. *Seattle Times:* https://www.seattletimes.com/seattle-news/william-clarks-descendants-right-a-wrong-with-chinook-tribe/.

Vocabulary for "A Stolen Canoe Returned"	
abandoned	Left behind
ancestors	Relatives from long ago who lived before you
apt	Appropriate or fitting
citizen	A member of a nation
Congress	The part of the U.S. government that writes up and votes on laws
descendant	A person related to you who lives after you
elk	A large deer with brown-red fur; Male elk have large antlers
expectations	Beliefs about how something should happen
frustration	Feeling annoyed or upset
goods	Items for trading such as beads, food items, and animal skins
hides	Animal skin treated to be used for making clothing
historian	A person who studies the past
in lieu of	In place of
malicious	Mean
merchants	British and American ships regularly stopped where the Columbia River meets the Pacific Ocean; Clatsop and Chinook peoples traded with British and Americans sailing the Pacific Ocean.
mistrust	Having doubts
National Park Service	An agency in the U.S. government in charge of the national parks
"Our preservation depends on never losing sight of this trait [treachery] in their character, and being always prepared to meet it in whatever shape it may present itself."	"Our lives depend on never forgetting their deception, and always expecting they will try to trick us."
potlatch	A ceremony that involves giving away food and gifts, a way to share wealth and resources with their community. In some communities, potlaches were banned (made illegal) because missionaries and government agents felt they were wasteful and a threat to society. Potlatch is a Chinookan word and means "to give."
reservation	An area of land managed by a tribal nation. Oftentimes, reservations were lands that were "reserved" for tribal nations through treaties that took away their homelands.
restoration	Return or recovery
strained relations	Conflict, lack of trust between two or more people
Supreme Court	The highest court in the United States that makes the final decision about laws
theft	Stealing
treaties	Written contracts between two nations

Student Handout B
5 Ws for "A Stolen Canoe Returned"

Directions: Read the article. While reading, underline or circle text that helps you answer the five questions. Then, record your notes in the chart.

5 Ws	"The Stolen Canoe"	"The Canoe Is Returned"
Who is the text about?		
Where is the setting?		
When do the events occur?		
What is the text about?		
Why do the events matter?		

CAPTION DRAWINGS

Directions: Draw a picture of something you want to remember about Canoe Journey, the Ten Rules of the Canoe, protocols for canoes arriving during Canoe Journey, or the story "A Stolen Canoe Returned." Include a caption for the picture to describe what is happening. Use word bubbles to show what people and objects in your picture are thinking and feeling.

A Closer Look at York's Life

Teaching Strategy: Close Reading and One-Pager

Purpose: Drawing from the Teaching Tolerance project *Teaching Hard History: American Slavery,* this lesson foregrounds key essential knowledges about freedom, enslavement, resistance, and families that help students learn about York within the context of the institution of slavery that he was born into and resisted.

Connection to the Standards

6 P's Framework	Power
C3 Framework	D2.His.16.3-5
	D3.3.3-5
	D3.4.3-5
	D4.1.3-5
Common Core State Standards	CCSS.ELA-LITERACY.RL.4.1
	CCSS.ELA-LITERACY.RL.4.2
	CCSS.ELA-LITERACY.RL.4.3
	CCSS.ELA-LITERACY.RL.4.4
	CCSS.ELA-LITERACY.RI.4.9

Introduction

York is given little attention within curriculum on the Corps of Discovery. Some texts omit him altogether; others mention him only briefly. And while some texts explicitly mention that York was enslaved, rarely are students encouraged to think deeply about York in the context of slavery.

Without knowledge of the institution of slavery, we worry that students will interpret passages about York that discuss him as Clark's childhood "companion" or that praise the fact that he was able "to vote," in ways that purport equality and minimize his enslavement. In many ways, York did experience more freedom than other enslaved people at that time. He was able to carry a gun on the military expedition when it was illegal for enslaved people to do so, for example. And although York, along with Sacagawea, were given the opportunity to vote on where the Corps of Discovery would build their winter fort when they had reached the Pacific Ocean, this act did not mean he was free.

Though upon his return York may have experienced "the warm welcome given all the returned explorers," he would have still been bound by the Code of 1804, under which "he would have been forbidden to leave Clark's temporary place of residence without a pass, forbidden to carry the firearm he had used on the expedition, forbidden to administer medicine to any white person . . . and, of course, forbidden to raise his hand, no matter how provoked, against any member of the white race" (Betts, 2000, p. 107). York may have experienced a degree of freedom on his journey, but he was not a free man; he remained, upon his return, enslaved by Clark for at least 10 years after the military expedition ended. York contested his own enslavement and requested his freedom on multiple occasions; however, Clark was adamant that York remain enslaved. Recent evidence from letters Clark wrote his brother Jonathan discovered in 1988 indicate that York's repeated requests for freedom and to be closer to his wife infuriated Clark, so much so that he beat York, sent him to jail on one occasion, and threatened to send him to a "more severe" master.

As discussed in Chapter 2, chattel slavery was an institution that was fiercely protected by those who benefitted from it. This lesson invites students to think about York in the context of slavery, making explicit York's resistance to his own enslavement, and Clark's insistence that he remain enslaved. Drawing from the Teaching Tolerance project *Teaching Hard History: American Slavery* (Teaching Tolerance, 2019), this lesson foregrounds key essential knowledges about freedom, enslavement, resistance, and families that help students learn about York in the context of the institution of slavery that he was born into and resisted. Our hope is that teachers have already introduced students to the concept of slavery, and that this lesson deepens student understanding of the institution of slavery by looking at the ways this institution shaped some aspects of the Corps of Discovery. Student Handouts A and B are derived from *Teaching Hard History: American Slavery* including several of their Essential Knowledge sections. Teachers should familiarize themselves with this framework prior to the lesson (https://www.tolerance

.org/frameworks/teaching-hard-history/american-slavery/k-5-framework#essential-knowledge).

Materials

- Copies of Student Handouts A, B, and C for all students

Duration

Each activity will take 30 to 40 minutes.

Procedures

Activity 1

1. Start the lesson by recording students' prior knowledge about York. Say to students, "Let's begin with what we know. Who is York? What do you know about York?" During the facilitation of the discussion, record students' answers on the dry erase board. Students may mention that York was "a slave." If they do, return to this point at the end of the conversation. If students do not mention this, say to students, "York was an important member of the Corps of Discovery. A key part of York's life was that he was enslaved. We say that York was 'enslaved' rather than he was 'a slave' because it is important when we are talking about slavery to remember that we are talking about people or human beings, not objects or things."

2. Say to students, "Sometimes textbooks do not even mention York at all. That is not fair, because he was important to the Corps of Discovery. Other times, they mention York, but say little about how he was enslaved. Today we are going to build on this knowledge that York was enslaved."

3. Distribute one copy of Student Handout A to each student. Say to students, "I am going to read a text to you about York. There are no records written by York himself. What is known about York is based on the journals of the Lewis and Clark Expedition and letters written by William Clark. As I read, follow along with your finger or a pencil. Circle or mark any words that are unfamiliar to you. After each passage, I will pause and answer any questions."

4. Read each passage, pausing after each section, and clarify any student questions. After each passage, ask students "What is one main

idea in this passage?" Take several student responses.

5. After reading the handout, invite students to discuss the following two questions in pairs: "What is one thing you learned about York that you did not know before? What is one thing you learned about slavery that you did not know before?" Facilitate a discussion for students to share their responses.

6. Collect Student Handout A or tell students to keep it for the next lesson.

Activity 2

1. On the dry erase board, create a chart with four columns, one for each big idea:

FREEDOM	ENSLAVEMENT	RESISTANCE	FAMILIES

2. Organize students into pairs and instruct students to prepare by gathering a pencil or highlighter and Student Handout A from the prior activity. Distribute copies of Student Handout B to all students.

3. Say to students, "Today we are going to look closer at the institution of slavery and how it impacted York. An institution is a custom, practice, or law that is accepted by many people. Slavery was an institution that was legal in the United States. This means that there were laws that said people could enslave others. However, even though slavery was legal, slavery was wrong, unfair, and unjust. Sometimes laws can be wrong. We are going to take a closer look at four big ideas about slavery."

4. Distribute Student Handout B. Provide an overview of the key concepts freedom, enslavement, resistance, and families.

5. Say to students, "In pairs, you will be assigned one of these big ideas. You and your partner will first review the description of the big idea you are assigned. Then, you will re-read the information about York's life featured in Student Handout A. As you re-read this information, look for evidence of your big idea. Highlight or underline evidence of your big idea. When you and your partner are finished highlighting or underlining, write three examples of key findings in the chart on Student Handout B. Be prepared to share a key point about your big idea with the class."

6. Model the Activity.

7. Assign pairs of students one of the big ideas. Allow students 15–20 minutes to work in pairs.

8. While students are working, circulate among the pairs to check for understanding and preparedness for sharing their findings with the class.

9. After pairs have completed the activity, facilitate a class discussion in which groups share the evidence they compiled in their handout. Begin with one big idea and ask various pairs, "What is one piece of evidence you found in the text for your big idea?" Record student comments in the chart on the dry erase board. Repeat the following process with each big idea and consider instructing students to complete the information for the remaining big ideas on Student Handout B. Keep the chart posted on the dry erase board for Activity 3.

10. After completing the chart on the dry erase board, ask students if they have any questions about York or about slavery. Record their questions for future inquiry.

11. Close the activity by having students share one word to describe a feeling they had during this activity.

Activity 3

1. On the chart posted on the dry erase board that was completed during Activity 2, add the following letters for the purpose of the one-pager.

A FREEDOM	B ENSLAVEMENT	C RESISTANCE	D FAMILIES

2. If students completed the information for the remaining big ideas on Student Handout B, instruct students to prepare by locating the handout. Distribute Student Handout C.

3. Say to students, "Today you will create a one-pager about York. In the center oval, you will represent York however you wish. You may draw him, or you may represent him through images, symbols, or words that you think are important. Remember, there are no actual photographs of York. Any image we see of him in books or online is from an artist or person who created an image based on descriptions or interpretations. Sometimes people drew him in stereotypical, hurtful, or dehumanizing ways. Dehumanizing means to make someone appear less than human. Be mindful of drawing York in a way that is respectful."

4. Say to students, "In each corner, you will represent one of the big ideas about slavery we have learned about, A) Freedom, B) Enslavement, C) Resistance, D) Families. You may use pictures, symbols, words, or information from Student Handouts A and B to represent each big idea."

5. Allow students time to complete their one-pager.

6. Post the one-pagers around the classroom and have students do a gallery walk and observe each other's work.

Extensions

- Give students the following scenario and invite them to complete the task individually, in pairs, or in small groups:
  » You are a historian. Your town is going to put up a statue to honor York and has asked you to create the informative plaque that will be featured below the statue. Write the caption that you think should be included with the statue.

- Read a textbook or children's book that features York, and have students critically analyze how York is represented. If no such book is available at your library, students could examine the following two passages from *I am Sacajawea, I am York: Our Journey West with Lewis and Clark* by Claire Rudolf Murphey (2005):

> They call me York, after my pappy, Old York, and the York River. On the plantation in Kentucky, Cap'n Clark and I used to play in the fields and go fishing. In my twelfth summer Master moved me into the big house and game me to his son. I've been by Cap'n's side ever since. On this long journey west to find a route to the Pacific Ocean, I am the only black man. (p. 4)

> Day and night the rain pours down. Finally, we reach the Pacific Ocean. Hallelujah! Cap'n Lewis asks each soldier and Charbonneau where to

build our winter fort. He records their votes in his book. Then my cap'n taps my shoulder. He wants me, a slave, to vote? My heart thumps! He points to Sacajawea, too. I smile at her. I am York. She is Sacajawea. For this one moment we are free. (p. 28)

» Facilitate a discussion of the book, or each passage, using the following questions: What does this book/passage tell us about York? What does this book/passage tell us about the relationship between York and William Clark? Is there evidence in this book that York was an enslaved person?

- Provide students with the following scenario: "After being read a book about York, in which the book says that Clark and York were childhood companions, a younger student asks you, 'Were Clark and York friends?' How would you respond to this student?" After a pair-share, lead a discussion. Encourage students to think about the younger student's question in light of what they learned about slavery. If needed, prompt students to think about power (i.e., Can you "own" a friend?)

Student Handout A
A Closer Look at York's Life

Born Enslaved

No one is sure the exact year York was born, since enslaved people often did not have birth certificates. York was likely born in the early 1770s on a **plantation** in Virginia. When York was born, he was already enslaved. York was born into slavery because York's parents, Old York and Rose, were also enslaved. Although enslaved people are human beings, when slavery was legal, enslaved people were viewed as **property**. Enslaved people were bought and sold, or passed down to family members, like property. Old York and Rose were enslaved by John Clark (William Clark's father), who **inherited** enslaved people from his father. After William Clark's father died, William learned from his father's **will** that he would inherit York, Old York, Rose, and five other enslaved people. Enslavers chose to enslave other people because they made money, or **profited** from, enslaved peoples' **labor**. Many people were enslavers, including presidents like Thomas Jefferson. Enslaved people did many kinds of work, but that work was often very difficult. Enslaved people, however, did not earn money for their work.

York's Life Before the Military Expedition

William Clark and York grew up together as children in the same house, but when York turned around 12 years old, he became Clark's personal "body servant." In 1784, the Clark family moved to Kentucky, along with about other 20 enslaved people who worked to set up a new plantation. York served on the plantation for many years. He also traveled places with Clark on business and accompanied Clark on several visits to meet with President Thomas Jefferson. Sometime before 1803, York married an enslaved woman, but there are no written records of her name, when they were married, or if they had children. York would have needed Clark's permission to visit her and marry her.

York During the Military Expedition

In 1803, Lewis and Clark were asked to put together a team for the military expedition. York, who was probably 31 or 32 years old and recently married, was chosen to join the **corps**. We do not know if York wanted to go on the military expedition. However, because he was enslaved, he did not have a choice. From the journals, there is evidence that York had many responsibilities, skills, and was a trusted member of the military expedition. He demonstrated courage when he risked his life to save Clark, and he was a skilled hunter and outdoorsman, provided medical care, and engaged in trade and creating **alliances** with Native nations. York was away from his wife, but he still thought about her. During the expedition, York was allowed to send home a gift package, which included two Mandan buffalo robes, to his wife and a friend named Ben (who was enslaved by Clark and freed in 1802). In some ways, York was treated like an equal member of the corps during the military expedition. For example, he carried a gun to hunt and voted on the location of Fort Clatsop. These were actions that other enslaved people could not do at that time. However, York was still written about in the journals of Lewis and Clark as "my boy York," "my servant," "my black servant," and "Capt. Clark's black man."

Freedom Denied

When the corps returned home, most of the men were awarded land and money. Lewis received $2,776.22 and Clark received $2,113.74. They also received 1,600 **acres** of land each. The other men each received double pay (approximately $333) and 320 acres of land. However, Sacagawea and York received no money or land. York also remained enslaved by Clark. York did not want to be enslaved. He wanted to be free and return to his wife in Kentucky, but Clark refused to give York freedom. "I am determined not to sell him," Clark wrote his brother Jonathan. Clark allowed York to visit his wife, but wrote that if York tried to run off, he would hire or sell him off to a "**severe** master." Clark allowed York to visit his wife for 4–5 weeks, but York stayed 4–5 months. Clark felt York was too concerned "about freedom" and did not "expect much from him as long as he has a wife in Kentucky." Clark **demanded** that York return home. When York returned, Clark noted that York was "disrespectful and **sulky**." However, after Clark gave him a "severe **trouncing**," and later put him in jail, he noted he was "a good fellow to work with." A month later, however, Clark became "**displeased** with him" again, and eventually hired him out to his brother, Edmund Clark. Edmund said no one liked York, possibly because he still wanted to be free. York was then sent to a more "severe" master in Louisville. In November 1815, Clark purchased a wagon and horses and York was the driver. Sometime after this, historians are not sure when, Clark eventually **granted** York the freedom he had always wanted, and he gave York the wagon business. It is unclear what happened to York after that. Some say he became ill with cholera and passed away in Tennessee. Others say he found a home in a Crow village and lived out his days there.

GLOSSARY

acre	A unit or measurement of land that equals 43,560 square feet
alliances	A union or relationship between people, groups, or countries
corps	A military group
demand	To say something in a forceful way
displeased	Unhappy
granted	To give or allow
inherit	To receive something from someone else, usually after they die
labor	Physical work
plantation	Large farms or plots of land that used enslaved peoples' labor to grow crops like cotton, rice, sugar, or tobacco
profit	To make money from something
property	Something someone can own and buy, sell, trade, or pass down
severe	Very bad or harsh
sulky	Quiet, angry, or upset about something
trouncing	To punish someone severely
will	A legal document that says what someone should do with their belongings when they die

Directions

1. To complete this activity, you will need Student Handout A, "A Closer Look at York's Life."
2. You and a partner will be assigned one of the four big ideas (freedom, enslavement, resistance, or families). In the first column, read the description of the big idea you were assigned.
3. Re-read Student Handout A, looking for evidence of your big idea. Use your highlighter or pencil to mark evidence in the text.
4. When you and your partner are finished marking the text, write three key findings in the second column. Be prepared to share your findings with the class.

The following themes are adapted from *Teaching Hard History: American Slavery* (Teaching Tolerance, 2019).

FREEDOM	Evidence
Being free means being able to choose what your life looks like without interference from others. Everybody wants to be free, but some people have more freedom and privileges than other people. People and institutions have the ability to restrict freedom by using power to make rules and punishment to make people obey the rules. People also restrict freedom by intimidating people into acting in certain ways. Key Questions: • Was York able to choose what his life looked like? • What evidence is there that York wanted his freedom? • What rules restricted York's freedom? How was intimidation or punishment used to try to force York to follow the rules?	1. 2. 3.

ENSLAVEMENT	Evidence
The main purpose of enslaving people is to make money. Enslaved people rarely earn money for their work. Many kinds of people can be enslaved, including children. Most enslaved people were in bondage for their entire lives. When enslaved parents had children, they were also enslaved. When people are enslaved, they do not have freedom. Their enslavers control their actions and can say where they move, what job they do, and whom they will live with. The founders of the United States and twelve presidents enslaved people. Key Questions: • Who benefited from York's enslavement? What were the benefits? • Who enslaved York's family? • What are examples of the ways York's life was controlled by enslavers?	1. 2. 3.

RESISTANCE	Evidence
Enslaved people hated being enslaved and resisted bondage in many ways. Although it was very difficult, some did manage to escape. Enslaved people resisted slavery to try and obtain some freedom in the midst of their enslavement. Everyday acts of resistance were common and took many forms, such as slowing down work, pretending to be ill or to not understand, running away, even armed rebellion. Key Questions: • What evidence is there that York hated being enslaved? • What are examples of how York resisted being enslaved?	1. 2. 3.

FAMILIES	Evidence
Enslaved people loved their families just like other people. Enslavers often separated families to make more money or as punishment. Once separated, families were rarely able to communicate or be reunited. About half of all enslaved people lived under the same roof as the families they worked for. Sometimes they ate the same food and wore the same clothes. Key Questions: • What evidence is there that York loved his family? • What evidence is there that York was separated from his family so his enslaver could make more money? • What evidence is there that York was separated from his family as punishment? • What evidence is there that York lived under the same roof, ate the same food, and wore the same clothes as his enslaver?	1. 2. 3.

Student Handout C

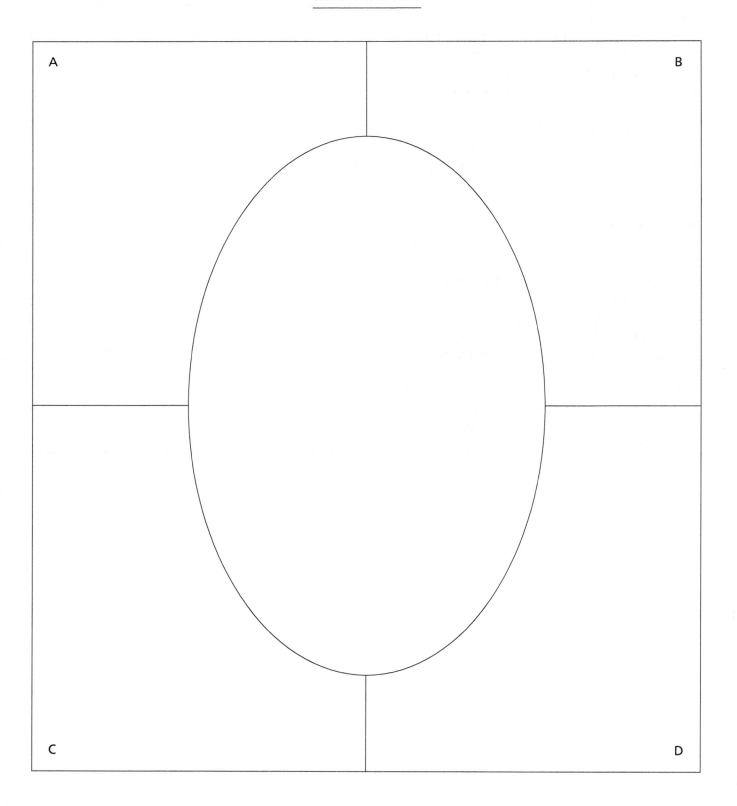

Part III

SECONDARY LESSON PLANS

The Stories Maps Tell

Teaching Strategy: Map Analysis

Purpose: This lesson plan introduces students to the ongoing presence and political sovereignty of tribal nations today.

Connections to the Standards

6 Ps Framework	Place
	Presence
	Perspectives
	Political Nationhood
	Power
C3 Framework	D2.His.1.6-12
	D2.His.5.6-12
	D2.His.7.9-12
	D3.3.6-12
Common Core State Standards	CCSS.ELA-Literacy.RH.6-12.1
	CCSS.ELA-Literacy.RH.6-12.6
	CCSS.ELA-Literacy.RH.6-12.7
	CCSS.ELA-Literacy.RH.6-12.9

Introduction

In the context of the Doctrine of Discovery, recorded observations about location, lists of the places Lewis and Clark named, and maps sketched during the Corps of Discovery helped enact the doctrine's principles. William Clark was the expedition's primary cartographer, using instruments, observations, and calculations to determine latitude and longitude. He sketched over a hundred detailed maps, noting landforms and location names. Clark created a map of the land and rivers from the Mississippi River to the Pacific Ocean, published in 1810, that also included new information from expeditions that took place after the return of Lewis and Clark's. The maps "became part of the evidence that the United States used for decades to prove its claim of first discovery and actual occupation of the Pacific Northwest" (Miller, 2008, p. 99). Further, the maps were useful for advancing the commercial interests of the United States with the intention of "beginning to bring the Indian Nations within the American

political and commercial orbit and strengthening the United States Discovery claim" (Miller, 2008, p. 99).

Clark and the mapmakers of his time understood they were not the first or only to chart land features. Historian James Ronda (1984) lists thirty entries from the Lewis and Clark journals that reference maps authored by Native mapmakers and used by the military expedition for route finding and information gathering. Ronda (1984) identifies three ways Native cartographers conveyed the landscape to the expedition: verbal descriptions, elaborate drawings on hides or on the ground, and the use of sand or other materials to draw relief maps. For the version published in 1810, Clark used details from these maps and included areas the military expedition did not visit but that were mapped for them by Native mapmakers. This lesson plan presents a map from 1805 drawn by Arikara leader Too Né that was featured in the May 2018 (Vol. 44, no. 2) issue of the Lewis & Clark Trail Heritage Foundation's periodical, *We Proceeded On*.

Lewis and Clark met Too Né on October 9, 1804, as they traveled through Arikara homelands. He continued with the Corps of Discovery through early November "providing a running ethnographic commentary and geographic lesson" (Jenkinson, 2018, p. 24) as the military expedition proceeded to the homelands of the Dakota and Ojibwe on the Upper Missouri River. Too Né, a speaker of 11 languages and Plains Sign Language, was a member of an Arikara delegation that traveled to Washington, DC, arriving in February 1806. He died in Washington, DC on April 6, 1806, and President Thomas Jefferson wrote a letter of condolence to the Arikara nation stating "we shed many tears over his grave, and we now mingle our afflictions with yours on the loss of this beloved chief."

In this lesson plan, students begin by viewing Too Né's map (1805) (*We Proceeded On*, p, 19 foldout) and Clark's map (2nd edition, 1814). As Clark may have done, when students examine Too Né's map they see "a device at once recognizable as a map and yet unfamiliar in structure and expression" (Ronda, 1984, p. 48). Too Né's map recorded geographical, political, mythical, and historical features (O'Briant, 2018). As described by O'Briant (2018), his map is organized by "the sacred water that flows through the literal middle of the Arikara universe. As the river bends, so does the map (in a very non-western scientific way) and all is oriented toward its new directional flow" (p. 13). In comparison to Clark's map conveying the story of "exploration and discovery" through western cartographic practices, Too Né's map represents "the entirety of the Arikara world, spanning the spiritual, but also the temporal: from the origins up to the present. He knew precisely where his people belonged in that world—geographically, politically, spiritually . . ." (p. 15). Comparing and contrasting the mapmaking styles of Too Né and William Clark is a way for students to respond to the question, "What stories do maps tell?" This activity models a process for examining maps using an analysis tool available for teachers and students from the Library of Congress (www.loc.gov/teachers /usingprimarysources/resources/Analyzing_Maps .pdf) in which investigative questions guide students through observation, reflection, and questioning.

Students repeat their use of the map analysis tool from the Too Né and William Clark exercise as they rotate through seven stations, viewing a variety of maps. These maps offer contemporary Native perspectives about homelands, tribal sovereignty, and political nationhood. Thus, the study of the Corps of Discovery is situated in the present as the maps are used to elicit discussion about the expedition's legacy. The lesson plan closes with a writing activity addressing the meaning of Roberta Conner's (Cayuse, Umatilla, and Nez Perce) presentation titled "We Must Tell Our Story" (2006b) from the Tribal Legacy Project that is featured in Station 1. (For more information about the Tribal Legacy Project, refer to Teaching Resource 4: Honoring Tribal Legacies, An Epic Journey of Healing.) As Roberta Conner states in the opening quote from her presentation titled "We Must Tell Our Story," the experiences of Native nations since contact with Lewis and Clark make a "a story that's not told very often." The maps curated for this lesson plan intentionally begin a study of the Corps of Discovery from the perspective that "we're still here."

Materials

- The lesson plan opens showing a visual of Too Né's (Arikara) map drawn in 1805. For background information, it is recommended teachers read: "Too Né's World: The Arikara Map and Native American Cartography" (Kevin O'Briant, 2018), www.lewisandclark .org/wpo/pdf/vol44no2.pdf#page=8.

- Copies of Student Handouts A, B, and C for all students
- Copies of "Stations 1–7" handouts for small groups visiting a station
- Computers for showing maps at Stations 1–7

Duration

This lesson plan takes approximately 90 minutes.

Procedures

1. Ask students to draw a map of a space they share (such as the school, streets surrounding the school, or the city). "Draw a map" is the only instruction given to students as the goal is to encourage a wide variety of maps. After students have finished, use the document camera to project examples for discussion (consider showing a map you have drawn). During the discussion, ask questions about what stories the maps convey about the space, how different experiences of the same space are conveyed, and about the meanings of symbols, and compare and contrast students' maps.

2. Distribute Student Handout A to all students. Say to students, "Today we are going to explore the different stories maps tell. We'll be using a protocol from the Library of Congress to help 'interview' these maps through observation, reflection, and questions." Review the instructions and questions for each column.

3. Project the image of Too Né's (1805) map: www.lewisandclark.org/wpo/pdf/vol44no2 .pdf#page=21. Say to students, "The first map is dated 1805 and was drawn by Too Né, an Arikara leader who traveled with the Corps of Discovery for two weeks and then visited Washington, DC to meet with President Thomas Jefferson and others." Zoom in/ out to provide students a detailed view of the map. Provide views of the geographic, political, temporal (past to present), and spiritual features Too Né included on the map (described in O'Briant, 2018). Facilitate a discussion for students to share findings they recorded in Student Handout A.

4. Next, project the image for William Clark's map dated 1814: www.loc.gov/item /79692907/. Say to students, "This is William Clark's completed map of the land traveled

by the Corps of Discovery from 1804 to 1806." Zoom in/out to provide students a detailed view of the map features. Consider a detailed view of the Fort Mandan region to show Clark's interpretation of the area drawn by Too Né. Facilitate a discussion for students to share their findings. Ask students, "How does this map compare and contrast to Too Né's map? What stories do these maps tell?"

5. Explain to students that they will visit seven stations featuring different maps and use the same process to examine the stories of the maps. Distribute Student Handout B to students and review the instructions. Remind students to refresh or re-upload the websites when they arrive at a station as some of the maps have important information or disclaimers to read prior to viewing.

6. In small groups, students rotate through the seven stations (approximately 8 minutes at each station). At each station, a document provides information about what is being viewed. Students record their findings in Student Handout B.

7. After students visit each station, facilitate a discussion of their findings. Emphasize concepts such as Native homelands, tribal sovereignty, and political nationhood. Ask students, "What stories do these maps tell? What do we learn about Native peoples today? What do we learn about Native perspectives? What do we learn about the legacy of the Corps of Discovery?"

8. Distribute copies of Student Handout C to all students. Refer to the handout to share about Roberta Conner and the instructions for listening to her presentation, "We Must Tell our Story." This video is from the Tribal Legacy Project (the website used in Station 1) (1 minute, 55 seconds) (www.lc -triballegacy.org/video.php?vid=744&query =Bobbie%20Conner). After students view the video, facilitate a discussion about what they annotated and why they identified these words or phrases as important. (Adobe Flash Player is required for the Tribal Legacy Project website.)

9. Next, review the instructions for the writing activity.

10. After completing the writing activity, ask students to share an excerpt with a partner. Then, ask for volunteers to share excerpts with the class.

Extension Activities

- Explore examples of maps from Indigenous perspectives by using the Decolonial Atlas website (decolonialatlas.wordpress.com/). Click on "Indigenous Perspectives" to see maps such as Minneapolis-St. Paul in Dakota and Ojibwe, North America from Lakota perspective, the Dakota Access Pipeline Indigenous Protest Map, a line drawing of the Shoshoni Map Rock, Inuit cartography, and Micronesian stick charts.

Directions: While viewing the maps, use the questions to help you observe, reflection, and question. Record your findings under each column.

	Observe What do you notice first? What graphical elements do you see? What places does the map show?	**Reflect** What does this map tell you about what was important to its author?	**Question** After viewing the map, what questions do you have? What are you curious about?
Too Né (1805)			
William Clark (1814)			

Student Handout B

Directions: During this activity, you will visit seven stations featuring a map. Refresh the website when you arrive at a new station. Just as we did with the maps drawn by Too Né (1805) and William Clark (1814), record your observations.

	Observe What do you notice first? What graphical elements do you see? What places does the map show?	**Reflect** What does this map tell you about what was important to its author?	**Question** After viewing the map, what questions do you have? What are you curious about?
Station 1 Tribal Legacy Project (National Park Service and the University of Montana, 2006)			
Station 2 Invasion of America (Claudio Saunt, 2014)			
Station 3 American Indians and Alaska Natives in the United States (U.S. Census Bureau, 2010)			
Station 4 Tribal Leaders Directory (U.S. Department of the Interior: Indian Affairs)			
Station 5 Jaune Quick-To-See Smith, *State Names* (Smithsonian American Art Museum, 2000)			
Station 6 Dakota Homelands Map Marlena Myles and Dawí (2019)			

	Observe	Reflect	Question
	What do you notice first? What graphical elements do you see? What places does the map show?	What does this map tell you about what was important to its author?	After viewing the map, what questions do you have? What are you curious about?
Station 7 Native Land (Victor Temprano, 2015)			

STATION 1

Map Title and Website	Tribal Legacy Project (lc-triballegacy.org/main.php)
Description	The Corps of Discovery took place in 1804–1806. Two hundred years later, in 2003–2006, the National Park Service organized a three-year commemoration of Lewis and Clark. The programming included a touring exhibit called the Tent of Many Voices. Presentations by Native speakers from Native nations along the Lewis and Clark National Historic Trail were recorded, organized, and archived as the Tribal Legacy Project. The map for this station is the homepage for the Tribal Legacy Project. Move the computer mouse over the map and click on different regions. For each region, move the computer mouse over the names of tribal nations to see their locations. If time allows, explore the presentations, flags of Native nations, and links to the tribal websites.

STATION 2

Map Title and Website	Invasion of America (Claudio Saunt, 2014) (usg.maps.arcgis.com/apps/webappviewer/index.html?id=eb6ca76e008543a89349ff2517db47e6)
Description	Claudio Saunt, a historian at the University of Georgia, created this map showing the dispossesion of Native homelands through treaty or executive order between 1776 and 1887. Click the clock icon at the bottom of the screen to change the speed of the animation. To view the animation in video, click the link at the top of the website next to the search bar.

STATION 3

Map Title and Website	American Indians and Alaska Natives in the United States (U.S. Census Bureau, 2010) (www2.census.gov/geo/maps/special/AIANWall2010/AIAN _US_2010.pdf)
Description	As mandated by the U.S. Constitution, the U.S. government counts the population every 10 years (referred to as the census). This map was created based on the 2010 census data and shows a population summary of American Indian and Alaska Native people in the United States.

STATION 4

Map Title and Website	Tribal Leaders Directory (U.S. Department of the Interior: Indian Affairs) (n.d.) (www.bia.gov/bia/ois/tribal-leaders-directory/)
Description	This map is provided by the Bureau of Indian Affairs (BIA). It is a directory of the leaders of tribal nations across the United States. You can switch views between BIA regions or states to see the federally recognized tribes in specific areas. For each tribal nation, the contact information, website, election information, and chair are listed.

STATION 5

Map Title and Website	Jaune Quick-To-See Smith, *State Names* (2000) (Smithsonian American Art Museum) (americanart.si.edu/artwork/state-names-73858)
Description	This is a painting by the artist Jaune Quick-to-See Smith. She is a member of the Confederated Salish and Kootenai Nation in Montana. Scroll down to the bottom of the website to watch a video of Jaune Quick-to-See Smith talking about *State Names*, how she became an artist, and her process of creating art.

STATION 6

Map Title and Website	Dakota Homelands Map (Marlena Myles and Dawí, 2019) (marlenamyl.es /project/dakota-land-map/)
Description	As described on the website, "this map tells the story of the past, present, and future of Dakota people and Dakota language in the Twin Cities (Minneapolis and St.Paul, MN). There are two maps to view along with audio pronunciation for all map features.

STATION 7

Map Title and Website	Native Land (Victor Temprano, 2015) (native-land.ca/)
Description	This map is an ongoing project by Victor Temprano of Vancouver, BC (Canada). On the website he writes, "I feel that Western maps of Indigenous nations are often inherently colonial, in that they delegate power according to imposed borders that don't really exist in many nations throughout history. They were rarely created in good faith, and often used in wrong ways." The purpose of this map is to educate people to recognize that wherever they are located, they are on Indigenous homelands. The interactive features include a search by location and the ability to switch or overlap views for territory, language, and treaty.

Student Handout C

Directions

1. View Roberta Conner's (Cayuse, Umatilla, and Nez Perce) presentation titled "We Must Tell Our Story" (2006) from the Tribal Legacy Project. The transcript of the presentation is presented below in the textbox. As she is speaking, underline words that are important to you. Roberta Conner is the director of the Tamástslikt Cultural Institute located on the Confederated Tribes of the Umatilla Indian Reservation. She served as the Vice President of the National Council of the Lewis and Clark Bicentennial Board of Directors and was a member of the Circle of Tribal Advisors.

> For many event planners and students and scholars, tribes are part of the backdrop to the Lewis and Clark Expedition story. Just part of the landscape through which they traveled. That's half right—we are part of the landscape. But the part that's wrong is that we're backdrop. I submit to you we are the story—the tribes and the land. This story has always been about land, it will always be about land.
>
> People who wonder why we're involved need to understand that we are here today and at every other signature event in Lewis and Clark planning meetings, not because it's fun necessarily but because we're still here. We are grateful to ancestors who made tremendous sacrifices so that we might be here. To tell you their history, to take care of the gift the Creator gave us that you moved on to. We can't tell that story if we don't go to the meetings, if we don't come to the conferences, and if we don't speak to audiences. That's why we're here because against incredible odds we have survived the last 200 years. Or, in the case of our friends from Monacan and other eastern tribes, the last 500 years. That's a story that's not told very often. We hope that the Bicentennial is that opportunity and most of you are in a position to help make that happen.

2. After watching Roberta Conner's presentation and underlining important words or phrases, what does this quotation mean to you? Reference specific maps and your findings from the station activity to support your answer.

What Were the Goals of the Lewis and Clark Corps of Discovery?

Teaching Strategy: Historical Investigation

Purpose: The purpose of this lesson is to challenge textbook simplifications of the goals President Thomas Jefferson outlined for the Corps of Discovery. Students analyze primary sources to answer the inquiry question, "What were the goals of the Corps of Discovery?"

Connection to the Standards

6 Ps Framework	Perspectives
	Power
C3 Framework	D2.His.16.6-12
	D3.3.3.6-12
Common Core State Standards	CCSS.ELA-Literacy.RH.6-12.1
	CCSS.ELA-Literacy.RH.6-12.4
	CCSS.ELA-Literacy.RH 6-12.5

Introduction

This lesson challenges the social studies textbook section often titled something similar to "The United States Expands West" in *The Americans* (Danzer, Klor de Alva, Krieger, Wilson, & Woloch, 2000), "The Lewis and Clark Expedition" in *The American Nation* (Davidson, 2005), "From Sea to Shining Sea" in *History Alive! Pursuing American Ideals* (Hart, 2013), or "Exploring the Louisiana Territory" in *American History: Beginnings through Reconstruction* (Davidson & Stoff, 2016). Remember from Chapter 3 that terms such as "expand," "expedition," or "exploring" are framed from a Eurocentric perspective, and tend to neutralize the militaristic aspect of the Corps of Discovery. These conventional textbook versions of the Corps of Discovery downplay the purpose, events, and consequences of the expedition's actions. Further, they omit the context of the Doctrine of Discovery that justified the military expedition, as well as the legacy this reconnaissance mission had on tribal nations. Contemporary experiences and perspectives about the legacy of the reconnaissance mission are not included. In this lesson plan, students compare and contrast the conventional textbook story of the Corps of Discovery with a series of primary documents. This teaching strategy, as the authors of *Reading Like a Historian* write,

> not only teaches students to take a critical approach to reading, it can show them the need to puzzle through historical sources in order to find out what really happened. This approach, what we refer to as "Opening Up the Textbook," changes the text from an inert authority, always issuing the final word, to one more historical source that must be critically evaluated like any other. (Wineburg, Martin, & Monte-Sano, 2013, p. 124)

Secondary Lesson Plan 2 challenges the textbook's "inert authority" by presenting students with six historical sources. Five of the sources are documents from 1803 and 1804 authored by President Thomas Jefferson and Meriwether Lewis. The sixth document is an interview with Gerard Baker (Mandan-Hidatsa) who worked for the National Park Service for 34 years and retired in 2010. He held significant positions such as Assistant Director for American Indian Relations and Superintendent of the Lewis and Clark National Historic Trail.

In addition to complicating the textbook section about the Corps of Discovery and extending student understanding about President Thomas Jefferson's intentions, this lesson plan prepares students for Secondary Lesson Plan 3: The Doctrine of Discovery. One of the activities in Secondary Lesson Plan 3 circles students back to a historical source examined in Secondary Lesson Plan 2 as they apply their knowledge of the Doctrine of Discovery by annotating the document with the doctrine's principles. As a result of these two lesson plans, student responses to the question, "What were the goals of the Lewis and Clark Corps of Discovery?" can go far beyond textbook distortions of Lewis and Clark.

Materials

- The following chart is posted on the dry erase board

What do we know?	How do we know?

- Teacher Handout A and B
- Copies of Student Handout A for each student.
- A packet of primary documents that includes one copy of Student Handouts B–F for each small group

Duration

This lesson takes approximately 60 to 90 minutes.

Procedure

1. Arrange students in small groups.
2. Begin the lesson by facilitating a class discussion to elicit students' prior knowledge about the purpose of the Corps of Discovery. Say to students, "Let's begin by considering what you already know about the Corps of Discovery. What were Lewis and Clark instructed to do by President Thomas Jefferson? Where did you learn this information?" As the discussion unfolds, record student answers on the chart under the columns "What do we know?" and "How do we know?"
3. Next, direct students to a specific passage in their textbook about the Corps of Discovery or project the excerpt featured in Teacher Handout A. After reading the excerpt with the class, facilitate a discussion with questions, such as: According to our text, what was the purpose of the expedition? How does the information from our text fit with what we already know about the expedition's goals?
4. Say to students, "Today we will compare and contrast what we know about the expedition's purpose, what our textbook tells us, and primary sources related to the expedition. As historical investigators, our goal is to answer the following question: What were President Thomas Jefferson's goals for the Lewis and Clark Corps of Discovery?"

5. Distribute copies of Student Handout A to each student and a packet of primary documents that includes Student Handout B–F for each small group. Explain to students, to complete Part 1 they will collaborate in small groups, reviewing a series of documents. The teacher or small groups can determine how students will collaborate (for example, small groups members select a document and share their findings with each other after becoming experts or small group members read each document together). The goal is to complete the chart (Part 1) on Student Handout A.
6. Using Teacher Handout B (Excerpts from President Thomas Jefferson's confidential letter to Congress; January 18, 1803), model how to do the activity by reading, annotating, and completing the first line of the chart.
7. While students are doing the activity, circulate among groups to check for understanding and completion of the chart. Project the image of the Jefferson Peace Medals to accompany Student Handout E (www.lewis-CLark.org/article/350).
8. When small groups have finished the chart, instruct small groups to continue collaboration as they finish by completing investigation questions (Part 2). Emphasize the need to use evidence from the documents when answering the questions. Circulate among groups to check for understanding and group preparedness for sharing findings with the class.
9. After students complete Part 2, facilitate a discussion using the following questions:

   - How did you answer our investigation question? What were the goals of the Corps of Discovery?
   - What documents provided the most compelling evidence? Why?
   - In what ways did the conclusions of groups compare and contrast?
   - How do our results compare and contrast with what the textbook presents to us?
   - Why does the textbook offer such a limited version of this story?
   - When you think of the Corps of Discovery as expansionist versus science information gathering, how does that change your view of the expedition?

10. Return to the chart on the dry erase board created at the beginning of the lesson. Ask students, "In what way has your understanding about the goals of the Corps of Discovery changed as a result of the historical investigation? What new questions are raised for you as a result of this investigation?"

studies textbooks with a variety of copyright dates. They make recommendations to a textbook publisher about what should be included and why. Or students write and illustrate their own textbook section about the Corps of Discovery to be shared with future students.

Extension Activities

- Students compare and contrast sections about the Corps of Discovery from several social

---
Teacher Handout A

Textbook Title: American History: Beginnings Through Reconstruction
Publisher: Pearson (Boston, MA); **Year:** 2016; **Page Numbers:** 200–201

EXPLORING THE LOUISIANA TERRITORY

Few Americans knew anything about the Louisiana territory. In 1803, Congress provided money for a team of explorers to study the new lands. Jefferson chose Meriwether Lewis, his private secretary, to head the expedition, or long voyage of exploration. Lewis asked William Clark to go with him.

Jefferson asked Lewis and Clark to map a route to the Pacific Ocean. He also told them to study the geography of the territory, including: ". . . climate as characterized by the thermometer, by the proportion of rainy, cloudy, and clear days, by lightning, hail, snow, ice . . . the dates at which particular plants put forth or lose their flowers, or leave, times of appearance of particular birds, reptiles, or insects" (Thomas Jefferson, letter to Meriwether Lewis, 1803).

Jefferson also instructed Lewis and Clark to learn about the Native American nations who lived in the Louisiana Purchase. These Native Americans carried on a busy trade with English, French, and Spanish merchants. Jefferson hoped that the Indians might trade with American merchants instead. Therefore, he urged Lewis and Clark to tell the Indians of "our wish to be neighborly, friendly, and useful to them."

Student Handout A

Part 1: Directions

As you examine each of the documents, record your findings in the chart.

Historical Investigation Question: What were the goals of the Corps of Discovery?

Document	List a minimum of 3 findings that help you answer the investigation question.
Example	Thomas Jefferson, Excerpts from confidential letter to Congress, January 18, 1803
Handout B	Thomas Jefferson, Excerpts from instructions to Lewis, June 20, 1803
Handout C	Thomas Jefferson, Excerpts from instructions to Lewis, January 22, 1804
Handout D	Meriwether Lewis, Excerpts from speech to the Yankton Sioux, August 30, 1804
Handout E	Form and Jefferson Peace Medal, 1804–1806
Handout F	Gerard Baker, interview

Part 2: Directions

After reading the documents, respond the following questions. Refer to evidence from the primary sources to support your answers.

1. What were the goals of the Corps of Discovery?

2. In what way has your understanding about the goals of the Corps of Discovery changed as a result of the historical investigation?

3. Why do you think textbooks offer such a limited version of this story?

Teacher Handout B
Thomas Jefferson, Excerpts from Confidential Letter to Congress

Description: This document presents excerpts from President Thomas Jefferson's confidential letter to Congress requesting $2,500 to fund the Corps of Discovery. As you read, note the language that gives insight into President Jefferson's vision for the development of the United States.

Source: Excerpt adapted from www.monticello.org/thomas-jefferson/louisiana-lewis-clark /origins-of-the-expedition/a-confidential-letter/

January 18, 1803

Gentlemen of the Senate, and of the House of Representatives

The Indian tribes residing within the limits of the United States, have, for a considerable time, been growing more and more uneasy at the reduction in the territory they occupy. In order to provide an extension of territory which the rapid increase of our numbers will call for, we will encourage two things. First, we will encourage them to turn to abandon hunting and turn to agriculture and domestic life. The extensive forests necessary in the hunting life, will then become useless, and they will see advantage in exchanging them for the means of improving their farms. Second, we will encourage them to multiply trading houses among them, and place within reach those things which will contribute more to their farming and domestic life. Experience and reflection will develop to them the wisdom of exchanging what they can spare and we want, for what we can spare and they want. In bringing together their and our settlements, and in preparing them ultimately to participate in the benefits of our government, I trust and believe we are acting for their greatest good.

The river Missouri, and the Indians inhabiting it, are not well known. It is understood that the country on that river is inhabited by numerous tribes, who furnish great supplies of fur. Beyond the river Missouri, there is the possibility of more trade and potential continued navigation to the Western Ocean.

An intelligent officer, with ten or twelve chosen men, fit for the enterprise, and willing to undertake it, might explore the rivers and land all the way to the Western Ocean. Their purpose would be to meet with the natives on the subject of trade, get admission among them for our traders, agree to trade, and return with important information about the tribes. Their arms, accessories to weapons, clothing, instruments for recording observations, and light and cheap presents for the Indians is all that they would carry. They would receive a soldier's portion of land on their return.

Other nations have done similar undertakings. The interests of trade are within the constitutional powers and care of Congress. In addition, the undertaking advances our geographical knowledge of our own continent. The appropriation of two thousand five hundred dollars, "for the purpose of extending external commerce of the United States," would cover the undertaking.

Student Handout B
Thomas Jefferson, Excerpts from Instructions to Lewis (1803)

Description: This document presents the instructions President Thomas Jefferson gave to Meriwether Lewis. As you read, note the language that gives insight into President Jefferson's vision and priorities for the Corps of Discovery.

Source: Excerpt adapted from www.monticello.org/thomas-jefferson/louisiana-lewis-clark /preparing-for-the-expedition/jefferson-s-instructions-to-lewis/

June 20, 1803

To Captain Meriwether Lewis, Captain of the 1st Regiment of Infantry, of the United States Army

The object of your mission is to explore the Missouri river to see if its primary stream and tributaries meet the Pacific Ocean and whether the Columbia, Oregon, Colorado or any other river may offer the most direct and practical water way across the continent for purposes of trade. Observe and record your routes along the rivers to the ocean.

Future trade with the people living along your route makes it important that you learn about those people. Make a point to learn the names of the nations; their population; their possessions; their language, traditions, monuments; their occupations in agriculture, fishing, hunting, war, arts; their food, clothing, and housing; their diseases and medicines; moral and physical circumstances that distinguish them from the tribes they know; their laws and customs; and items they have for trade they can offer or want from us.

Because all nations want to grow bigger and stronger in terms of power and authority, it will be useful to find out what you can about their morals, values, religion, and other information among them. This information will help those who try to civilize and teach them.

Also pay attention to the land and soil, the growth of vegetables, especially those not of the United States. Pay attention to the animals, especially those not known in the United States. Also, the mineral productions of every kind, but more particularly metals and volcanic appearances. Finally, pay attention to the climate and record the weather.

In all your interactions with the natives, treat them in a friendly manner and tell them of your journey's innocence. Make them acquainted with the position, character, and peaceful commercial interests of the United States. Share our wish to be neighborly, friendly, and useful to them.

Given under my hand at the city of Washington this 20th day of June 1803.

Student Handout C
Thomas Jefferson, Excerpts from Instructions to Lewis (1804)

Description: This document presents instructions President Thomas Jefferson gave to Meriwether Lewis *after* the Louisiana Purchase was completed. As you read, note the language that gives insight into President Jefferson's vision and priorities for the Corps of Discovery.

Source: Excerpt adapted from memory.loc.gov/service/mss/mtj/mtj1/029/02909570958.pdf.

January 22, 1804

Dear Sir,

My letters since your departure have been of July 11 & 15. Nov. 16 and Jan. 13. Yours received are of July 8, 15, 22, 25; Sep. 25, 30; & Oct. 3. Since the date of the last we have no certain information of your movements. With mine of Nov. 16., New Orleans was delivered to us on the 20th of Dec. and our troops and government established there.

When your instructions were penned, this Louisiana Purchase was not complete and it was not known how acquiring this land would affect your instructions. Now that we are sovereigns of the country, we are allowed to set up trade with the natives.

You should inform those through whose country you will pass, or whom you may meet, that their late fathers the Spaniards have agreed to withdraw all their troops from all the waters and country of the Mississippi and Missouri. The Spaniards have surrendered to us all their subjects, posts, and lands. Now, we have become their fathers and friends. They will have no cause to lament this change. We have sent you to find out about the country and the nations inhabiting it so we can establish places, times and goods to trade. As soon as you return with the necessary information, we shall prepare supplies of goods and persons to bring them so we can be acquainted with them as soon as possible. They will find in us faithful friends and protectors.

Although you will pass through no settlements of the Sioux, you will probably meet with parties of them. On that nation we wish most particularly to make a friendly impression, because of their immense power, and because we learn they are very desirous of being on the most friendly terms with us.

Accept my friendly salutations and assurances of affectionate esteem and respect.

Student Handout D
Meriwether Lewis, Excerpts from Speech to Yankton Sioux

Description: This document is Meriwether Lewis' speech introducing the military expedition to the Yankton Sioux. This text of this speech was repeated to all Native nations during the journey. As you read, note what information Lewis is delivering on behalf of President Thomas Jefferson and the United States.
Source: Excerpt adapted from www.nps.gov/mnrr/planyourvisit/upload/L&CSpeech.pdf

August 30, 1804

Children.—It gives us much pleasure to have met you here this day in council. We salute you as the children of your Great Father the great Chief of the United States of America . . . Now open your ears that you may hear his words, and clear your minds to understand them.

Children.—We have come to inform you, as we go also to inform all the native nations who inhabit the borders of the Missouri, that a great Council was lately held between this great Chief of the United States of America, and your Old fathers the French and Spaniards. In this council it was agreed that all the white men on the waters of the Missouri and Mississippi, should obey the commands of the Great Chief of America, who has adopted them as his children, and they now form one common family with us. Your old traders are no longer the subjects of France or Spain, but have become the citizens of the United States of America, and are bound to obey the commands of their great chief the President, who is now your only great father.

Children.—You will perceive from what has been said, that the Great Chief of the United States of America has become your only father; he is the only friend to whom you can now look for protection, or from whom you can ask favor or receive good counsel. He will take care that you shall have no just cause to regret the change; he will serve you and not deceive you.

Children.—Know that the great chief who has thus offered you the hand of friendship, is the Great Chief of the United States of America, whose cities are as numerous as the stars of the heavens, and whose people, like the grass of the plains, cover with their cultivated fields and wigwams, the wide extended country reaching from the western border of the Mississippi to the Great Lakes of the East, where the land and the Sun rises from the face of the Great Waters.

Children.—Follow the counsels of your great father, and the great spirit will smile upon your nation, and in future years will make you to outnumber the trees.

Student Handout E
Form and Jefferson Peace Medal

Description: Lewis and Clark carried 89 Jefferson Peace Medals on the expedition. There were five sizes of medals and they were made of silver. The medals were given to leaders of Native nations during a ceremony in which Lewis delivered a speech. When the medals and gifts were presented, this form was used by the expedition. View an image of the Jefferson Peace Medals using this link: www.lewis-clark.org/article/350.
Source: brbl-dl.library.yale.edu/pdfgen/exportPDF.php?bibid=2002511&solrid =3519971&imgid=1008642

1804–1806

THOMAS JEFFERSON, PRESIDENT OF THE UNITED STATES

From the powers vested in us and _____ by the above authority: To all who shall see these presents, Greetings:

Know ye, the chief of the _____ NATION is now attached to the UNITED STATES; also his welcome has proven his desire to cultivate peace, harmony, and good neighborhood with the said States, and the citizens of the same; we do by the authority vested in us, require and charge, all citizens of the United States, all Indian Nations, in treaty with the same, and all other persons whomsoever, to acknowledge and treat the said _____ and his _____ in the most friendly manner, declaring him to be the friend and ally of the said States: the government of which with at all times be extended to their protection, so long as they do acknowledge authority of the same.

Having signed with our hands and affixed our seals
this _____ day of _____ 180

Student Handout F
Gerard Baker, Interview

Description: This interview is posted on the Public Broadcasting Service (PBS) website supporting the 1997 Ken Burns-directed film, *Lewis & Clark: The Journey of the Corps of Discovery*. Gerard Baker, Mandan-Hidatsa, worked for the National Park Service for 34 years and retired in 2010. He held significant positions such as Assistant Director for American Indian Relations and Superintendent of the Lewis and Clark National Historic Trail.

Source: Excerpt adapted from www.pbs.org/lewisandclark/living/idx_6.html

---

1997

When Lewis and Clark talked about a new "Great Father" in Washington, how did the Indians react?

I think, by then, they had been visited by quite a few people and so it wasn't a big thing. I think they realized it was a routine that they had to go through. They would listen to the speeches and accept the medals, accept different gifts, and in fact, the tribe at the time expected gifts. They expected everybody to get something.

What was Lewis and Clark's routine for interacting with the Indians?

You could call their Indian diplomacy the great traveling medicine show. They really did have a pattern that they had inherited from generations of Indian policy. The traveling medicine show worked like this, first there was a parade in which the European style technology was shown off. You wanted to show Indians uniforms and guns and the objects of the Industrial Revolution to impress them and then you wanted to show Indians trade goods and so the great country store was wheeled out. You wanted to show Indians all of those objects that they might gain if they became part of an industrial world that grew out of St. Louis. Then came the serious negotiation because Lewis and Clark represented not only military power, commercial power, but also diplomatic power. And then there was always a showing of the flag, the great American symbol of sovereignty and power.

What did the peace medal symbolize?

Peace medals symbolized two very different things. And they represented two different things on two different sides of the cultural divide. For Euro-Americans, for Thomas Jefferson's captains, the peace medal represented a recognition of American sovereignty. If I give you a peace medal, it means that you are now one of mine. That you've accepted the sovereignty of the American president. On the other hand, for native people, accepting a peace medal might simply mean recognition that we are equals. We are not fathers and sons, not fathers and children, but we're all one. And the peace medal also represented a source of power. Native people often believed that the power that the Europeans has were not in their own bodies, but in their objects. And so the peace medal is a wonderful symbol of difference.

Johnson v. McIntosh (1823) and the Doctrine of Discovery

Teaching Strategy: Historical Investigation

Purpose: The purpose of this lesson is to introduce students to the Doctrine of Discovery by examining Chief Justice John Marshall's ruling in *Johnson v. McIntosh* (1823). Then students revisit documents from the prior lesson to investigate President Jefferson's use of the principles of the Doctrine of Discovery.

Connection to the Standards

6 Ps Framework	Presence
	Perspectives
	Political Nationhood
	Power
C3 Framework	D2.His.1.6-12
	D2.His.3.6-12
	D2.His.16.6-12
	D3.3.6-12
	D4.6.6-12
	D4.7.6-12
	D4.8.6-12
Common Core Standards	CCSS.ELA-Literacy.RH.6-12.1
	CCSS.ELA-Literacy.RH.6-12.2
	CCSS.ELA-Literacy.RH.6-12.4
	CCSS.ELA-Literacy.RH.6-12.9

Introduction

During the closing discussion and writing activity in Secondary Lesson Plan 2, students share their new knowledge and understanding concerning the goals of the Corps of Discovery. Sometimes during this discussion, a student asks, "What gave President Jefferson the idea that he could take the land by sending Lewis and Clark to the Pacific Ocean?" Unbeknownst to the student, this pivotal question sets the frame for a new look at social studies curriculum about the Corps of Discovery—and Manifest Destiny—through the Doctrine of Discovery. Chapter 2 of *Teaching Critically*

About Lewis and Clark presents background knowledge for teachers related to the Doctrine of Discovery and its ten elements as described by Miller (2008). The purpose of this lesson is to highlight the centrality of the Doctrine of Discovery and its significance to the Corps of Discovery. The lesson undertakes this purpose by focusing on Chief Justice John Marshall's application of the Doctrine of Discovery in the ruling of *Johnson v. McIntosh* (1823)—the first of three Supreme Court cases referred to as the Marshall Trilogy.

The case of *Johnson v. McIntosh* (1823) was presented to the Supreme Court 20 years after President Jefferson sent a confidential letter to Congress on January 18, 1803, requesting $2500 for support of "an intelligent officer, with ten or twelve chosen men, fit for the enterprise, and willing to undertake" a military expedition supplied with "arms and accoutrements, some instruments of observation, and light and cheap presents for the Indians." One reason offered by President Jefferson for the request is that "other civilized nations have encountered great expense to enlarge the boundaries of knowledge by undertaking voyages of discovery . . . our nation seems to owe to the same object, as well as to its own interests, to explore this, the only line of easy communication across the continent, and so directly traversing our own part of it." Miller (2008) argues that President Jefferson's deliberate use of language regarding expansion, civilization, discovery and finding a route across the continent are evidence of "a working day-to-day knowledge" of the principles of the Doctrine of Discovery (p. 2).

The Supreme Court case *Johnson v. McIntosh* (1823) is notable because it was the first time the Doctrine of Discovery is encoded in U.S. law. Developing an understanding of Chief Justice Marshall's ruling and the principles of the Doctrine of Discovery provides students with critical knowledge to then revisit Thomas Jefferson's documents from Secondary Lesson Plan 2. Students apply this new understanding by reexamining these sources through the lens of the Doctrine of

Discovery. The result is understanding that the dispossession of Native homelands was not simply due to actions of a few "bad" people, but was normalized in the practices, and eventual policies, of the Founders and their descendants, and the bedrock of Constitutional law. Some students may be aware of the racist language and assumptions that are embedded into U.S. law. Others may be surprised by the explicitness of these racist assumptions within the doctrine and the ready acceptance of those assumptions by Chief Justice John Marshall.

Materials

- Copies of Student Handout A and B for all students
- Teacher Handout A and B
- Video: "Testimony of the Iroquois (Haudenosaunee): Doctrine of Discovery" www.digitalwampum.org/doctrine-of -discovery
- Lesson Plan 1 Student Handouts B, C, or D

Duration

Activity 1 takes approximately 20–30 minutes. Activity 2 and 3 each take approximately 20–40 minutes.

Procedures

Activity 1

1. To set the foundation for understanding the "Ten Elements of the Doctrine of Discovery" (refer to Chapter 2, Table 2.1, p. 16), begin the lesson by facilitating a visualization exercise. Say to students and pause as necessary, "I am going to ask you a series of questions and we are going to do a visualization activity. The purpose of the activity is to evoke the themes of today's lesson. If you are comfortable, close your eyes or find a place in the room to focus, listen carefully, and try to relax. Breathe deeply, slowly. Imagine a specific place that is important to you, where you feel safe and most comfortable. Imagine the details and allow yourself to experience what it feels like to be at this important place. Imagine that this important place is not only significant to you, but has been important to generations of the people closest to you. Now, imagine that I arrive and declare ownership of this important place because I discovered it. Because

I made this discovery, I am entitled to take possession. In addition, my discovery allows me to take possession of all the places that are in proximity to your important place. I can set the terms for everything that happens there. Pay attention to how this makes you feel. Pay attention how this compares to your feelings before I arrived and discovered your important place. When you are ready, open your eyes."

2. After students have opened their eyes, debrief the visualization activity by facilitating a discussion with the following questions: When I asked you to imagine an important place, what came to your mind? What makes these places important to you? How do you feel when you visit the important place? How did it feel when I "discovered" your important place? (Refer to the end of this lesson plan for an extension activity related to the places students identified.)

3. Say to students, "Our purpose today is to learn more about the meaning of discovery to the Lewis and Clark Expedition. Our goal is to understand why President Thomas Jefferson would believe it possible to give the instructions that we examined in yesterday's historical investigation. Today's question is: What was the context that made those instructions possible? To help us answer this question, we are going to jump to 1823— 20 years after President Jefferson issued instructions to Meriwether Lewis. Our focus is the Supreme Court case titled *Johnson v. McIntosh* (1823)."

4. Distribute Student Handout A to all students. Read the case summary to the class. In small groups, students discuss the question: How should the Supreme Court decide the case? Facilitate a discussion for groups to share their opinions and rationale.

5. Project Teacher Handout A to reveal the Supreme Court ruling. Read the ruling to the class. Say to students, "Chief Justice Marshall's use of the Doctrine of Discovery is the reason why we are focusing on this court case. The doctrine is a series of papal bulls—laws authored by the Pope—that became accepted international law among European powers to determine which country had the `Discovery' right to colonize. One example was written by Pope Alexander VI in 1493 to give Spain the right to claim the territory of the Americas and

justify the actions of Christopher Columbus. President Thomas Jefferson, and others, understood the principles of the Doctrine of Discovery. Chief Justice Marshall's use of the doctrine is significant because it became encoded in U.S. law and remains in U.S. law today."

6. Instruct students to look at the reverse side of Student Handout A, and project Teacher Handout B showing excerpts from the ruling. Say to students, "Let's look at the Ten Elements of the Doctrine of Discovery and see if we can find Chief Justice Marshall's use of the doctrine in his ruling." As a class, annotate the quotes by applying the principles of the Doctrine of Discovery. For example, after reading out loud the first sentence, ask students if they think principles from the doctrine are applicable and why. Then, indicate which element(s) by number or name by writing it on the document the class is viewing. (Consider the option of distributing the quotes to small groups and having students annotate collaboratively.) Use the following questions to extend the discussion and student understanding:

   a. Return to the opening activity of today's class. According to the Court, did the I have the right "by discovery" to take claim your important place and set the terms for everything that happens there? Why?

   b. Consider the 5th Amendment statement that "no person shall . . . *be deprived of life, liberty, or property, without due process of law; nor shall private property be taken for public use, without just compensation.*" How does the decision in *Johnson v McIntosh* (1823) fit with the 5th Amendment in relation to tribal nations? What does it say about the claim that the United States was built on "everyone is equal before the law?"

   c. What problems might occur for Native nations if they could only sell or trade with the United States?

   d. Why do you think this law has yet to be overturned?

Activity 2

1. To reference the Doctrine of Discovery, students will need Student Handout A from Activity 1. Say to students, "To understand how the Doctrine of Discovery is used today to justify the taking of land from Native nations, let's view a six-minute video titled 'Testimony of the Iroquois (Haudenosaunee): Doctrine of Discovery' (www.digitalwampum.org /doctrine-of-discovery/). As you listen to Oren Lyons, a traditional Faithkeeper for the Turtle Clan of the Onondaga Nation, and Sydney Hill, the Tadodaho (traditional leader) of the Haudenosaunee and member of the Onondaga Nation, consider the relevance of the Doctrine of Discovery today."

2. After viewing the video, facilitate a discussion of student responses. This is the point in the lesson plan in which connection is made to the Corps of Discovery by asking students, "Given our understanding of the Doctrine of Discovery (its use since 1493 and encoded in law since 1823), what does our knowledge of the Doctrine of Discovery add to our understanding of the purpose of the Corps of Discovery? Let's dig deeper into our response to this question by annotating a source from yesterday's lesson by applying the Ten Elements of the Doctrine of Discovery. We'll do the same thing we did earlier when we applied the elements to the sentence from Marshall's ruling; now we will use a source from the Corps of Discovery."

3. From Secondary Lesson Plan 1, select Student Handout B, C, or D. Distribute copies to small groups to annotate using the Doctrine of Discovery. While students are doing the activity, circulate to check for understanding and preparedness for sharing findings with the class.

4. When students have finished, facilitate a discussion of student findings and the way in which today's lesson adds to their understanding.

Activity 3

1. Explain to students that people have challenged the Doctrine of Discovery in primarily three ways: denouncing and/ or attempting to revoke, educating, and overturning. Read Chapter 2 for further background knowledge. Share with students some of the following examples:

   a. Long March to Rome (longmarchtorome .com/)

   b. The Sisters of Loretto (Rotondaro, 2015; www.ncronline.org/news/justice /doctrine-discovery-scandal-plain-sight)

    c. Interfaith action occurring at the Standing Rock Sioux Reservation during the demonstrations against the Dakota Access Pipeline (Roewe, 2016; www .ncronline.org/blogs/eco-catholic/larger -faith-community-comes-standing-rock -solidarity)

    d. Mitch Walking Elk and his students from St. Paul, MN (Hopfensberger, 2018; www .startribune.com/american-indian-teens -head-to-vatican-hoping-to-overturn -historic-papal-decrees/477183033/)

    e. Supreme Court ruling in *Washington State Department of Licensing v. Cougar Den* (2018) (Agoyo, 2019; www.indianz .com/News/2019/03/19/supreme-court -delivers-slim-victory-in-y.asp)

2. Facilitate a discussion in which students brainstorm ways they can contribute to these efforts.

3. Student Handout B presents an example of a possible action by writing a letter advocating for including the Doctrine of Discovery in curriculum about the Corps of Discovery.

Students can choose who to address the letter to, such as textbook publishers, district curriculum coordinators, state education committees in charge of social studies standards, and so on.

Extension Activity

- During debrief of the visualization exercise in Activity 1, students share important places they selected. Point out to students that these places are located on Native homelands. For Native students, this activity may be difficult as it reflects their family's recent history of dispossession. For non-Native students, it is important to point out that the feelings and loss they experience during the activity were lived by Native peoples. Design a research assignment in which students learn the story of the important place they identified, how they can educate others about its shared history, and how they can contribute to efforts of Native peoples to care for this important place.

Student Handout A

Directions: After reading the case summary, your goal is to decide the case. How should the Supreme Court rule in *Johnson v. McIntosh* (1823)? Be prepared to explain and share your answer with classmates.

SUPREME COURT CASE SUMMARY: *JOHNSON V. MCINTOSH* (1823)

Plaintiff: Thomas Johnson
Defendant: William McIntosh
Date Argued: February 14–18, 1823
Chief Justice: John Marshall

- In 1773, William Murray purchased two tracts of land from the Kaskaskia, Peoria, and Cahokia Nations. In 1775, Murray purchased more land from the Piankeshaw Nation. The land Murray purchased became part of the U.S. territory in 1776. In 1803 and 1809, the U.S. government established treaties with the same tribal nations involved in the land transactions of 1773 and 1775. Thomas Johnson, descendant of William Murray, inherited the land in 1819. There was no title to the land because the purchase was in violation of the Royal Proclamation of 1763 and the land was transferred to the U.S. government.
- In 1815, William McIntosh purchased the same land from the U.S. government. He received title to the land in 1818. McIntosh sued to have Johnson removed from the land.
- Thomas Johnson argued he was entitled to the land because the Kaskaskia, Peoria, Cahokia, and Piankeshaw Nations had lived on the land since Time Immemorial. This gave them the natural right to sell it to anyone they wanted. William Murray bought the land fair and square and his heirs should be entitled to it.
- William McIntosh argued because the Kaskaskia, Peoria, Cahokia, and Piankeshaw Nations were discovered by England and the land was passed on to the United States, they had no permanent right to the land and thus no right to sell the land to private individuals—only to the country that had discovery rights. Therefore, William Murray's purchase was not valid and thus he did not own the land and could not pass it to his descendant, Thomas Johnson. McIntosh argued that his purchase from the United States was the only valid contract.

Questions:

- Who does the land "belong" to? Johnson? McIntosh? Kaskaskia, Peoria, Cahokia Nations? Piankeshaw Nation?
- How should the Supreme Court rule? Why? (Choose one.)
  a. Thomas Johnson is entitled to the land because Murray made the purchase directly from Native nations.
  b. William McIntosh is entitled to the land because he made the purchase directly from the United States.

Ten Elements of the Doctrine of Discovery

1	First discovery	The first European country to "discover" lands unknown to other Europeans gets the land.
2	Occupancy	To claim the land, the European country must live on the land by building forts and settlements.
3	Preemption/ European Title	The European country that discovers and occupies the land is the only entity that can buy land from a Native nation.
4	Indian Title	The land that is not sold to the European country is considered land that a Native nation can continue living on.
5	Trade	The European country that discovers and occupies the land is the only country the Native nation can engage in trade.
6	Contiguity	The European country that discovers and occupies the land can claim all the land that they can see and reach by waterways.
7	Terra nullius	Latin word meaning "land belonging to no one." If lands are not being used in ways a European country recognizes, that country can claim the land.
8	Christianity	Non-Christians do not have the same rights as Christians to own land.
9	Civilization	European ways of living are "advanced," and this gives them a right to the land.
10	Conquest	Military victory is a way to claim land.

Adapted from Robert J. Miller (2008), pp. 3–4.

Supreme Court Case Summary: *Johnson v. McIntosh* (1823)

What happened?
Date Decided: February 28, 1823 (unanimous)
Chief Justice: John Marshall

- In the case of *Johnson v. McIntosh* (1823), the Supreme Court decided in favor of William McIntosh.
- Chief Justice John Marshall relied on the Doctrine of Discovery for the ruling. The following key ideas from the Doctrine of Discovery were applied to the case:
  » First discovery: The first European country to "discover" lands unknown to other Europeans gets the land.
  » Preemption/European Title: The European country that discovers and occupies the land is the only country that can buy land from Native nations.
  » Christianity: Non-Christians do not have the same rights as Christians to own land.
  » Civilization: European ways of living are "advanced," and this gives them a right to the land.
- Based on Doctrine of Discovery and the Supreme Court's use of the doctrine's principles, Native nations had no right to sell property to private individuals, only to a "discoverer," such as England or the United States.
- Therefore, the original sale to William Murray was invalid, and Thomas Johnson had no ownership of the land. William McIntosh's purchase was valid.
- This decision has never been overturned, so it is still the law of the land.

Teacher Handout B
Johnson v. McIntosh (1823) 21 U.S. 543 (8 Wheat. 543, 5 L.Ed. 681)

Chief Justice: John Marshall

From the unanimous opinion written by Chief Justice Marshall:

The United States, then, have unequivocally acceded to that great and broad rule (Discovery) by which its civilized inhabitants now hold this country. They hold, and assert in themselves, the title by which it was acquired. They maintain, as all others have maintained, that discovery gave an exclusive right to extinguish the Indian title of occupancy, either by purchase or conquest; and gave also a right to such a degree of sovereignty, as the circumstances of the people would allow them to exercise. . . .

Conquest gives a title which the Courts of the conqueror cannot deny. . . . The British government, which was then our government, and whose rights have passed to the United States, asserted a title to all the lands occupied by Indians. . . . It asserted also a limited sovereignty over them, and the exclusive right of extinguishing the title which occupancy gave to them. . . .

But the tribes of Indians inhabiting this country were fierce savages, whose occupation was war, and whose subsistence was drawn chiefly from the forest. To leave them in possession of their country was to leave them in wilderness. . . .

However extravagant the pretension of converting the discovery of an inhabited country into conquest may appear; if the principle has been asserted in the first instance, and afterward sustained; if a country has been acquired and held under it; if the property of the great mass of the community originates in it, it becomes the law of the land and cannot be questioned.

Excerpted from /cdn.loc.gov/service/ll/usrep/usrep021
/usrep021543/usrep021543.pdf

Student Handout B
Informed Action: Writing Activity

Directions: Write a letter advocating for why it is important to include the Doctrine of Discovery in curriculum about the Corps of Discovery. Choose who you want this letter to be addressed to (textbook publishers, district curriculum coordinators, state education committees in charge of social studies standards, teachers, future teachers, local school board, newspaper, school newspaper, etc.). Use the following outline for a formal letter.

Insert the recipient's address (Street, City, Zip Code)
Date
Your Address (Name, Street, City, Zip Code)
Dear (insert the recipient's name),

A. In the first paragraph, introduce yourself. End the paragraph by finishing the following sentence: "The purpose of my letter is to . . ."

B. In the second paragraph, explain how learning the Doctrine of Discovery added to your understanding of the Corps of Discovery.
   a. Example 1
   b. Example 2

C. In the third paragraph, explain why the Doctrine of Discovery is relevant today.
   a. Example 1
   b. Example 2

D. In the fourth paragraph, explain why you think students should learn about the Doctrine of Discovery.
   a. Reason 1
   b. Reason 2

E. End the letter by restating your purpose. Thank the reader for their time.

Sincerely,

Insert your name

Questioning *American Progress* (John Gast, 1872)

Teaching Strategy: Painting Analysis

Purpose: Students apply their knowledge of the Doctrine of Discovery to critically examine paintings and make connections to the underlying purpose of the Corps of Discovery.

Connections to Standards

6 Ps Framework	Presence
	Perspectives
	Power
C3 Framework	D2.His.1.6-12
	D2.His.6.6-12
	D4.6.6-12
Common Core State Standards	CCSS.ELA-Literacy.RH.6-12.1
	CCSS.ELA-Literacy.RH.6-12.2
	CCSS.ELA-Literacy.RH.6-12.6
	CCSS.ELA-Literacy.RH.6-12.7
	CCSS.ELA-Litearcy.RH.6-12.9

Introduction

This lesson is designed for students to analyze illustrations that are commonly included in textbook chapters sometimes titled "Westward Expansion" or "Manifest Destiny," similar to how they critically examined textbook sections about the Corps of Discovery in Secondary Lesson Plan 2. The painting *American Progress* by John Gast (1872) is frequently published in textbooks. George Crofutt, a publisher of a journal called *Crofutt's Western World* and of tourist guides to the American West, commissioned *American Progress* from painter John Gast and distributed the image widely as a poster and cover image for the guidebooks. The Autry Museum of the American West in Los Angeles, CA, holds the original painting and its description includes the following remarks:

> With so many images of the western landscape already in circulation, Crofutt decided to create a new design. He discussed his ideas with Gast, and together they came up with this image, which Crofutt described as a: . . .

> *beautiful and charming female . . . floating westward through the air, bearing on her forehead the "Star of Empire" . . . In her right hand she carries a book . . . the emblem of education and . . . national enlightenment, while with the left hand she unfolds and stretches the slender wires of the telegraph, that are to flash intelligence throughout the land.* (collections .theautry.org/mwebcgi/mweb.exe?request=record;id =M545330;type=101)

American Progress illustrates Manifest Destiny and its themes of modernization, advancement, technology, possession, expansion, and civilization. The ideology of Manifest Destiny is deeply rooted in the Doctrine of Discovery's assumptions and in the application of its principles. This lesson lets students apply their knowledge of the doctrine from the prior lesson plan to analyze *American Progress*.

After students discuss their interpretations of *American Progress*, paintings depicting the Corps of Discovery become the focus of their critical examination. Paintings of the military expedition by Charles Russell and Edgar Paxson are often included in textbooks. Paxson's 1912 mural *Lewis and Clark at Three Forks* is installed in the Montana House of Representatives' lobby in the State Capitol building in Helena. It was also used as the cover image for *Undaunted Courage: Meriwether Lewis, Thomas Jefferson, and the Opening of the American West* by Stephen Ambrose (1996). Like Edgar Paxson, Charles Russell has a painting in the Montana State Capitol building; it is titled *Lewis and Clark Meeting Indians at Ross' Hole* (1912). For this lesson we look at another Russell painting, *Lewis and Clark on the Lower Columbia* (1905), which illustrates events recorded in the military expedition journals on October 28, 1805. The analysis tool from the Library of Congress used in Secondary Lesson Plan 1 is revisited to prompt students to observe, reflect, and question as they view the paintings by Paxson and Russell and to note how these are in relationship to Gast's image.

To make a link between Lewis and Clark, the Doctrine of Discovery, Manifest Destiny and the present, this lesson includes the perspectives of contemporary Native artists. During the bicentennial of the Corps of Discovery, the Montana Museum of Art & Culture curated a nationwide traveling exhibition titled *Contemporary Native American Art: Reflections after Lewis and Clark*. Jim Denomie's (Lac Courte Oreilles Band of Ojibwe) painting *Manifold Destiny* (2000), in the MMAC's collection, was included in the exhibition and is featured in this lesson plan to extend student analysis of *American Progress*. *Manifold Destiny* presents students with humor, imagination, and lived experience in the images that reference themes students examined when viewing *American Progress*. Also included in this lesson plan is Wendy Red Star's (Apsáalooke) annotated photographs of the Crow Peace Delegation of 1880. The portraits were taken in Washington, DC, when the six tribal leaders from the Crow Nation were forced to sign a treaty ceding land to the U.S. government for the purpose of railroad development. In her 2014 work (in the Portland Art Museum, Portland, OR), Red Star uses red ink to explain details of regalia, assert identity, and offer commentary that is sometimes humorous. In describing the annotated portraits, she states, "The images represent a human being, a reservation era chief, the forming of the Crow Indian reservation, the loss of Crow lands, the changing of a people, and the resilience of a culture." *Manifold Destiny* (Denomie, 2000) and "Medicine Crow & The 1880 Crow Peace Delegation" (Red Star, 2014) provide students with examples of Native artists disarming Manifest Destiny and colonization through works of art.

Materials

- Project the following images:
  - » *American Progress* (John Gast, 1872) collections.theautry.org/mwebcgi/mweb .exe?request=record;id=M545330;type=101
  - » *Manifold Destiny* (Jim Denomie, 2000) (montanamuseum.pastperfectonline.com /webobject/6A9FE134-3778-4D1E-9BE6 -000422433390)
- Video: "Medicine Crow & The 1880 Crow Peace Delegation" (Wendy Red Star & Steven Zucker r,2018) smarthistory.org/seeing -america-2/peace-delegation/ (6 minutes, 40 seconds) OR www.wendyredstar.com /medicine-crow-the-1880-crow-peace -delegation
- Copies of Student Handout A for all students
- Computers for small groups

Duration

This lesson takes approximately 45–60 minutes.

Procedures

1. Arrange students into small groups and have one or two computers for each group.
2. Review with students the concepts of the Doctrine of Discovery and Manifest Destiny. Say to students, "Today's focus will be on viewing how these concepts were expressed in visual arts."
3. Project the image of *American Progress*. Click on the image and use the "zoom in" feature to make it larger. Say to students, "*American Progress* was painted in 1872 by John Gast. It was widely reproduced as an image of the dominant cultural view of the expansion of the United States."
4. Distribute copies of Student Handout A and review the instructions. Emphasize that there are no "right" answers and the goal is for students to observe and interpret.
5. While students are doing the activity, circulate and check for understanding and preparedness for sharing findings with the class.
6. When groups have finished, facilitate a discussion eliciting a variety of interpretations. Consider the following discussion questions:
   a. How does the painting relate to the Doctrine of Discovery?
   b. How does the painting relate to the idea of Manifest Destiny?
   c. The painting was commissioned (ordered and paid for) by George Crofutt, who published travel guides about the West. Why do you think he commissioned *American Progress*?
7. Say to students, "The next step is to view paintings depicting the Corps of Discovery and to compare the images to *American Progress*." Instruct students to see the reverse side of Student Handout A and review the instructions. Consider asking students to look at the images in their textbook depicting the Corps of Discovery.
8. While students are doing the activity, circulate and check for understanding and preparedness for sharing findings with the class.
9. When groups have finished, facilitate a discussion in which students share their findings.
10. Project the image of *Manifold Destiny* (Denomie, 2000). Say to students, "Now let's

view *Manifold Destiny*, painted in 2000 by Jim Denomie, who is from the Lac Courte Oreilles Band of Ojibwe." Explain to students that this painting was included in a touring exhibit titled *Contemporary Native American Art: Reflections after Lewis and Clark* organized by the Montana Museum of Art & Culture (University of Montana, Missoula). Read the following excerpt about *Manifold Destiny* (Denomie, 2000) from the exhibition's publication:

> In his painting, *Manifold Destiny*, not only does he play with an inspired pun in his title making a joke of the Vanishing Indian myth and Manifest Destiny, but he creates a world where Indian women on horseback hunt VW buffaloes by painting horns on an old, green VW bug. The women hunt this mechanical beast in a lushly colored landscape where a railroad crossing sign, a buffalo skull and telephone poles mark a world transformed. Denomie chooses women as hunters to ". . . acknowledge that in today's society, women have adopted roles of leadership." He writes, ". . . today's women are doctors, lawyers, teachers, artists, writers, military personnel, mothers (both single and partnered), tribal leaders, and more." But clearly these warriors must deal with a world out of balance. (Montana Museum of Art & Culture, 2005, p. 27)

Facilitate a discussion of *Manifold Destiny*, repeating the use of the analysis tool prompting students to observe, reflect, and question. Encourage students to compare and contrast *Manifold Destiny* with other images viewed during the prior activity.

11. Say to students, "We have one additional artist response to view. Let's view a film of Apsáalooke artist Wendy Red Star talking about the annotated photographs titled 'Medicine Crow & The 1880 Crow Peace Delegation.'" Show the video. (NOTE: At 3:54 in the video, the words "kick your ass" are visible in the annotated photograph and briefly discussed by the artist. As an alternative, individually show the annotated portraits from Wendy Red Star's website: wendyredstar.com/medicine-crow -the-1880-crow-peace-delegation.) Facilitate a discussion of "Medicine Crow & The 1880 Crow Peace Delegation," repeating the use of the analysis tool prompting students to observe reflect, and question. Emphasize connections to prior lessons.

Extension Activities

- Share other works by artists Jim Denomie and Wendy Red Star. Consider revisiting the painting *State Names* (Jaune Quick-to-See Smith, 2000) used in the station activity from Secondary Lesson Plan 1 and showing other work by Jaune Quick-to-See Smith (Confederated Salish and Kootenai Nation). Students select a painting they would include in a textbook section about Manifest Destiny and write an extended caption.
- Ask students to annotate or draw a revised *American Progress* given what they learned from the discussion of the other paintings. One specific instruction could be: "Inspired by Wendy Red Star's annotated portraits, pick at least 3 features from *American Progress* and add word bubbles to show what people or objects are thinking and feeling."
- For a lesson using Visual Thinking Strategies to facilitate student discussions about paintings depicting Sacagawea, read Elementary Lesson Plan 6: Sacagawea: Beyond Interpreter and Guide. Level the content and procedures for teaching to secondary students.

Student Handout A
American Progress (John Gast, 1872)

Directions: This painting is known as *American Progress* and was painted by John Gast in 1872. View the painting and discuss your observations. Answer the questions. There are no "right" answers and your goal is to observe and interpret.

1. Look first at the "Spirit" or "Goddess" of Progress in the middle.
   a. What is she holding or carrying?

   b. What do you think is the meaning of those?

   c. What else do you see in the image of the "Spirit"?

2. Now look at the left side of the painting.
   a. What people and animals do you see?

   b. What are they doing? How do you think they are feeling? What makes you say that?

   c. What do you think is the meaning of the people and animals on the left?

   d. What colors do you see? What do you think they represent?

3. Now look at the rest of the painting.
   a. What people do you see?

   b. What are they doing? Where are they going?

   c. What technology do you see?

   d. What does the technology represent?

   e. What else do you see and what does it mean to you?

   f. What colors do you see? What do you think they represent?

4. Describe in a few sentences what you think the painter is intending to say in the painting.

Directions: View the paintings depicting the Corps of Discovery and read the descriptive information for each of the paintings. Then, using the analysis tool from the Library of Congress, complete the chart. Prepare to share your findings.

	Charles Russell (1905) *Lewis and Clark on the Lower Columbia* www.cartermuseum.org/ artworks/339	Edgar S. Paxson (1912) *Lewis and Clark at Three Forks* mhs.mt.gov/education/Capitol /Art/House-Lobby
OBSERVE What do you notice first? What people and objects are shown? How are they arranged? What other details do you see?		
REFLECT What is happening in the image? Who you think was the audience for this image? What do you learn about the Corps of Discovery from this image?		
QUESTION After viewing the painting, what questions do you have? What are you curious about?		

Standing Rock and the "Larger Story"

Teaching Strategy: Mystery

Purpose: Using this student-centered teaching activity, students participate in a collaborative process examining the Corps of Discovery as part of the historical context for the events at Standing Rock.

Connections to the Standards

6 Ps Framework	Presence
	Perspectives
	Political Nationhood
	Power
	Partnerships
C3 Framework	D2.His.1.6-12
	D2.His.2.6-12
	D2.His.3.6-12
	D2.His.16.6-12
	D4.2.6-12
	D4.3.6-12
	D4.6.6.-12
	D4.7.6-12
Common Core State Standards	CCSSE.ELA-Literacy.RH.6-12.2
	CCSS.ELA-Literacy.RH.9-12.3

Introduction

Beginning in April 2016, people began answering LaDonna Brave Bull Allard's (Lakota) call to come to the Standing Rock Sioux Reservation to resist the construction of the Dakota Access Pipeline. Thousands of Indigenous peoples and allies gathered in solidarity to protect Oceti Sakowin homelands through February 2017. Scenes from the camps were circulated widely and included footage of private security, federal, state, and local law enforcement using violence to suppress the Water Protectors' acts of resistance. In writing about the historical significance of Standing Rock in the context of the Whitestone Massacre (1863), Allard stated,

> We must remember we are part of a larger story. We are still here. We are still fighting for our lives, 153 years after my great-great-grandmother Mary watched as our people were senselessly murdered. We should not have to fight so hard to survive on our lands. (Allard, 2016)

Understanding the "larger story" of Standing Rock means recognizing how "Indigenous resistance draws from a long history, projecting itself backward and forward in time" (Estes, 2019, p. 18). Thus, Standing Rock is simultaneously viewable as "colonial déjà vu" (Whyte, 2019, p. 329) and as ongoing actions of justice toward a decolonial future.

The purpose of this lesson plan is to address the questions: How is a pipeline connected to the legacy of the Corps of Discovery? How is the present related to the past? The lesson takes up this purpose by using the mystery teaching strategy. Rather than the teacher conveying information through lecture, the mystery teaching activity presents students with a series of clues they collaboratively put together to answer a set of questions. Students engage with subject matter content through teamwork and problem-solving skills in figuring out a process to answer the mystery questions. This lesson plan is not an exhaustive history of Standing Rock and settler colonialism. It is intended to prompt students to make connections across the lesson plans from *Teaching Critically About Lewis and Clark* as one way to set Standing Rock in a historical context. The writing activity at the end of this lesson is intended to support students in critically reflecting on contemporary events in light of this longer history of settler colonialism.

This lesson plan uses an image of an advertisement for 76-brand gas stations as an introduction to the mystery activity. In 2018, the advertising firm Carmichael Lynch received a silver Jay Chiat Award for Strategic Excellence for ad campaigns promoting the three gas station brands owned by Phillips 66 (Conoco, 76, and Phillips 66). The 76 gas station campaign was titled "Gene and Jean's Awesome Adventure Road Trip" and featured seven short video stories about Gene and Jean's life traveling in their Volkswagen van. Graphic T-shirts, stickers, and patches were designed to accompany the video segments with slogans like "Thataway Awaits" and "Drive West." In developing the campaign, Carmichael Lynch "honed in on a single cultural insight: that while people hate stopping to fill up for gas, they love what a full tank allows them to do. A full tank of gas is a catalyst for adventure and possibility" (www.carmichaellynch.com/carmichael -lynch-wins-silver-strategic-excellence-2018-jay -chiat-awards/). A series of small signs were posted at 76 gas stations to reference the campaign and its themes. One of the signs stated, "Let's Lewis and Clark this thing." This shortsighted slogan advances the dominant narrative of the Corps of Discovery as an adventure story and erases the legacy of land theft and the displacement of Native peoples that followed in its wake. In addition, the "fun-seeker focused campaign" seemingly absolves the role of Phillips 66 in the story of land theft as the campaign was rolled out a year after the Water Protectors' actions against the Dakota Access Pipeline (DAPL) at Standing Rock. Since 2014, Phillips 66 maintains 25% ownership of the DAPL project.

Before and after participating in the mystery activity, students view this sign and are asked to consider the meaning of the phrase, "Let's Lewis and Clark this thing." In doing so, students examine how the Carmichael Lynch advertisement campaign for Phillips 66 is an example of how settlers

> take great pains to forget or cover up the inevitable violence of settlement. Settlement is deeply harmful and risk-laden for Indigenous peoples because settlers are literally seeking to erase Indigenous economies, cultures, and political organizations for the sake of establishing their own. (Whyte, 2019, p. 324)

When viewed from the historical context of the Corps of Discovery, the settler colonial logics within the phrase "Let's Lewis and Clark this thing" are made visible. President Thomas Jefferson identified "the Sioux" by name in the January 22, 1804 instructions to Meriwether Lewis (refer to Secondary Lesson Plan 2, Student Handout C). He wrote, "We wish most particularly to make a friendly impression, because of their immense power, and because we learn they are very desirous of being on the most friendly terms with us." The Corps of Discovery encountered members of the Oceti Sakowin on September 23, 1804, as they traveled upriver on the Missouri. What followed was eight days of tension, conflict, and the expedition's diplomatic blunder as Lewis and Clark refused the demands of the Oceti Sakowin for upriver passage and failed to understand the historical, political, and economic interests of the Oceti Sakowin peoples (Howe, 2004). In writing about these events in the military expedition journal, Clark described the Oceti Sakowin as "the vilest miscreants of the savage race." In relationship to the events of September 1804, "Let's Lewis and Clark this thing" has multiple meanings beyond adventure. It references the expedition's "aggressive and deceptive behavior" (Howe, 2004, p. 56) during the eight days with the Oceti Sakowin in September 1804, including deception, intimidation, threats, taking hostages, the use of alcohol in an attempt to gain advantage, and a refusal to negotiate. For this lesson, the 76 gas station advertisement is used to connect the Water Protectors' actions at Standing Rock to the legacy of the Corps of Discovery.

Special Note: Oceti Sakowin

The name "Sioux" is abbreviated from the French word *Nadouessioux*. This word is derived from the Ojibwe word *natowessiwak* that means "little snakes," used to describe the Ojibwe's enemies to the west. As Estes (2019) writes, "the Dakota, Nakota, and Lakota nations never called themselves 'Sioux'" (p. 69). Following Estes, we use the name Oceti Sakowin meaning People of Seven Council Fires. For further information and to hear the pronunciation, refer to the page "Nation: Oceti Sakowin" at the website *Native Knowledge 360°* by the National Museum of the American Indian (americanindian.si.edu/nk360/plains-belonging-nation/oceti -sakowin).

Duration

This lesson plan takes approximately 60–80 minutes.

Materials

- For teachers interested in background information and additional reading, it is recommended teachers they read:
  » *Our History Is the Future: Standing Rock versus the Dakota Access Pipeline and the Long Tradition of Indigenous Resistance* by Nick Estes (2019)
  » *Standing with Standing Rock: Voices From the #NoDAPL Movement* edited by Nick Estes and Jaskiran Dhillon (2019)
  » "Fighting for Our Lives: #NoDAPL in Historical Context" by Nick Estes (2016) in *Red Nation* (https://therednation

.org/2016/09/18/fighting-for-our-lives
-nodapl-in-context/)

» "The Dakota Access Pipeline,
Environmental Injustice, and US Settler
Colonialism" by Kyle Powys Whyte (2019)
in *The Nature of Hope: Grassroots Organizing,
Environmental Justice, and Political Change*

» "Lewis and Clark among the Tetons:
Smoking out What Really Happened"
by Craig Howe (2004), *Wicazo Sa Review*
(Vol. 19, No. 1, p. 47–72)

» *Standing Rock: Greed, Oil, and the Lakota's
Struggle for Justice* by Bikem Ekberzade
(2018)

» Standing Rock Syllabus
(nycstandswithstandingrock.wordpress.
com/standingrocksyllabus/)

- Teacher Handout A
- Copies of Student Handout A and C for all
students
- Two copies of Student Handout B

Procedure

1. Prior to class, cut one copy of the clues
(Student Handout B) into individual clues and
shuffle the cut clues. Keep one complete copy
for yourself.

2. As a pre-activity exercise, show students the
image of the 76 gas station billboard that reads,
"Let's Lewis and Clark this thing" (Teacher
Handout A). This was a 2018 ad campaign
by the corporation. Use the Think-Pair-
Share discussion format to facilitate students'
response to the following questions: What does
the saying posted on this billboard mean? Why
do you think the gas company is referencing
Lewis and Clark? What is the message? After
discussion, explain to students that the 76
chain of gas stations is owned by the Phillips
66 Company, one of the corporations funding
the Dakota Access Pipeline. In 2016–2017,
thousands of people organized and gathered
to protect the traditional homelands and
waters of the Oceti Sakowin. Tell students the
purpose of the activity is to learn about the
social movement and connections to the legacy
of the Corps of Discovery.

3. Next, show the video "Mni Wiconi: The Stand
at Standing Rock" (Divided Films, 2016) (8:26,
www.youtube.com/watch?v=4FDuqYld8C8).
This video provides a summary of the events

at Standing Rock. Prior to viewing, prepare
students by explaining the video shows images
that include dog attacks, pepper spray, and
physical confrontation.

4. Tell students they are going to try to solve a
mystery. The mystery question is, "How is a
pipeline connected to the legacy of the Corps
of Discovery? How is the present related to
the past?" Explain that they are going work
together as a class to answer a set of questions.
Each student will have a clue (class size will
determine if students will have more than one
clue or one clue for a pair of students) that is
necessary to fully solve the mystery. Explain
that part of the point of the lesson, beyond the
content, is to practice group discussion, problem solving, and collaboration skills.

Alternative process: If students have trouble working in a large group or if the learning
community is not ready for a whole-class
activity, divide students into small groups of
4–5. Provide a copy of all the clues (cut up)
to each group and run the mystery as a small
group activity. The small groups will sort the
clues to answer the questions. If a small group
is struggling, provide support by identifying
two or three questions to answer. The closing
discussion can include a compare/contrast
of small group findings and mystery solving
strategies.

5. Distribute Student Handout A. Explain the
rules for the process: (1) each of the questions
needs to be answered, (2) an adequate answer
must be a narrative that answers the question,
not a list of clues, and (3) the only way to
share clues is by the person with the clue
reading it aloud (this maintains the process as
a class). Point out that the class will first need
to decide how to work together to answer
the questions. Emphasize that every clue
must be used in order to correctly answer the
questions, and that it is acceptable for clues
to be used multiple times. If students have
difficulty getting organized, consider offering
examples of how classes solve the mystery:

    a. After clues are distributed, individual
students read their clue silently and
determine which question they think it
best fits. One student takes on the role
of calling out a question. Students who
determined their clue fits this question
stand or raise hands. One at a time these

students read their clues to the class. The class works together to come up with a summary/narrative of these clues.

b. After clues are distributed, individual students read their clue silently and determine which question they think it best fits. Student volunteers tape the questions to the dry erase board and walls with separation space for small groups to meet. Then, students form small groups by moving to the question they think best fits their clue. One at a time, small groups read their clues to the class. The class works together to come up with a summary/narrative of the clues.

c. Students stand in a circle. Clues are distributed. Individual students read their clue silently and determine which question they think it best fits. One student takes on the role of calling out a question. Students who determined their clue fits this question enter the circle. One at a time these students read their clues to the class. The class works together to come up with a summary/ narrative of these clues. Then students leave the center to rejoin the circle.

Note that once students begin, you will step back and let them run the class unless they need help.

6. Distribute the clues from Handout B. For this mystery lesson plan, there are forty clues. Hand out one clue per student or as appropriate for your class size. Ask for any questions, remind them that you are stepping back, and let students begin.

7. Monitor the class process. If students are having trouble getting organized, you may need to help. If particular clues are left out of the discussion, you may want to point out that there are more clues for the question. If students appear to be simply listing clues rather than answering the question, nudge them to propose a narrative answer. Otherwise, do your best to let the students work on their own.

8. When students have completed the mystery, project Teacher Handout A and say to students, "Let's return to the image of the 76 gas station billboard used at the beginning of the lesson. Think about the ways in which this sign has new meaning." Distribute copies of

Student Handout C to all students. Review the instructions for the writing activity.

9. After they complete the writing activity, ask students to share an excerpt with a partner. Then ask for volunteers to share excerpts with the class.

Extension Activities

- Ask students if they know of other examples of activism by Indigenous peoples that are similar to what occurred at Standing Rock in 2016–2017. Point out to students that there are many examples of historical and contemporary acts of resistance by Indigenous peoples and those in solidarity with them. Explain to students that the purpose of this activity is to explore the activism of Native nations related to contemporary land conflicts and sovereignty. Each group is assigned a different Native nation currently engaged in action similar to what happened at Standing Rock. The examples in Teaching Resource 1 can be used for this activity. The small groups research and create a poster providing classmates with information about the action. After all groups have finished and the posters are on the wall, time is designated for viewing and learning from the posters as a gallery walk. After students have completed the gallery walk, they share their reactions and reflections with a partner. Then facilitate a class discussion about possible actions informed by student interest and choice. Examples include writing letters to stakeholders, contributing to the efforts of the Water Protector Legal Collective to support those arrested at Standing Rock, conducting a teach-in to educate peers, arranging a guest speaker (in person or via video chat) to share updates and ways to get involved, writing a class position statement or resolution, writing articles for the school newspaper, or creating a special issue.

- Ask students, "Is there a time you or someone you know stood up for something you believe in? Or do you know of examples of young people standing up for something they care about?" Share that the youth Water Protectors at Standing Rock were significant to the momentum and visibility of the events that occurred. Explain to students that the purpose of this activity is to explore the activism of the youth Water Protectors. Show all or sections of the ABC news feature, "Meet the youth at the heart of the Standing Rock protests against the Dakota Access Pipeline" (2017) (abcnews.go.com/US/meet-youth-heart -standing-rock-protests-dakota-access/story ?id=45719115). This video features the stories of Native youth activists with footage of life in the camps and at the protests. Prior to viewing, prepare students by explaining that the video includes images that may be difficult to watch. Consider creating a viewing guide for students to complete while watching the video. After viewing, facilitate a discussion in which students share their reactions and reflections with a partner. Then facilitate a class discussion about possible actions informed by student interest and choice.

- Another option to explore Native youth activism and Standing Rock is to use a lesson plan offered by public radio station KQED of northern California. The lesson plan offers video, radio excerpts, a timeline, reading, and teaching procedures to explore the youth activists at Standing Rock. Opportunity for student action is included (ww2.kqed.org /lowdown/wp-content/uploads/sites/26 /2017/05/Youth-of-Standing-Rock-lesson -plan.pdf).

- To teach about the encounter of September 1804 between the Corps of Discovery and the Oceti Sakowin, consider using the lesson plan and materials titled "Lewis and Clark on the Upper Missouri," from the North Dakota Studies program at the State Historical Society of North Dakota (documents at www.ndstudies.gov/gr8/content/unit-ii -time-transformation-1201-1860/lesson-4 -alliances-and-conflicts/topic-2-diplomacy -trade-and-war/section-3-lewis-and-clark -upper-missouri).

Student Handout A
Mystery Questions

Directions: Each person in our class has 1 or 2 clues needed to answer the questions below. Work together to answer all of the questions. Using the clues, build a narrative to answer each question. The only way to share a clue is by a person reading it aloud. The clues can be used multiple times to answer the questions.

1. Who wanted to build the Dakota Access Pipeline?

2. Why did they want to build the pipeline?

3. Who gathered to oppose the pipeline and protect the lands and waters from pipeline construction?

4. What were the objections to the pipeline?

5. How did the Water Protectors challenge pipeline construction?

6. How did the local and federal agencies respond to the Water Protectors?

7. Why do Native peoples see the Dakota Access Pipeline as part of a legacy broken treaties and land theft?

8. What connections can we make to the Corps of Discovery?

Student Handout B
Mystery Clues

Energy Transfer Partners is the corporation that built and manages the Dakota Access Pipeline. They partner with the following other oil and gas companies: Phillips 66, Enbridge, and Marathon Petroleum.

Oil and gas companies, along with individuals and groups supporting the industry, contributed $102,209,039 to Republican and Democrat candidates in the 2016 election.

On January 24, 2017, President Trump signed the executive order to approve construction of the Keystone XL and Dakota Access pipelines.

The 1,172-mile-long underground pipeline allows for a more direct transfer of oil from the Bakken oil fields of North Dakota to an oil distribution center in Patoka, IL.

Energy Transfer Partners argues that the pipeline is a safe, economic, efficient, and reliable way to transfer oil from the fields to the market.

The pipeline project is a $3.78 billion investment that will result in 8,000–12,000 jobs related to construction and manufacturing. Dakota Access, LLC (a company within Energy Transfer Partners) estimated a total of 40 permanent operating jobs.

The pipeline project will result in an estimated total of $156 million in sales and income tax revenue for the four states along the pipeline route (North Dakota, South Dakota, Iowa, and Illinois).

On April 1, 2016, LaDonna Brave Bull Allard and other leaders from the Oceti Sakowin started the Sacred Stone Camp on land owned by Allard within traditional Oceti Sakowin territory.

The people from Native nations who came to Sacred Stone Camp called themselves "Water Protectors," not protestors. They called themselves Protectors because they weren't just organizing *against* the pipeline; they were also organizing *for* the protection of lands and waters.

As the number of Water Protectors increased, additional camps were established nearby: Rosebud Camp, Red Warrior Camp, and Oceti Sakowin Camp.

From April 2016 through February 2017, thousands of people, sometimes as many as 10,000, gathered at the camps. Members from over 300 federally recognized Native nations gathered to protect Oceti Sakowin homelands from the pipeline.

Environmentalists, politicians, celebrities, veterans, and Black Lives Matters activists were among the thousands who joined in solidarity with the Standing Rock Sioux Tribe to oppose construction of the Dakota Access Pipeline.

Indigenous youth were significant to the social movement. Young people organized to inform, educate, and advocate against pipeline construction.

Water Protectors argue a leak or spill could damage the Missouri River, which is the main source of water for the Standing Rock Sioux Tribe. Greenpeace USA and the Waterkeeper Alliance revealed that the Energy Transfer Partners reported 527 pipeline spills from 2002–2017. The Dakota Access Pipeline leaked four times in 2017.

The words, "Water is Life," unify the Water Protectors. "Water is life" signifies the sacredness of water, the belief that water is a living being with its own rights, and our dependence on water for survival.

The original route proposed for the pipeline to cross underneath the Missouri River 10 miles north of Bismarck, ND. Bismarck is the capital of North Dakota with 92% of the population identifying as white.

After concerns were raised by the residents of Bismarck about the potential danger to the water supply, a new pipeline route was identified.

The new pipeline route (after Bismarck) crossed the Missouri River under the Oahe (oh-WAH-hee) Reservoir—a half-mile upriver from the Standing Rock Sioux Tribe.

Tribal leaders from the Standing Rock Sioux Tribe argued the U.S. Army Corp of Engineers violated treaty agreements and tribal sovereignty by not consulting with the Sioux nation's government about the new pipeline route, and failed to conduct thorough studies of the route's impact.

Construction of the pipeline resulted in the desecration of ancestral burial grounds and sacred sites on the homelands of the Standing Rock Sioux Tribe.

The land used for pipeline construction was never ceded by treaty to the U.S. government by the Standing Rock Sioux Tribe. That means the land remains in their control and the U.S. government is violating agreements between nations.

Ceremony and prayer were important to the Water Protectors as they challenged the pipeline construction.

At the camps, trainers from groups such as the Indigenous People's Power Project (IP3) led daily workshops for Water Protectors teaching non-violent direct action principles and strategies.

The Water Protectors used a variety of non-violent direct action strategies, such as marches, blockades, education, social media campaigns, court cases, and demonstrations.

Energy Transfer Partners hired private security officers to ensure the construction of the pipeline would continue.

On August 19, 2016, in response to the Water Protectors, North Dakota Governor Jack Dalrymple declared a state of emergency.

The state of emergency allowed North Dakota and other states to share resources and emergency personnel. Most often, this is used as a response after a natural disaster.

As a result of the state of emergency declared by North Dakota Governor Jack Dalrymple, the police department near the Standing Rock Sioux Reservation received law enforcement support from 10 states, 24 counties, and 16 cities.

Intimidation strategies by law enforcement included: use of military-grade equipment, pepper spray, rubber bullets, attack dogs, water cannons during winter subzero temperatures, tear gas, and concussion grenades; surveillance; and crowd containment by police in formation. Over 300 Water Protectors were injured.

Law enforcement responses included over 760 arrests. The Water Protector Legal Collective was established at the Oceti Sakowin Camp during the Standing Rock actions. This organization provides legal support to Water Protectors arrested during the events.

Prior to contact with European and U.S. traders, explorers, and settlers, the Oceti Sakowin lived in a complex society alongside other Native nations in the Great Plains.

In 1803, the United States paid France $15 million for the Louisiana Purchase. The United States did not consult with or seek the consent of the Oceti Sakowin or other Native nations whose homelands were within in this area.

In 1804, President Thomas Jefferson instructed the Corps of Discovery "to make a friendly impression" with the "the Sioux . . . because of their immense power."

In September 1804, the Corps of Discovery encountered the Lakota while traveling upriver on the Missouri. After they refused to pay for passage, tensions escalated, resulting in the military expedition taking two Lakota leaders, Black Buffalo and Buffalo Medicine, as hostages to secure continued travel on the Missouri River.

After a week of tension and failed diplomacy in September 1804, William Clark described the Lakota as "the vilest miscreants of the savage race, [who] must ever remain the pirates of the Missouri, until such measures are pursued, by our government, as will make them feel a dependence on its will for their supply of merchandise."

The 1851 Treaty of Fort Laramie set boundaries between the Native nations of the Great Plains on an area of about 134 million acres. The 1868 Treaty of Fort Laramie reduced these lands to 25 million acres and forced multiple tribes into the Great Sioux Reservation.

In 1866–1867, the U.S. government launched a series of military campaigns for access to and ownership of the gold located in the Black Hills.

The U.S. Congress passed the Indian Appropriations Act of 1876, which included legislation referred to as "sell or starve." The Native nations defending their homelands in the Black Hills were cut off from supplies and rations (starve) until the lands were ceded to the U.S. government (sell).

In 1889, the U.S. Congress passed the Sioux Bill, splitting the Great Sioux Reservation into six small reservations. The Standing Rock Sioux Reservation was allotted 2 million acres.

Another example of stolen land occurred in 1962 when the Army Corps of Engineers completed construction of the Oahe Dam on the Missouri River. The Standing Rock Sioux Reservation lost over 56,000 acres and four communities were permanently flooded, forcing people to relocate.

Student Handout C
Mystery Reflection

Directions: After completing the mystery activity, write your response to the reflection questions.

1. Return to the image of the advertisement for 76 gas stations that reads, "Let's Lewis and Clark this thing." What new responses do you have to this sign?

2. What do you think Phillips 66 needs to know about this ad campaign and its connection to the legacy of the Corps of Discovery?

3. As a class, what do you think we did well together while solving the mystery questions?

Role Play: The Bicentennial of the Lewis and Clark Corps of Discovery

Teaching Strategy: Role Play

Purpose: The purpose of this lesson plan is for students to understand the different perspectives and concerns of stakeholders planning the bicentennial of the Corps of Discovery.

Connections to the Standards

6 Ps Framework	Presence
	Perspectives
	Political Nationhood
	Power
	Partnerships
C3 Framework	D2.His.1.6-12
	D2.His.4.6-12
	D2.His.5.6-12
	D4. 6.6-12
Common Core State Standards	CCSS.ELA-Literacy.RH.9-12.3
	CCSS.ELA-Literacy.RH.6-12.6
	CCSS.ELA-Literacy.RH.6-12.8
	CCSS.ELA-Literacy.RH.6-12.9

Introduction

Planning for the 2003–2006 bicentennial commemoration of the Corps of Discovery began in 1994. That year, three Native leaders—Lawrence Wetsit (Assiniboine), Jeanne Eder (Dakota), and Allen V. Pinkham, Sr. (Nez Perce)—were elected as the first of 14 Native members of the National Council of the Lewis & Clark Bicentennial's Board of Directors (Circle of Tribal Advisors, 2006). The National Park Service was the lead federal agency, organizing and coordinating with other federal agencies, non-profit organizations, Native nations, states, cities, and rural communities. In 1996, as a result of Native advocacy, the National Council officially adopted "the term commemoration instead of celebration to describe forthcoming bicentennial activities" (Circle of Tribal Advisors, 2006, p. 92). The National Council also "voted early, and unanimously,

to make 'tribal involvement' its number one priority for the commemoration" (p. 73).

The primary goals for the bicentennial included: emphasizing the perspectives and contributions of Native peoples, resource stewardship, education, and establishing partnerships. As noted in the executive summary report about the bicentennial, "revisiting the Lewis and Clark story 200 years later required the strength of partnerships but also the openness to share multiple views" (National Park Service, 2008, p. 7). David Sarasohn's (2005) *Waiting for Lewis and Clark: The Bicentennial and the Changing West* chronicles how "the power of the story and the power of the moment" were experienced during the planning and implementation of the commemoration (p. 5). Informed by Sarasohn's account of the bicentennial, this lesson plan is designed for students to consider how the National Park Service represented the Corps of Discovery informed by multiple perspectives.

This lesson plan reflects the role playing teaching strategy practiced in Rethinking Schools and the Zinn Education Project. Carefully planned role plays present students with the opportunity and challenge to examine a historical question from a variety of viewpoints. Students are not asked to replicate history, which results in what Nikki Mandell and Bobbie Malone (2007) describe as "a false understanding or what may be characterized as imagined history" (p. 73). In contrast to imagined history, role plays can elicit historical imagination when designed to "help students understand that the course of past events was not inevitable, but was shaped by the interaction of people, ideas, motives, material culture and differences in power to effect change" (p. 73). For this role play, the goal is for students to understand the different perspectives and concerns of stakeholders planning the bicentennial of the Corps of Discovery. The setting is a bicentennial planning meeting facilitated by the teacher in the role of the National Park Service. In small groups, students present the roles of Native leaders interested in participating in the bicentennial,

Native leaders questioning participation, a delegation of environmental and conservation groups, heritage tourists, and a delegation from the travel and tourism industry. After debriefing the events of the role play, the teacher shares an account of actual events from the bicentennial.

Duration

This lesson plan takes approximately 90–120 minutes.

Materials

- Teacher Handout A (Role Play Introduction) and Teacher Handout B (What Really Happened?)
- Student Handouts C, D, E, F, and G, representing five roles, each assigned to one of five groups. Each student receives a copy of the role assigned to their group. On the back of each role handout, print Student Handout A (Role Play Questions).
- Student Handout B (Logo), one copy per group
- A nameplate for each group (groups can do this)
- Teacher Handout C (Extension Activity) to read aloud in class (and copies for students as needed)

Procedures

1. Tell students they are going to do a role play about the bicentennial of Lewis and Clark that took place from 2003–2006. If students have not participated in a role play before, point out that they may have a role they disagree with. Ask them to do their best to play the role, noting that nobody will assume that is what they actually believe and there will be time to debrief the experience of role play. Remind students that the roles are based on actual events and lived experiences; referencing stereotypes to perform roles is unacceptable. Say to students, "The National Park Service partnered with many groups to support the three-year, national touring exhibit called the 'Lewis and Clark Bicentennial: Corps of Discovery II.' Today's role play is an early planning meeting facilitated by the National Park Service. The central question of the role play is: How should the Corps of Discovery be represented for the bicentennial?"

2. Divide students into groups and assign each group a role. Provide groups with a name plate or have students create a name plate for their group. Give students copies of their role and the role play questions (Student Handouts C, D, E, F, and G with Student Handout A copied on the other side). Give each group one copy of the logo (Student Handout B).

3. Begin the role play by calling the meeting to order. Introduce yourself as the National Park Service Chair of the Lewis and Clark Bicentennial Planning Committee. Welcome each group to the meeting: Native Leaders Considering Participation in the Bicentennial, Native Leaders Questioning Participation in the Bicentennial, the Environmental and Conservation Delegation, the Heritage Tourist Delegation, and the Travel and Tourism Delegation. Project the opening statement (Teacher Handout A) and read it to the class. Explain to students that they will first work in groups to understand their roles and develop their positions. Then they will have the opportunity to negotiate with other groups before the main meeting begins. In that meeting, the group will need to decide on three main standards/priorities for the Bicentennial exhibits.

4. Give time for students to silently read their roles, or they can be read aloud within groups. Tell students to underline key sentences they find helpful or significant to their role.

5. Next, review the role play questions (Student Handout A). Point out that Question 5 will not be part of the large group discussion during the meeting but is designed to help them plan how to work with other groups. Explain that students will need to answer Question 4 at the end of the meeting. Also, encourage small groups to draft an alternative logo (Question 3).

6. Give time for small groups to prepare for the meeting and negotiations by answering the role play questions and discussing the logo (Student Handout A and Student Handout B). Circulate the room to check for understanding and preparedness.

7. After the small groups complete the role play questions and recommendations for the logo, ask students to select 2 or 3 people (no more than half the group) who will visit other table groups to negotiate during the

negotiation session. Point out that those who do not travel will remain at their tables and be primarily responsible for discussing their group's position during the role play meeting.

8. When all groups are ready, instruct the "travelers" to meet with the sitting members of other groups for the purpose of compromise, alliance building, and so on. To avoid travelers forming a group in the middle of the room, emphasize they can only talk to the remaining seated group members. Remind students that they will need to decide on three goals, so they need to think about their own top priorities and who they can make a deal with. Give students at least 15 minutes for this session—longer if they are engaged. Have students return to their home groups and give them a few minutes to finalize their positions.

9. Call the meeting to order. As the chair, you facilitate the meeting. Ask each group to make a short statement of their three goals for Question 1. Record the goals on the dry erase board and group them as appropriate. Next, explain that you will take proposals, vote on them, and when three priorities have reached a majority vote, that part will be considered complete. Next, lead a discussion and vote on Questions 2 and 3. After the three questions are resolved, officially close the meeting, and ask each group to state its final decision on whether to continue participating (Question 4).

10. Facilitate debrief of the role play. Consider the following questions for discussion or writing.
    » Staying in role, what do you think of the final decisions?
    » Stepping out of your role, how do you think the Bicentennial will go forward? What might it look like?

    » What did the role play help you understand about the complications of representing the Corps of Discovery in the stories we tell?

11. Using the document camera, project Teacher Handout B to summarize the actual events of the bicentennial.

12. As an exit ticket, ask students to write a response to the following questions: Compare the actual events with the results from the role play. What similarities were there? What differences were there? Why do you think those differences occurred?

Extension Activities

- Using the recommendations published by the Circle of Tribal Advisors in *Enough Good People: Reflections on Tribal Involvement and Inter-Cultural Collaboration 2003–2006* (Circle of Tribal Advisors and BNI, n.d.), students plan the tricentennial of the Corps of Discovery. Use the following link to access the publication: cms.lc-triballegacy.org/book. Click on "Recommendations."

- Read students the story "We Don't Need Those Anymore," written by Rachel Cushman, a Tribal Council Member of the Chinook Indian Nation, who reflects on her participation in the bicentennial commemoration. After reading the story, facilitate a discussion with students by asking the following questions: Why was Rachel hesitant to participate in the "Flight of Discovery"? How did she participate in this event on her own terms? Think of a time you were hesitant to participate in something, but chose to do so on your own terms. How have you embodied this idea of participating on your own terms, or of creative resistance, in your own life?

Teacher Handout A
Role Play Introduction

NATIONAL PARK SERVICETHE BICENTENNIAL OF THE CORPS OF DISCOVERY

On behalf of the National Park Service, it is my honor to welcome you to the first planning workshop for the bicentennial of the Corps of Discovery. The National Park Service is drafting plans for a three-year, national touring exhibit for the bicentennial of Lewis and Clark. The title of the traveling exhibit is "Lewis & Clark Bicentennial Corps of Discovery II."

The National Park service received $26 million to support projects along the 3,700-mile Lewis & Clark National Historic Trail. The traveling exhibit will stop at 95 locations with 15 signature events starting in Monticello (the home of President Thomas Jefferson), reaching to Astoria (the lower Columbia River where the Corps of Discovery reached the Pacific Ocean), and ending in St. Louis (the returning point of the expedition). It is estimated over 500,000 people will visit the exhibit and attend signature events during the three years of activity.

Our purpose today is to discuss and take action on the following:

1. Agree upon three goals for the bicentennial traveling exhibit and signature events.
2. Decide if the bicentennial will be referred to as a celebration or commemoration.
3. Agree upon the words and images of the logo design.
4. The groups participating today will decide to continue participation in the bicentennial or to withdraw.

Student Handout A
Role Play Questions

Directions: Using the perspective of the role assigned to your group, prepare for the meeting by responding to the following questions.

1. The bicentennial programming will include a traveling exhibit and signature events during the three-year event. What are your group's three goals for this programming? For example, "Develop a strategy for restoration of environmental resources."

   a.

   b.

   c.

2. You will have the opportunity to negotiate with other groups before the meeting. Who will you negotiate with? What are your common interests, concerns, goals? Use the chart before and during negotiations to prepare for the meeting.

Groups	Our Shared Interests, Concerns, Goals
Native Leaders Considering Participation	
Native Leaders Questioning Participation	
Delegation of Environmental and Conservation Groups	
Heritage Tourist Delegation	
Travel and Tourism Delegation	

3. Some have proposed the bicentennial be referred to as a celebration; others prefer using the word commemoration. What is your recommendation? Why?

4. There has been discussion about redesigning the bicentennial logo (refer to Handout C); that is, whether to keep or to change the imagery and words. How do you feel about the logo? What phrases and or images would you add or change?

5. Will you participate as partners with the National Park Service in Lewis & Clark Bicentennial Corps of Discovery II? Why or why not?

Student Handout B
Role Play: Bicentennial Logo

Directions: Using the perspective of the role assigned to your group, give your recommendations for whether to keep or change the imagery and words of the bicentennial logo.

The logo is an adaptation of the Jefferson peace medals presented by members of the Corps of Discovery to leaders of Native nations. The handshake represents friendship and establishment of friendly relations between the military expedition and the tribes met along the way. The pipe, often used during Native ceremonies, indicates peace and approval. The downward facing tomahawk is symbolic of achieving peace by laying down weapons. "Peace and Friendship" were the words on the original Jefferson peace medal. "Corps of Discovery II" and "200 Years to the Future" embody the spirit of the project: to visit the past, to acknowledge the present, and to envision the future of the Lewis and Clark story.

National Park Service Logo	Your Recommended Changes

Adapted from National Park Service, 2008, p. 61

Student Handout C
ROLE: Native Leaders Considering Participation in the Bicentennial

You are part of a delegation of tribal advisors from Native nations along the Lewis and Clark National Historical Trail. While each of your communities is unique, your group members share the inclination to support involvement in the bicentennial events. However, you want to make sure that the National Park Service and the other groups participating are willing to make Native perspectives central to the programming. Many previous historical "celebrations" have excluded Native perspectives, perpetuated stereotypes about Native peoples, and portrayed Native peoples as only in the past. This is not acceptable.

First, it's important that the event be called a "commemoration," not a "celebration." To celebrate the military expedition implies that it is unquestioned as a positive event. Allen Pinkham, Nez Perce, said it best: "To us, Lewis and Clark aren't heroes." In the wake of the expedition, Native peoples experienced theft of homelands, the forced decline of Native languages, and pervasive problems that communities continue to wrestle with today (for example, inadequate employment, healthcare, and housing). The word "commemoration" allows for a more balanced representation and story of the Corps of Discovery and its legacy.

The main theme you want others to understand is "We're still here." Native peoples are not just history, but are thriving today. Therefore, you want Native perspectives along the trail to be heard, and you want an emphasis on the contributions of Native peoples, both historical and today. As Leonard Maker, Osage, said, "We're not a museum piece. We're vibrant and living people."* You want participants to know that Native peoples survived—you are resilient, strong, you are here.

Another key goal for your group is the protection of cultural resources. The National Park Service is estimating hundreds of thousands of tourists. Often, tourists are disrespectful, damage sacred places, and steal belongings. Even though the Native American Graves Protection and Repatriation Act (1990) was supposed to prevent this, it is a pervasive problem today. You want tribal advisors from Native nations to review and approve all maps designed for tourists to ensure that sacred sites are not opened to tourists. You also want to include specific language authored by tribal advisors to give guidelines for visiting places with respect.

However, since there will be tourists, you want tribal nations to benefit from it. You see the bicentennial as a way to generate income and outside interest in Native businesses. Daphne Richards-Cook, Oglala, said, "We can use it not to honor them [Lewis and Clark], but to market us."* Also, anything that represents itself as "Native" should be designed by Native peoples, and earnings should go to tribes. This is not only a protection provided by the Indian Arts and Crafts Act (1990), but also the right thing to do.

Finally, you are certainly concerned about the damage done to the ecosystems along the trail. Dams along the rivers have flooded communities and made lakes where there were rapids. The dams have also caused a catastrophic decline in the numbers of salmon along the Columbia watershed. Stewardship of land should certainly be a theme of the commemoration. However, you do not want the focus on stewardship to outshine the focus on Native perspectives of the Corps of Discovery and its legacy.

NOTE

* Quotations from Sarasohn (2005).

Student Handout D
ROLE: Native Leaders Questioning Participation in the Bicentennial

You are part of a delegation of tribal advisors from Native nations along the Lewis and Clark National Historic Trail. While each of your communities is unique, your group members share skepticism and question the National Park Service's call to partner for the bicentennial of the Corps of Discovery. The only way you would consider participating is if all of your concerns are addressed.

For you, the bicentennial is not a celebration. Tim Giago, Oglala Lakota journalist, wrote that Native nations should not be "grabbing on and riding the coattails of an expedition that only brought them destruction."[1] The bicentennial is another reminder of the legacy of the Corps of Discovery that includes the theft of homelands, the forced decline of Native languages, and pervasive problems that your communities continue to wrestle with today (for example unemployment, health, and housing). Your communities are working tirelessly to restore your lands, languages, and health and well-being. As leaders of Native nations, you do not have the time or funds to contribute to Lewis and Clark events. This is not your priority.

Second, one key goal is for the National Park Service and the government of the United States to engage all Native nations in a nation-to-nation relationship—as equals. You believe the bicentennial call for "partnership" is for show. There are two problems. For Native nations that are federally recognized, you have yet to feel treated as equals. For Native nations that are not federally recognized, you face the complicated choice of partnering with the federal government, which does not see you as a sovereign nation. For example, the Lemhi Shoshone, the tribal nation Sacagawea was born into and was reunited with during the expedition, were forced 200 miles south of their homelands. The Lemhi Shoshone are not a federally recognized tribal nation. They refuse to participate until the process of federal recognition and establishing a reservation on their homelands is started. You support them in this demand.

Third, you are not convinced participating in the bicentennial will benefit Native nations. You worry that the bicentennial events will be just like previous historical "celebrations" that excluded Native perspectives, perpetuated stereotypes about Native peoples, and portrayed Native peoples as in the past while ignoring the presence of your communities today. This is not acceptable. You want Native perspectives to be the focus of the bicentennial. "It was two men—two men who encountered at least 48 different tribes," said Judy BlueHorse Skelton, a Nez Perce/Cherokee instructor at Portland State University. "And yet it's always a story about these two men."[2]

Finally, you want limits to the tourist impact on land and cultural resources that are important to Native nations. You have heard a story that many of the Native belongings brought back by Lewis and Clark ended up in the fraternities of the University of Virginia, near President Jefferson's house. You do not want thousands of tourists to disrespect, vandalize, or loot important sacred and cultural sites.

NOTES

1. Giago, T. (2004, June 18). Should Indians Celebrate Lewis and Clark? *Yankton Daily Press & Dakotan*. https://www.yankton.net/opinion/article_e894fec7-5aee-574c-9fc9-4cc87593b760 .html. Also, refer to Sarasohn, 2005, p. 23.

2. Olsen, K. (2006). Discovering Lewis and Clark. *Teaching Tolerance*, Issue 29, https://www .tolerance.org/magazine/spring-2006/discovering-lewis-and-clark.

Student Handout E
ROLE: Delegation of Environmental and Conservation Groups

You are a coalition of environmental groups, such as the Sierra Club and American Rivers. Your goal is for the bicentennial to focus on ecological concerns. In particular, you want the events to recognize how much the ecosystems along the Lewis and Clark National Historic Trail have been changed—damaged—since the original expedition. Certainly, the bicentennial should not be called a celebration—perhaps it should be called a memorial, in honor of the many losses.

Lewis and Clark would not even recognize many stretches of the rivers they paddled down. Both the Missouri and the Columbia river systems have been changed by the construction of multiple dams, which turn huge sections of what were once wild rivers into giant lakes. For example, an entire set of falls and rapids on the Columbia, known as Celilo Falls, was flooded by the dam at The Dalles. Dam construction, and other human actions, completely change the ecosystems along the river.

These actions have caused catastrophic declines in salmon runs in the Columbia watershed. In Lewis and Clark's time, there were so many salmon in the Columbia that it was said that you could walk across the river on the backs of salmon and not get your pants wet. Today the runs are less than 1% of what they were before white civilization came along. This decline is due to dams, to habitat loss from human changes to the creeks and rivers, and from pollution due to industrial and pesticide runoff. The Lands Council of Spokane, WA, said it best: "As America prepares to celebrate the Lewis and Clark bicentennial, the decisions about salmon will also be decisions about the bicentennial—celebration of efforts to restore the river of life, or eulogy for what has been lost in the past 200 years after Lewis and Clark."

The upper Missouri is also constrained by dams, reducing sturgeon runs, while the lower Missouri has been turned into a giant transportation mechanism for barges shipping grain, destroying habitats along the way. It runs so fast that Lewis and Clark would not be able to paddle up the river if they were here today. Rebecca Wodder, president of American Rivers, said, "What the bicentennial brings to us is a stage to tell the story of what the rivers were like 200 years ago, and what we can do now."

You are concerned that the hordes of tourists who are expected to come to the sites along the Lewis and Clark trail will worsen ecological damage. You would like to see strict limits on where tourists can go.

Further, while you understand that the bicentennial events will recognize history, you believe they should focus on environmental education—teaching tourists about the ways humans affect ecosystems. The goal of the bicentennial events should encourage stewardship—how we can restore and maintain the rivers, forests, and grasslands on which we depend to live.

NOTE

* Quotations from Sarasohn (2005).

Student Handout F
ROLE: Heritage Tourist Delegation

When the National Park Service and their partners imagine what type of tourist will participate in the bicentennial of the Corps of Discovery, they imagine you. The tourism industry calls you a heritage tourist. You are interested in the stories of places and you expect a personal, unique, and authentic experience. The National Park Service estimates that 500,000 of you will visit bicentennial exhibits and attend signature events during the three years of activity.

Research conducted by the tourism industry provides a profile of your group to the National Park Service and their partners. Heritage tourists are college educated and employed. You are typically between the ages of 45 and 65. You are often at the height of your career and you have income to spend during your vacation time. Many of you have children and your goals are to have an adventure, to learn, and to enjoy a family vacation. In comparison to other types of tourists, your vacations are longer and you will spend more money while traveling. You will be eating at restaurants, shopping at local stores, paying for tours, buying souvenirs, engaging in recreational activities, and paying entry fees to visit tourist sites.

You have read books and watched documentaries about Lewis and Clark. The documentaries presented powerful images of the land with the words of the journals from the expedition. Marietta Castle, from Rock Island, IL, said, "We kept reading more and just said, 'We've got to see the trail'." The themes capturing your interest are adventure, heroism, leadership, connection to land, and the historical contributions of Native peoples. Nik Yeager, from Palmyra, MO, said, "It's a unique journey in history. [The bicentennial is] something you can only do once. It's a nice way to relive it." Recently, you learned about the bicentennial events through advertisements on television. You believe this is a wonderful opportunity to see the sites you viewed in the documentaries and learn more about the stories told in the books.

You are aware the bicentennial will stretch over three years. You have heard the most about events planned in Montana, Oregon, Missouri, and North Dakota. You are thinking about planning a trip to bicentennial events in one of those states. For some of you, if your trip is enjoyable and meets your expectations, you will consider planning another vacation to participate in the bicentennial programming. If you do not enjoy the trip, you will likely not participate in other bicentennial events.

NOTE

* Quotations from Sarasohn (2005).

Student Handout G
ROLE: Travel and Tourism Delegation

You live in a city located on or near the Lewis and Clark National Historical Trail and serve as the Travel and Tourism Director for your community. You are joined by people who serve in the same role from communities all along the Lewis and Clark National Historical Trail—from Astoria, OR, to St. Louis, MO. While each of your communities is unique, you share a common interest in the potential economic benefit of tourism from the bicentennial.

Members of the Travel and Tourism delegation are interested in developing tourist attractions that will lure heritage tourists. Heritage tourists are interested in the stories of places and expect a personal and authentic experience when they visit. Betsy Baumgart, head of the Promotion Division of Travel Montana, said, "Heritage tourism is the fastest growing part of the business and cultural tourists are better-educated and higher income." Your goal is for tourists to contribute to the local economies during their stay.

Many of the communities along the Lewis and Clark National Historical Trail need an economic boost from tourism as the economic stability from industries such as logging, fisheries, agriculture, and manufacturing is no longer guaranteed. Your delegation is excited by the opportunity to receive National Park Service funds to support travel and tourism projects. The National Park Service is promising several hundred thousand visitors—this is exactly what your communities need! David Borlaug, President of the Lewis and Clark Fort Mandan Foundation in Washburn, ND, said, "For generations, our strategy has been to slow people down on their way somewhere else. For the first time ever, we are a destination. . . . Now we've got America's attention."

The goal of the Travel and Tourism delegation is to develop and market tourist-friendly content. You want the tourism messaging to be celebratory, positive, and welcoming. You believe tourists are attracted to story lines that depict Lewis and Clark as heroes and emphasize the theme of adventure. You are wary of raising issues that cause tourists to feel discomfort or conflict. Lorraine Roach, a business consultant from Grangeville, ID, said, "If we get too provocative, we might alienate the people we need."* Environmental issues or painful histories are subjects important to include for raising awareness, but should not be the central focus of the tourist experience.

You are aware that some groups in attendance hesitate to promote and embrace tourism. There are concerns about impacts on environmental and cultural resource areas. You believe such concerns are solvable problems and the economic benefit is a priority. More tourists result in more money to benefit all interests!

NOTE

* Quotations from Sarasohn (2005).

Teacher Handout B
The Lewis and Clark Bicentennial: What Really Happened?

Planning began in 1994. The bicentennial programming started in 2003 and ended in 2006. It required massive collaboration and coordination involving Native nations, federal agencies, states, cities, and rural communities.

In 1996, representatives from Native nations persuaded the National Park Service to refer to the bicentennial as a commemoration.

In 2000, the National Park Service named Gerard Baker, Mandan-Hidatsa, the Superintendent of the Lewis and Clark Historic Trail. Widely respected and recognized within the National Park Service and Indian Country, Superintendent Baker was key to planning and collaborating with Native nations.

The National Park Service and partners organizing the bicentennial were informed by four primary goals: emphasizing the perspectives and contributions of Native peoples, resource stewardship, education, and establishing partnerships.

The Circle of Tribal Advisors (COTA) was established in 2000 and was a delegation of representatives from Native nations. COTA's goals for the bicentennial included: ensuring the accuracy and completeness of bicentennial programming, promoting respect and understanding of tribal sovereignty, and promoting the protection and restoration of Native homelands.

Over 48 Native nations participated in the bicentennial. All nations, regardless of federal recognition status, were included.

Throughout the bicentennial, Native nations' decision to participate was complicated and sometimes charged with conflict. For example, the Chinook Nation withdrew and hosted their own events after disagreeing with bicentennial organizers about recognition of their homelands. Also, citizens of the Oglala Sioux nation confronted reenactors during an event. They demanded the reenactors turn around because the military expedition resulted in the devastation of Indian Country. COTA respected these actions and committed to increasing awareness about the reasons why Native nations did not support the bicentennial.

COTA published *A Guide to Visiting the Lands of Many Nations* to educate tourists how to respect the property, privacy, and traditions of Native places; provide guidance for buying Native art; and offer facts and contact information for Native nations. COTA printed 250,000 brochures, and it was available for download. Of all printed brochures available during the bicentennial, the *Guide to Visiting the Lands of Many Nations* was highest in demand.

Circle of Conservation Advisors (COCA) was established in 2000 and was joined by organizations such as the Sierra Club and American Rivers to advocate and raise awareness for stewardship during the bicentennial. Organizers were not able to meet fundraising goals, resulting in fewer events focused on the environment than expected.

The handout in the role play featured the first version of the bicentennial logo released by the National Park Service in 1999. In 2004, the National Park Service designed an updated logo to reflect the commitment to include Native perspectives in the commemoration.

The Circle of Tribal Advisors (COTA) also designed a logo. Read about the meaning of the words and the images of the COTA logo in *Enough Good People* (p. 134; available online through the Tribal Legacy Project website, cms.lc-triballegacy.org/book).

The traveling exhibit stopped in 95 locations during the three-year commemoration. One of the exhibit highlights was the Tent of Many Voices—a performance space for Native presenters to share their perspectives about the history, legacy, and contemporary experiences and contributions of Native peoples.

The Tent of Many Voices made 14 visits to American Indian communities and reservations. More than 400 Native people gave more than 1,800 hours of presentations, stories, history, cultural demonstrations, music, dance, plays, films, and more in the Tent of Many Voices.

In addition to the traveling exhibit, fifteen signature events were organized starting in Monticello (January 2003), reaching the lower Columbia (November 2005), and ending in St. Louis (September 2006). Three of the commemoration's fifteen National Signature Events were hosted by tribal nations (Great Sioux Nation, Nez Perce Tribe, Mandan-Hidatsa-Arikara Nation).

The National Park Service estimates over 500,000 tourists participated in bicentennial events between 2003 and 2006 with peak attendance occurring in 2005 and lowest attendance in 2006.

Six million dollars of National Park Service Challenge Cost Share funding was awarded to tribes for bicentennial projects, language preservation, educational efforts, and more.

Teacher Handout C
"We Don't Need Those Anymore"

A story about one Native student's creative resistance during the Lewis and Clark Bicentennial

Written by Rachel Cushman, Tribal Council Member of the Chinook Indian Nation

I was in high school when the bicentennial events were being planned and taking place. I was a member of the Portland Public School Native Youth Leadership Program and we were invited to participate with the Flight of Discovery, a cross country flight, following the path that Lewis and Clark took on their "expedition" across what would become the United States. I was hesitant about participating, because my tribe, the Chinook Indian Nation had recently, at that time, been granted federal acknowledgment by the United States Department of the Interior, just to have it rescinded 18-months later. My people were the ones that had helped Lewis and Clark survive their journey, but my people were still being neglected by the same government that had sent Lewis and Clark to map out the west. After some thought, I decided to participate. I got to ride in a 4-seater plane and view the Columbia River from the air. It was beautiful. It was home. I saw all the landmarks from our creation stories that have been passed down from generation to generation, since Time Immemorial.

Prior to the event, we were asked to prepare items that we would huy huy (Chinook for trade) with the participants of the flight. Trading well is extremely important to my people. Chinookan people of the Columbia River are considered expert traders. For thousands of years, people from throughout the Americas came to the trading villages on the Columbia River, because of our expertise. When Lewis and Clark traveled through our territory, we were not impressed by the items they offered. I thought long and hard about what my contribution to the trade would be. I wanted to make a statement. I wanted my gifts to mean something. I prepared a basket with plants, native to the area, as well as, salves, teas, and some tule weaving. These items showed that Chinook Indian Nation's culture is still thriving despite broken promises by the US governments.

I also included curtain rings. Of the hundreds of items Lewis and Clark packed and traded throughout their journey, they traded over 400 curtain rings. My people don't forget bad trades, and they pass that information down from one generation to the next. My Leadership Program advisor asked me why I included curtain rings. I told her, "because they thought they were good enough for us in 1805, when in reality, they were ridiculous. They can have them back." She laughed, and replied, "well, that's very thoughtful."

When the trade took place, the participants offered the Native youth leaders large, old, beautiful trade beads, along with other assorted articles. Afterward, we presented them our items. At first, they were happy to see our contributions to the trade, but then they saw the curtain rings. I don't know if they knew what to think. Their eyes glazed over a little, and I could see that they were puzzled. My only comment to them was, "we don't need those anymore." I made a statement. It wasn't big. I resisted.

SECONDARY LESSON PLAN 7

Revisiting What We Know About York

Teaching Strategy: Historical Investigation and Mock Hearing

Purpose: Students examine a timeline of York's life and letters authored by Clark describing York's desire for freedom by applying four themes from the Teaching Tolerance project *Teaching Hard History: American Slavery:* freedom, enslavement, resistance, and families. The purpose of this lesson is for students to learn about York within the context of the institution of slavery that he was born into and resisted. This lesson is an adaptation of Elementary Lesson Plan 7 for secondary students.

Connections to the Standards

6 Ps Framework	Power
C3 Framework	D2.His.16.6-12
	D3.3.6-12
	D4.6.6-12.
Common Core State Standards	CCSS.ELA-Literacy.RH.6-12.1
	CCSS.ELA-Literacy.RH.6-12.2
	CCSS.ELA-Litearcy.RH.9-12.3
	CCSS.ELA-Literacy.RH.6-12.4
	CCSS.ELA-Literacy.RH.6-12.7
	CCSS.ELA-Literacy.RH.6-12.9

Introduction

In 1988, 47 letters written by William Clark and addressed to his brothers and nephew were found in the attic of Temple Bodley, great-grandson of Jonathan Clark (William's brother). On October 29, 1990, the Jonathan Clark Papers-Temple Bodley Collection were gifted to the Filson Historical Society. The letters were a significant addition to the historical record as they are dated from 1792 to 1811—before, during, and after the Corps of Discovery. Clark is recognized for meticulous detailed reporting in the Corps of Discovery journals. The letters in the Jonathan Clark Papers-Temple Bodley Collection add new perspective about Clark as they

> allow the reader to see beneath the persona of a famous explorer and territorial administrator and are a vital

source for any biography or study of him. The letters are written in such a personal and informative style that sometimes it seems almost as if you are peeking over Clark's shoulder at the people and scenes he describes. (Holmberg, 2002, p. 4)

Among the topics Clark addressed is York, who is mentioned in 11 of the letters (Holmberg, 1992). The letters clearly state that York was not passive about his enslavement as Clark writes about York's desire for his freedom. These requests frustrated and infuriated Clark as he narrates physically punishing York, on one occasion putting him in jail, threatening to send him to a more "severe master," and eventually leasing him to another enslaver. As discussed in Chapter 2, the added historical record from Clark's letters draws attention to the ways slavery is intertwined with the Corps of Discovery. This is the focus of Secondary Lesson Plan 7, which is an adapted version of Elementary Lesson Plan 7 for secondary students.

Our hope is that teachers have already introduced students to the concept of slavery, and that this lesson deepens student understanding of the institution of slavery by looking at the ways this institution shaped some aspects of the Corps of Discovery. Drawing from the Teaching Tolerance project *Teaching Hard History: American Slavery* (Teaching Tolerance, 2019), this lesson foregrounds key essential knowledges about freedom, enslavement, resistance, and families that help students learn about York within the context of the institution of slavery that he was born into and resisted. Teachers should familiarize themselves with the framework prior to teaching this lesson (www.tolerance.org/frame works/teaching-hard-history/american-slavery). The opening activity is a historical investigation featuring a timeline of York's life and excerpts from Clark's letters about York. Students read and mark evidence for each of the themes (freedom, enslavement, resistance, and families) and corroborate findings across the documents. In discussing their findings, students often report being taken aback by Clark's writing. With this additional knowledge of York's resistance to his own enslavement, and Clark's adamant refusal to free him, students have also felt frustrated with textbook accounts about York that gloss over his enslavement. The lesson plan ends with a mock hearing activity based on President Bill Clinton's recognition of Clark, Sacagawea, and York by posthumously honoring the three members of the Corps of Discovery with new Army titles in 2001. As historians with expertise in the content of the letters authored by Clark, students provide testimony and recommendations at a mock hearing facilitated by the teacher. The primary question students address is: What does it mean to honor York and Sacagawea for their contributions to the Corps of Discovery, which was intertwined with slavery and led to the dispossession of Native homelands?

Duration

Each activity takes approximately 45–60 minutes.

Materials

- Copies of Student Handout A and F for each student
- A packet of primary documents for each group of students that includes one copy of Student Handouts B, C, D, and E

Procedures

Activity 1

1. Organize students into small groups of four.
2. Start the lesson by recording students' prior knowledge about York. Say to students, "Let's begin with what we know. Who is York? What do you know about York?" During the facilitation of the discussion, record students' prior knowledge on the dry erase board. Students will likely mention that York was "a slave." Say to students, "York was an important member of the Corps of Discovery. A key part of York's life is that he was enslaved. We say that York was 'enslaved' rather than he was 'a slave' because it is important when we are talking about slavery to remember that we are talking about people or human beings, not objects or things."
3. Say to students, "Sometimes textbooks do not even mention York at all. That is not fair, because he was important to the Corps of Discovery. Other times, they mention York, but say little about how he was enslaved. Today we are going to look closer at the

institution of slavery and how it impacted York through four key themes: freedom, enslavement, resistance, and families. These themes will help us think about ways to extend the historical record about York, Clark, and the Corps of Discovery in the context of slavery."

4. Distribute one copy of Student Handout A to each student and the packet of documents that include Student Handouts B, C, D, and E to each small group. Instruct students in each small group to select one of the documents (Student Handout B, C, D, or E).
5. Direct students' attention to Student Handout A and overview the definitions of the four themes. Explain that students will read the document they selected and find evidence for each of the themes by using different symbols or colors. For example, a star or the color red is assigned to the theme of "freedom," and evidence in the document for this theme is marked accordingly. Explain to students that language Clark uses in the letters may be deeply hurtful as they will encounter derogatory terms and reaffirm expectations for how the words will be addressed.
6. Facilitate a process for assigning a symbol or color to each theme. Options for this process include: the teacher, class, small groups, or individuals determine symbols or colors for each theme. When symbols or colors are decided, instruct students to record this in column one of Student Handout A for each theme.
7. Next, model annotating a document using symbols or colors for each theme. Consider organizing students into pairs sharing the same document so they can read and annotate collaboratively. Remind students their goal is to become an expert about their document and they will share findings with their small group. (If necessary, remind students they are not writing information on the chart posted on the reverse side of Student Handout A. This will happen later in step 9.)
8. While students are reading and annotating the documents, circulate to check for understanding and preparedness for sharing findings in their small groups.
9. After students finish annotating, say to students, "It is time to share your findings with members of your small group. Flip

to the reverse side of Student Handout A. Share examples of evidence you found for each theme. Try to find agreement between documents. For example, is there evidence in the timelines that is also found in the letters? Your goal is to list three significant findings for each theme and identify the documents where the evidence is found. Sometimes you will list more than one document." Model the activity providing one or two examples.

10. While students are sharing their findings and recording evidence in the chart, circulate to check for understanding and preparedness for class discussion.

11. After small groups complete the chart, facilitate a discussion using the following questions:

> » Return to our prior knowledge we recorded on the dry erase board. What new information did you learn about York?
> » After learning more about York, Clark, and the context of slavery, how does this add to your understanding of the Corps of Discovery?

12. Close by having students share one word to describe a feeling they had during or after the lesson.

Activity 2

1. Organize students into the same small groups from the previous activity. Small groups will need the handouts from Activity 1 (Student Handouts A, B, C, D, and E). Student Handout A is necessary for Activity 2 and Student Handouts B–E are supportive for Activity 2.

2. Begin the lesson by asking volunteers to summarize what was learned in the prior activity.

3. Distribute Student Handout F and project the document. Say to students, "Today's activity begins with a scenario. On January 17, 2001, President Clinton posthumously honored William Clark, Sacagawea, and York. William Clark was promoted to Captain of the Regular Army so that his rank was equal to Meriwether Lewis. Sacagawea and York were each given the title Honorary Sergeant. Imagine you are a historian as I read Student Handout F out loud."

4. After reading the scenario, direct students to the reverse side of Student Handout F and project the document. Provide an overview of the activity. Explain to students they will use the findings they recorded in Student Handout A to write the statement. Additionally, explain that there will be a mock hearing in which groups will be able to read their statements.

5. While students are doing the activity, circulate among groups to check for understanding, group preparedness, and ensure they have identified a group member to speak.

6. When groups are ready with their statements, call the hearing to order. Say to students, "Hear ye, hear ye! I call this hearing to order. The purpose of these proceedings is to hear testimony from historians about President Clinton's plan to posthumously honor William Clark. Is there a group that would like to begin? Thank you. Please rise, state your name, and read your statement." To avoid redundancy, after three groups share their statements, say to students, "Are there groups with unique evidence to add to the record? Are there groups with different recommendations?" Once groups have responded, close the meeting by stating, "Thank you for your statements today."

7. To facilitate a discussion of the mock hearing, begin by projecting the article "Fallout Over Freedom" from the website, "Discovering Lewis and Clark" (www.lewis -clark.org/article/3355#toc-3). Explain to students the website was published three years prior to President Clinton's recognition of Clark, York, and Sacagawea. Scroll to the section titled, "Whose Hero? Whose Victim?" Read this section out loud to students. Then, ask students the following questions:

> » What does it mean to honor York and Sacagawea for their contributions to the Corps of Discovery, which was intertwined with slavery and resulted in dispossession of Native homelands?
> » During the mock hearing, what recommendations do you think were helpful to thinking about how to honor York?
> » What new questions are raised for you?

Extension Activities

- Follow this lesson by adapting Elementary Lesson Plan 6 Sacagawea: Beyond Interpreter and Guide for secondary students.
- In the book *In Search of York*, Betts (2000) traces how narratives of York are distorted to forward racist ideologies. These depictions are "a creation of prejudice masquerading as history" (Betts, 2000, p. 64). Black Studies scholar David Millner (2003) adds to this analysis by noting that in "each generation since 1805–1806, the York story has been presented in a form that reflects the interracial behaviors, politics, and dynamics of that generation" (p. 306). Millner focuses on two specific forms: Sambo and Superhero. Using the evidence and analysis featured in Betts (2000) and Millner (2003), design a historical investigation comparing and contrasting representations of York sampled across time to uncover the racist ideologizes underlying the representations. After the inquiry, students apply their knowledge by developing a critical reading tool for children's books about York.

Student Handout A

Directions: The chart presents four themes from *Teaching Hard History: American Slavery* (Teaching Tolerance). When reading a document for this historical investigation, your goal is to identify and mark text that matches these themes. Determine a symbol or color that you will use for each of the themes and indicate this in Column 1.

Freedom	Being free means being able to choose what your life looks like without interference from others. Everybody wants to be free, but some people have more freedom and privileges than other people. People and institutions have the ability to restrict freedom by using power to make rules and punishment to make people obey the rules. People also restrict freedom by intimidating people into acting in certain ways. *Was York able to choose what his life looked like? What evidence is there that York wanted his freedom? What rules restricted York's freedom? How was intimidation or punishment used to try to force York to follow the rules?*
Enslavement	The main purpose of enslaving people is to make money. Enslaved people rarely earn money for their work. Many kinds of people can be enslaved, including children. Most enslaved people were in bondage for their entire lives. When enslaved parents had children, they were also enslaved. When people are enslaved, they do not have freedom. Their enslavers control their actions and can say where they move, what job they do, and whom they will live with. The founders of the United States and twelve presidents enslaved people. *Who benefited from York's enslavement? What were the benefits? Who enslaved York's family? What are examples of the ways York's life was controlled by enslavers?*
Resistance	Enslaved people hated being enslaved and resisted bondage in many ways. Although it was very difficult, some did manage to escape. Enslaved people resisted slavery to try and obtain some freedom in the midst of their enslavement. Everyday acts of resistance were common and took many forms, such as slowing down work, pretending to be ill or to not understand, running away, even armed rebellion. *What evidence is there that York hated being enslaved? What are examples of how York resisted being enslaved?*
Families	Enslaved people loved their families just like other people. Enslavers often separated families to make more money or as punishment. Once separated, families were rarely able to communicate or reunited. About half of all enslaved people lived under the same roof as the families they worked for. Sometimes they ate the same food and wore the same clothes. *What evidence is there that York loved his family? What evidence is there that York was separated from his family so his enslaver could make more money? What evidence is there that York was separated from his family as punishment? What evidence is there that York lived under the same roof, ate the same food, and wore the same clothes as his enslaver?*

Small Group Directions

1. Now that you have read and marked the document, share information you highlighted with group members. See if you can find agreement between different documents.
2. In column 2, identify three findings for each theme. List the documents where the evidence is found. If the evidence is found in more than one document, list multiple documents.

List of sources:

- Document 1: Timeline of York's Life: Born Enslaved, Early Life, and During the Corps of Discovery
- Document 2: Timeline of York's Life: After the Corps of Discovery
- Document 3: Letters from William Clark to Jonathan Clark (November–December 1808)
- Document 4: Letters from William Clark to Jonathan Clark (December 1808–August 1809)

Freedom Was York able to choose what his life looked like? What evidence is there that York wanted his freedom? What rules restricted York's freedom? How was intimidation or punishment used to try to force York to follow the rules?	1. 2. 3.
Enslavement Who benefited from York's enslavement? What were the benefits? Who enslaved York's family? What are examples of the ways York's life was controlled by enslavers?	1. 2. 3.
Resistance What evidence is there that York hated being enslaved? What are examples of how York resisted being enslaved?	1. 2. 3.
Families What evidence is there that York loved his family? What evidence is there that York was separated from his family so his enslaver could make more money? What evidence is there that York was separated from his family as punishment? What evidence is there that York lived under the same roof, ate the same food, and wore the same clothes as his enslaver?	1. 2. 3.

Student Handout B
Timeline of York's Life: Before and During the Corps of Discovery

Description: This document presents a timeline of York's life before and during the Corps of Discovery. As you read the document, use different colors to underline or highlight examples for each of the themes (freedom, enslavement, resistance, and families).

Source: The timeline was adapted from three sources: "'I wish you to see and know all:' The recently discovered letters of William Clark to Jonathan Clark" by James J. Holmberg in *We Proceeded On*, November 1992, Vol. 18, No.4, p. 4–12; *In Search of York* by Robert Betts (2000), and *York's Adventures with Lewis and Clark: An African-American's Part in the Great Expedition* by Rhoda Blumberg (2004).

York: Timeline

Born Enslaved: York's Life Before the Corps of Discovery

1733 John Clark, William Clark's father, inherits Old York and other enslaved upon *his* father's death.

Early 1770s York is born. William Clark is born in 1770 and it is known that Clark is a little older than York. They grow up together in the same house.

1784 At around the age of twelve, York is assigned by John Clark to be a "body servant" to William Clark (age fourteen). The Clark family move from Virginia to Kentucky. The people they enslave are taken with them.

1799 John Clark dies and William inherits the family plantation (Mulbury Hill in Louisville, KY) consisting of equipment, livestock, thousands of acres of land, and eight enslaved including York, his parents (Old York and Rose), and siblings (Nancy and Juba).

1800–1802 York accompanies Clark on visits to see President Thomas Jefferson. President Jefferson was a neighbor to the Clark family in Virginia.

Before 1803 Clark gives permission for York to marry a woman enslaved by a family living near Mulbury Hill (the marriage is not considered legal); her name, date of marriage, and whether they had children is unknown.

York's Life During the Lewis and Clark Corps of Discovery

1803 Clark receives a letter from Meriwether Lewis inviting him to be a co-captain on the Lewis and Clark Expedition. As an enslaved person, York is to accompany Clark on the three-year expedition.

1803–1806 The journals document York's contributions as a trusted member of the Corps of Discovery. Evidence from the journals indicates York is an expert hunter, a skilled outdoorsman, provides medical care, engages in trade, and creates alliances with Native nations. York carries a gun and votes to determine the location of Fort Clatsop (two actions enslaved people could not do at the time). On one occasion he is allowed to send home a gift package that included two Mandan buffalo robes to his wife and a friend named Ben (who was enslaved by Clark, freed in 1802 and still working for the family). Disregarding the Native names of geographic locations, Clark renames two places after York: York's Eight Islands and York's Dry Creek.

In the journals, words used to refer to York include: "I ordered my Black servant to dance," "my boy York," "my little Negro boy, York," "my servant," and "Captain Clark's Black man." York is not listed on the official roster of expedition members Clark submits to the War Department (Sacajawea and John Baptiste are also not listed).

After the expedition, most of the men were awarded land and money. Lewis received $2,776.22 and Clark received $2,113.74, and 1,600 acres of land each. The other men received double pay (approximately $333) and 320 acres of land. York and Sacagawea received no money or land. York remained enslaved by Clark.

Student Handout C
Timeline of York's Life: After the Corps of Discovery

Description: This document presents a timeline of York's life after the Corps of Discovery. As you read the document, use different colors to underline or highlight examples for each of the themes (freedom, enslavement, resistance, and families).

Source: The timeline was adapted from three sources: "'I wish you to see and know all:' The recently discovered letters of William Clark to Jonathan Clark" by James J. Holmberg in *We Proceeded On*, November 1992, Vol. 18, No.4, p. 4–12; *In Search of York* by Robert Betts (2000), and *York's Adventures with Lewis and Clark: An African-American's Part in the Great Expedition* by Rhoda Blumberg (2004).

York: Timeline

York's Life After the Lewis and Clark Corps of Discovery

1808	Clark is named Brigadier General and Indian agent for the West. Clark and Julia Hancock marry and the family relocates from Louisville, KY, to St. Louis, MO, for Clark's new job. The people they enslave are moved with them and York is separated from his wife.
1808–1809	In letters to his brother, Clark writes about York's desire to be freed as a result of his service during the expedition. York wants to return to his wife in Kentucky. Clark refuses to give York freedom. He allows York to visit his wife for four to five weeks and he stays four or five months. When York returns, Clark describes him as "disrespectful and sulky" and recounts physically punishing York and sending him to jail. Later, he hires out York to his brother, Edmund Clark.
1811	York learns that is wife is forced to relocate to Natchez, MS, with the family that enslaved her.
1815	Clark and John Hite Clark (his nephew) enter a business agreement to purchase a wagon and team to be operated in Louisville, KY. York is the driver.
After 1815	Clark frees York. York is given the wagon transport business and reportedly hauls goods between Nashville, TN, and Richmond, KY.
1832	The writer Washington Irving interviews Clark and asks about York. Clark states that York lost the business because he was lazy, agreed to bad business deals, and he did not take care of the horses. Clark adds that York was unable to cope with freedom and returned to domestic service because he needed a master. Finally, Clark states that York was returning to him when he died of cholera in Tennessee. Others say York found a home in a Crow village and lived out his days there.

Student Handout D
Letters from William Clark to Jonathan Clark (November–December, 1808)

Description: This document presents excerpts from letters written by William Clark addressed to his brother, Jonathan Clark. Using the different color highlighters you selected to represent the themes, highlight examples of freedom, enslavement, resistance, and families.

Source: Adapted from "'I Wish You to See and Know All:' The Recently Discovered Letters of William Clark to Jonathan Clark" by James J. Holmberg in *We Proceeded On*, November 1992, Vol. 18, No. 4, p. 7–8.

November 9, 1808 (William Clark writing to Jonathan Clark)

I will send York and permit him to stay a few weeks with his wife. He wishes to stay there altogether and hire himself which I have refused. He prefers being sold to returning here. He is serviceable to me at this place and I am determined not to sell him to gratify him. I have directed him to return by being included in my nephew's shipment of goods. If any attempt is made by York to run off, or refuse his duty as a slave, I wish him sent to New Orleans and sold or hired out to some severe master until he thinks better of such conduct. I do not wish him to know my directions if he conducts himself well. This choice I must request you to make if his conduct deserves severity.

November 22, 1808 (William Clark writing to Jonathan Clark)

While York is waiting to return St. Louis, if my nephew has any thing for him to do—he does not like to stay in St. Louis on the account of his wife being in Louisville. He is serviceable to me here and perhaps he will see his situation there more unfavorable than he expected and will, after a while, prefer returning to this place.

December 10, 1808 (William Clark writing to Jonathan Clark)

I did wish to do well by him, but as he has got such a notion about freedom and his immense services, that I do not expect he will be of much service to me again. I do not think with him, that his services have been so great or my situation would permit me to liberate him. I must request you do for me as circumstances may seem best or necessary and I will support your actions. He could be of service to me and save me money, but I do not expect much from him as long as he has a wife in Kentucky. I find it is necessary to look out a little and must get in some way of making a little. You will not disapprove of my inclinations on this score. I have long discovered your wish (even before I went [on] the Western trip) to induce me to believe that there might be a rainy day. Clouds seem to fly thicker than they use to do and I think there will be a rainy day.

Student Handout E
Letters from William Clark to Jonathan Clark (December, 1808-August, 1809)

Description: This document presents excerpts from letters written by William Clark addressed to his brother, Jonathan Clark. Using the different color highlighters you selected to represent the themes, highlight examples of freedom, enslavement, resistance, and families.

Source: Adapted from "'I Wish You to See and Know All:' The Recently Discovered Letters of William Clark to Jonathan Clark" by James J. Holmberg in *We Proceeded On*, November 1992, Vol. 18, No. 4, p. 8–9.

December 17, 1808 (William Clark writing to Jonathan Clark)

I do not care for York's being in this country. I am a little displeased with him and intended to have him punished, but Governor Lewis has insisted on my only hiring him out in Kentucky which, perhaps, will be best. This I leave entirely to you, perhaps if he has a severe master awhile he may do some service. I do not wish him again in this country until he applies himself to come and get over that wife of his. I wished him to stay with his family four or five weeks only and not four or five months. Dear Brother, I give you a great deal of trouble about my concerns, shall I ever compensate you?

May 29, 1809 (William Clark writing to Jonathan Clark)

York brought my horse. He is here but of very little service to me. He is insolent and sulky. I gave him a severe trouncing the other day and he has minded his ways. Since he could be hired for anything at or near Louisville, I think if he was hired to serve a severe master he would see the difference and do better.

July 22, 1809 (William Clark writing to Jonathan Clark)

I have taken York out of the Caleboos [jail] and he has for two or three weeks been the finest Negro I ever had.

August 26, 1809 (William Clark writing to Jonathan Clark)

Since I confined York, he has been a good fellow to work.

August 26, 1809 (William Clark writing to Jonathan Clark)

I have become displeased with him and shall hire or sell him. On the fifth of next month, I shall set him off in a boat to Wheeling as a hand. On his return to the falls, I wish much to hire him or sell him. I can't sell Negros here for money.

Student Handout F
The White House President Clinton: Celebrating the Legacy of Lewis and Clark

---

On January 17, 2001, President Clinton will posthumously honor three members of the Lewis and Clark Corps of Discovery in recognition of their courage and contributions to our nation's history:

- On the recommendation of the Secretary of Defense, and by congressional authorization, President Clinton will posthumously present William Clark his rightful military commission by promoting him from Lieutenant of the Corps of Artillerists and Engineers to Captain in the Regular Army, with an effective date of March 26, 1804. On the expedition, Lewis and Clark shared equally the responsibilities of command, and although President Jefferson sought the rank of Captain for Clark, the promotion was denied by the War Department and Clark was instead given the rank of Lieutenant.
- The President will present the title of Honorary Sergeant, Regular Army to Sacagawea, a young Lemhi Shoshone woman who served as Lewis and Clark's guide. Sacagawea was the only woman to accompany the explorers to the Pacific Ocean and back, and her interpretation and navigation skills proved invaluable to the expedition.
- The President will present the title of Honorary Sergeant, Regular Army to York, Clark's personal slave who accompanied the expedition party. York was the first black man to cross the continent, and although relatively unknown, was instrumental in the success of the exploration.

(Adapted from clintonwhitehouse5.archives.gov/WH/new/html/Wed_Jan_17_101131_2001.html)

You are a group of historians preparing testimony for a hearing that will address President Clinton's plans to recognize the contributions of William Clark, York, and Sacagawea. You want the President to take into consideration new information entered into the historical record about William Clark. In 1988, 47 letters written by Clark and addressed to his brothers and nephew were found in the attic of Temple Bodley, great-grandson of Jonathan Clark (William's brother). On October 29, 1990, the Jonathan Clark Papers-Temple Bodley Collection were gifted to the Filson Historical Society.

You think it is important to inform the White House of the implications of the posthumous honor in the context of the recent update to the historical record about William Clark. Your goal is to collaboratively write a statement presenting your recommendation to the President that is supported by evidence from the historical record (a timeline of York's life and excerpts from the letters). Use the reverse of this handout to write your statement.

Dear President Clinton and Interior Secretary Babbitt,

We are historians of the Lewis and Clark Expedition specializing in the historical record about York and William Clark. We are here today to provide a statement about the decision to posthumously honor William Clark by promoting him from Lieutenant to Captain.

Summarize your position	**We believe**
Support your position with evidence from the documents. Explain how the evidence supports your position.	**First,**
Support your position with evidence from the documents. Explain how the evidence supports your position.	**Second,**
Support your position with evidence from the documents. Explain how the evidence supports your position.	**Finally,**
State what action you think should happen.	**Given this evidence, we recommend**

Respectfully,
[SIGN YOUR NAMES]

Part IV

TEACHING RESOURCES

Native Lands Under Siege

A variety of historic and contemporary examples of Native Nations advocating for the protection, restoration, or repatriation of their homelands provides students a starting point for inquiry into contemporary issues of land dispossession and struggles for self-determination and sovereignty. In addition to this selective list, we recommend the Indian Land Tenure Foundation website (iltf.org/).

Bears Ears National Monument

Hopi Tribe, Navajo Nation, Ute Mountain Ute Tribe, Pueblo of Zuni, and Ute Indian Tribe

On December 28, 2016, President Barack Obama used his authority under the Antiquities Act to establish the Bears Ears National Monument. This announcement was a victory for the Bears Ears Inter-Tribal Coalition (five nations listed above), and all of the tribal nations nations declared support for protecting the 1.3 million acres of land. The Bears Ears National Monument is the first co-managed effort between the federal government and the five nations coalition. In the 2016 publication "Bears Ears: A Native Perspective," Regina Lopez-Whiteskunk, Ute Mountain Ute Council, said, "We bring to the table direct ties to the land; with many of the tribal customs it all lies in the verbal delivery of what was. It's very important that we take every step in protecting our heritage. We are of the land, we don't quite own it but we're here as caretakers" (p. 10). Under President Donald Trump, on August 24, 2017, Interior Secretary Ryan Zinke recommended shrinking and changing the management conditions of Bears Ears (and other monuments established by President Obama). Carleton Bowekaty, Zuni Councilman and Bears Ears Inter-Tribal Coalition Co-Chair, responded, "Secretary Zinke's recommendation is an insult to Tribes. He has shown complete disregard for Sovereign Tribes with ancestral connections to the region, as well as the hundreds of thousands of people who have expressed support" (Bears Ears Coaltion, 2017). On December 4, 2017, President Donald Trump signed an order reducing Bears Ears from 1.3 million acres to 220,000 acres.

Web resource:

- Bears Ears Inter-Tribal Coalition: bearsearscoalition.org

Mauna Kea and the Thirty Mile Telescope

Kanaka Maoli

Mauna Kea, the highest mountain in Hawai'i with an elevation of 13,796 feet, is a sacred site for Kanaka Maoli (Native Hawaiian people). In the creation story of the Hawaiian island chain, Mauna Kea is the first born of Papahanaumoku (earth mother) and Wakea (sky father). In the documentary *Mauna Kea—Temple Under Siege* (2006), Dr. Pualani Kanaka'ole Kanahele describes Mauna Kea as "where our roots start. That's where our island begins. That's where the first rain from Wakea hits. . . . That's where the first sunlight that rises every morning hits. That mountain is the first for everything we have." This helps explain the decades of resistance to the use of Mauna Kea as a site for telescopes. Resistance against the most recent proposal to build the Thirty Mile Telescope (TMT) atop Mauna Kea resulted in court hearings. On October 30, 2018, the Hawai'i Supreme Court ruled in favor of building the telescope project. With approval from the state of Hawai'i, construction began in June 2019 when law enforcement agencies cleared structures built by protectors. Since July 2019, Kanaka Maoli and allies—who refer to themselves as kia'i, or protectors—have gathered and camped at the base of Mauna Kea to protect the mountain from unwanted construction. Many, included Elders, have been arrested during this process. Still, kia'i have remained steadfast in their resistance, even establishing a university at camp, Pu'uhonua o Pu'uhuluhulu Maunakea, to center and promote Hawaiian values and teachings throughout the process, and ensure that kia'i remain committed to kapu aloha, a Hawaiian concept and practice of centering compassion and aloha, even in the face of opposition. As of 2020, protectors continue to camp at Mauna Kea to oppose the desecration of the mountain.

After over five months of demonstrations, Governor David Ige removed state law enforcement, announcing on December 20, 2019, that construction would not proceed for the time being while those opposing the telescope project vowed to remain organized and vigilant to protect Mauna Kea.

Web resource:

- Truthout: truthout.org/articles/mauna-kea
  -protests-are-part-of-a-long-fight-against
  -colonialism

Shasta Dam

Winnemem Wintu

On May 1, 1941, the U.S. Congress passed legislation to seize the land of the Winnemem Wintu for the purpose of building a dam to support the agricultural development of the Central Valley in California. In 1945, construction of the Shasta Dam was completed and 4.5 million acre-feet of water flooded the traditional lands of the Winnemem Wintu. On July 29, 2015, the federal Bureau of Reclamation released a proposal to increase the height of Shasta Dam by 18.5 feet to meet the needs of population growth and water shortage. Construction will cost $1.3 billion and will result in further flooding of the cultural and historical resources of the Winnemum Wintu. The short film "Don't Drown Our Culture" (www.youtube.com/watch?v=wpU5hEPSkNA) opens with tribal member Betti Comas standing beside Chief Caleen Sisk asking, "I ask the public—where do you want us to be? I ask the government—where do you want us to be? Do you have plans for us?"

Web resource:

- Winnemem Wintu: www.winnememwintu.us

Reversing Loss of Land

Osage Nation

The Osage Nation owned nearly 1.5 million acres in the 1900s. After 200 years of losing land through treaty negotiation and white settlement, the tribal nation currently owns 5 percent of its original acreage. In 2016, the Osage Nation purchased the 43,000-acre Bluestem Ranch from media mogul Ted Turner in an effort to reverse the loss of land. In a letter addressed to Ted Turner, Principal Chief Geoffrey Standing Bear writes, "These plains are part of the Osage people's original homelands. Our ancestors lived on these lands as hunters and as people who chose to enjoy life exactly on the location of the Bluestem Ranch. At least we have the ability and opportunity to once again own this much land in one place."

Web resource:

- Letter, Standing Bear to Turner, Jan. 21, 2016: www.osagenation-nsn.gov/news-events/news /letter-chief-standing-bear-ted-turner

Celilo Falls (Wy-am)

Yakama, Umatilla, Warm Springs, and Nez Perce

Celilo Falls was an enormous set of falls and rapids on the Columbia River about 10 miles east of The Dalles, OR. For thousands of years, it was a central, and sacred, fishing ground for the Yakama, Umatilla, Warm Springs, and Nez Perce. In fact, the richness of the fishing made Celilo Falls a meeting and trading center where as many as 5,000 people came together from hundreds of miles. After World War II, the push for use of the Columbia for hydropower led to a vast expansion of large dams on the river. One of those dams was built at The Dalles. When the dam was completed in 1957, the rising waters behind the dam completely drowned Celilo Falls and much of the land around the falls. Members of the tribal nations watched in grief as their sacred site disappeared. The federal government promised in the 1950s to build replacement fishing villages. The first rebuild project occurred in 2016 with the construction of 15 permanent homes at Celilo Village. After a delay in funding for the second rebuild project, the tribal nations and Oregon Senator Jeff Merkley and Washington Senator Patty Murray pressed to have the funding restored.

Web resource:

- Columbia River Inter-Tribal Fish Commission: www.critfc.org

Our Shared Responsibility

Lummi Nation

Since 2013, members of the Lummi Nation have organized an annual Totem Pole Journey in which totem poles created by the House of Tears Carvers are transported hundreds of miles and presented to tribal nations and local communities. Each journey addresses environmental issues, focusing on fossil fuel terminals, oil and coal trains, pipelines, endangered animals, and other matters. The routes bring together a coalition of Native nations, environmental groups, religious leaders, ranchers, fishery representatives, and community activists with shared interests for water and land protection/restoration. The 2019 journey began in Miami, FL, calling for the restoration of the Salish Sea, protection of the Southern Resident orcas from extinction, and demand that Seaquarium release an orca, Tokitae, that was taken from the Salish Sea 47 years ago, A

15-foot-long totem pole honoring the orca traveled 7,700 miles, raising awareness of the Lummi Nation's Salish Sea Campaign. Lummi Nation Chairman Jay Julius stated, "This is a vision of resilience, truth, belonging, and healing for *qwe 'lhol mechen* [orca]. This is a battle for the soul of Xwullemy, the Salish Sea" (Salish Sea Sentinel, 2019).

Web resource:

- Salish Sea Campaign: sacredsea.org

Book Review

Piecing Me Together by Renée Watson (2017)

When accepting the 2018 Coretta Scott King Author Award for *Piecing Me Together*, Renée Watson said,

> I wonder how the #MeToo and #TimesUp movements, the #BlackLivesMatter movement, and the call to #SayHerName are impacting what girls believe about their worth. How are they making sense of the world they inherited? Are they taught black history only through the lens of sorrow and pain? Are they allowed to be their whole selves and live at the intersection of their lives, not having to compartmentalize who they are at school, or in spaces that may not see them as whole beings? When the world chips away at their souls, breaks them into pieces because of racism, sexism, and classism, who will help them piece themselves back together? (Watson, 2018)

These questions are central to *Piecing Me Together* as Watson (2017) conveys the experiences of an African American high school student named Jade who attends a mostly white and affluent private high school outside of her neighborhood where she navigates the complexity of being an outsider. Jade's self-discovery is an exploration of place, identity, and intersectionality, and she expresses her voice through collage. Through her artwork, Jade pieces together a sophisticated statement of self-reflection and activism as she makes meaning of her own experiences, her understanding of history, and an incident of police brutality that reverberates through the city in which she lives.

Jade's interest in history, particularly the Corps of Discovery, is how *Piecing Me Together* fits within the scope of *Teaching Critically About Lewis and Clark: Challenging Dominant Narratives in K–12 Curriculum*. Jade first learns about York from her friend Lee Lee. From Jade's perspective, Watson writes,

> "What did York do?" I ask.
>
> "Mrs. Phillips said he was a good hunter and he set up the tents and managed the sails. Once, he even saved Clark from drowning. . . . When they needed to decide on where to go next or how to handle a challenge, York got to vote. Sacagawea, too. The first time a black man and a woman were ever given that privilege."
>
> Lee Lee tells me that Lewis and Clark came with gifts and that it was a ritual to have a meeting ceremony. At that meeting, Lewis and Clark told the tribal leaders that their land was now the property of the United States, and that a man in the east was their new great father.
>
> They did not tell them York was Clark's slave.
>
> They did not tell them that their new great father owned slaves . . .
>
> I have so many more questions, but Lee Lee is on to the next topic. She starts telling me about all the Northside drama—who's broken up, who's gotten back together. I know so many of them because we all went to middle school together.
>
> The whole time Lee Lee is talking, I am thinking about York and Sacagawea, wondering how they must have felt having a form of freedom but no real power. (pp. 22–24)

Through her growing awareness of historical context, Jade begins to question what is and is not taught in school and she begins to reassess her relationship to place. For example, Jade questions the Native stereotype of a local professional sports team mascot, she begins to see references to the Corps of Discovery throughout her city in critical way, and she develops an understanding of how Thanksgiving is experienced by Native communities. In addition, Jade is drawn to York's story as she seeks to understand how her own sense of freedom is mediated by race, class, and gender. Watson depicts Jade's imagining of York traveling west years after the Corps of Discovery by writing,

> I see York traveling west again, knowing which way to go this time. I see him crossing rivers, crossing mountains, seeing the Native Americans who were so awed by him. This time he is no one's servant or slave. This time he tells them the whole story, tells how he is the first of his kind.
>
> This time he speaks for himself.

Of the art I've been making lately, this is the only one where I've included myself. I am with York, both of us with maps in our hands. Both of us black and traveling. Black and exploring. Both of us discovering what we are really capable of. (pp. 260–261)

Through Jade's story, Watson weaves references to issues raised by the Black Lives Matter and Say Her Name movements together with the racial politics of the Corps of Discovery.

In this way, *Piecing Me Together* explicitly connects the past and the present and as such, the novel adds to a social studies unit about the Corps of Discovery in unique and significant ways. Teaching ideas for using *Piecing Me Together* to complement lessons about the Corps of Discovery include:

- The teaching guide published to accompany the book provides activities and discussion prompts organized by theme to explore intersectionality. It is available at: media.bloomsbury.com/rep /files/Piecing%20Me%20Together%20Guide .pdf. Teachers can use this teaching guide to facilitate a class reading of the novel.
- Students can examine Jade's self-expression through collage and how she connects the present to the past in her artwork. Then students can create their own collages, reflecting how they make meaning of the Corps of Discovery in the context of today.

- Similar to the benefit organized by Jade and Lee Lee at the end of the book, the students' collage projects can be featured in a public showing where students share the meaning of their collages and their knowledge about the legacy of the Corps of Discovery.

Jade's critical awareness leads her to see references to the Corps of Discovery in her city in new ways. Students can brainstorm a list of place names, monuments, and signs they see as part of their daily lives and research the stories of the sites they list. Based on their findings, students present ways to annotate or change the sites to provide a more inclusive and responsible story of place. As an example, it is recommended teachers share the story of the unanimous vote of the San Francisco Unified School District to remove the 1936 fresco mural "Life of Washington" from the walls of George Washington High School (www.cnn.com /2019/06/26/us/san-francisco-mural-slaves-native -americans-trnd/index.html). Another example is the vote by the Charlottesville, VA, City Council to stop celebrating a a local holiday for Thomas Jefferson's birthday and replace it with Freedom and Liberation Day (www.dailyprogress.com/news/council-sets-vote -on-jefferson-s-birthday-as-a-city/article_2b6f67c2 -9169-11e9-9c99-4f6ceedbee31.html and www.daily progress.com/news/local/city-nixes-jefferson-s-birth day-as-holiday/article_cbe05f4f-7165-5420-8f40-521 cebbd66e8.html).

Partnerships Realized
The Confluence Project

I want to connect you back to the landscape, make you pay a little closer attention to where you are, maybe who you are. Two hundred years from now, we might be living in a better place. Right now, we're at a huge crossroad.

—Maya Lin (Bock, 2005)

In 1999, Antone Minthorn, Chairman of the Confederated Tribes of the Umatilla Indian Reservation was rewatching a documentary about Maya Lin when he was struck with an idea. What if Maya Lin designed a series of public art installations along the Columbia River to tell the story of land, river, and resilience? Coincidentally, Jane Jacobsen, from the Vancouver National Historic Reserve Trust, had the same idea. Both independently called David Nicandri, Director of the Washington State Historical Society and charged with organizing the state's events of the Lewis and Clark bicentennial, to share their vision; thus the Confluence Project was started. The collaborative effort to persuade Lin to accept the proposal spanned a year and required patience as she initially said no. The efforts to change her mind included a chance meeting at her office in New York City, the involvement of Washington State Governor John Locke, and a package that included books and maps along with an item from each installation site (a stone, feather, shell, stick, and handful of earth). In 2000 Lin committed to the Confluence Project, and the first of six installations was dedicated on May 7, 2006, at Cape Disappointment State Park in Washington State.

Today the Confluence Project is a well-established nonprofit guided by the mission "to connect people to the history, living cultures and ecology of the Columbia River system through Indigenous voices" (www.confluenceproject.org/). The five installations spanning 438 miles of the Columbia River system are presented on the website with special features, such as audio tours, virtual tours, and interviews, to describe each of the sites.

- Cape Disappointment State Park (Ilwaco, WA). The installation includes multiple elements: a boardwalk leading to the beach inscribed with text from the journals to mark the beginning and end of the journey at the Pacific Ocean; a trail made of crushed oyster shells with concrete pavers inscribed with the lyrics of a Chinook praise song shared on November 18, 2005, to commemorate the arrival of the Corps of Discovery 200 years earlier; a basalt fish cleaning table inscribed with the Chinook origin story; and a viewing platform of Baker Bay with text from the journals describing the view (Dedicated in May 2006).
- Land Bridge at Fort Vancouver (Vancouver, WA). As visitors walk the Land Bridge connecting Fort Vancouver to the Columbia River waterfront, they learn about indigenous plants and view several installations by artist Lillian Pitt (Confederated Tribes of the Warm Springs). Johnpaul Jones (Choctaw/Cherokee) was the architect for the project (Dedicated in August 2008).
- The Bird Blind at the Sandy River Delta (Troutdale, OR). The 1.2-mile trail to the Bird Blind provides visitors a walk through the restored Sandy River Delta. The plants and animal species observed in the military expedition journals, many of which are threatened or endangered today, are inscribed on the slats of the Bird Blind (Dedicated August 2008).
- The Story Circles at Sacajawea State Park (Pasco, WA). For more than ten thousand years Native peoples have gathered at this site of the confluence of the Columbia and Snake rivers. The seven circles are inscribed with text from the military expedition journals and the stories of Native peoples (Dedicated in August 2010).
- The Listening Circle at Chief Timothy State Park (Clarkston, WA). Chief Timothy State Park is located on an island in the Snake River near the confluence with the Clearwater River.

A path leads to the Listening Circle, which is an amphitheater in a shape informed by a Nez Perce blessing ceremony performed at the site. The location and positioning of the Listening Circle are intended to highlight visitors' experience of the setting. According the Confluence Project, the landscape at the Listening Circle is the only installation resembling what Lewis and Clark viewed as they traveled through the homelands of the Nez Perce (Dedicated in May 2015).

Describing the intention of the Confluence Project's art and landscape installations, Roberta Conner (Cayuse, Umatilla, and Nez Perce), Director of the Tamástslikt Cultural Institute located on the Confederated Tribes of the Umatilla Indian Reservation, stated,

As a consequence of these memorials we would hope people would begin to understand . . . that we have within our culture a cycle of renewal with places, and people, with species of this landscape. And that cycle of renewal is one that we have maintained, but we invite other people to join because that is how we have sustained the place that sustains us. (Grabow, 2011)

The Confluence Project is a program of partnerships between Northwest Native nations, Maya Lin, architect Johnpaul Jones, private and organization contributors, federal government agencies, and state government agencies in Oregon and Washington. The hope is that after experiencing the installations, visitors leave with a new appreciation for the meaning of the word *confluence*. In addition to meaning rivers coming together, confluence is the coming together of the visitor's experience, the environment, historical context, and the perspectives of Native peoples.

The good faith of these partnerships is exemplified in a statement released on February 8, 2019, announcing the postponement of the sixth installation at Celilo Falls on the Columbia River near The Dalles, OR. The U.S. Army Corps of Engineers manages the part at Celilo Falls. The Confederated Tribes of Warm Springs, the Confederated Tribes of the Umatilla Indian Reservation, and the Nez Perce Tribe supported the construction of Lin's plan for the site at Celilo Falls. Despite the support of three tribal nations, the Yakama Nation informed the U.S. Army Corps of Engineers that their nation did not support public access and requested the park be decommissioned. As noted by JoDe Goudy, Yakama Nation Tribal Council Chairman, "Continued use of this location by the public risks further destruction of the Yakama Nation's cultural resources" (Banse,

2019). After a series of meetings with tribal councils and advisors to discuss ways to continue with the project at Celilo Falls, Confluence Project Executive Director Colin Fogarty (2019) wrote,

We have taken this as an opportunity to listen respectfully and reflect. Our guiding principles for moving forward are to listen first to our tribal partners and respect all voices along the Columbia River. We also remember our commitments. At this moment, it is more important to do this right than it is to do it right now. . . . The mission of Confluence is to connect people with the history, living cultures and ecology of the Columbia River system through Indigenous voices. We will continue to advance that mission through five completed art landscapes, educational programming and community gatherings. This work remains as important as ever.

There will be no installation constructed at Celilo Falls until the Yakama Nation agrees. Meanwhile, the Confluence Project continues partnership with the Yakama Nation through other initiatives related to the project's mission. The Confluence Project is an example of how to meaningfully cultivate and sustain partnerships with and between Native peoples, nations, and organizations.

The education programming and community gatherings are initiatives that carry forward the mission of the Confluence Project beyond the installation sites. The education program connects K–12 classrooms with Native artists and tradition keepers to create meaningful projects about the Columbia River system. The purpose of the residency is to connect students to place through art and education. The Confluence Project arranges 20 hours of contact time for Native artists in the classroom to facilitate students' expressions of what they are learning. The culminating experience is a public sharing of the students' projects. In addition to classroom residencies, field trip experiences are organized for students to learn from Native perspectives about the places where they live. One example of a Confluence Project field trip is artist Toma Villa and storyteller Ed Edmo's work with 4th-grade students from White Salmon, WA. Students visited the site of the famous petroglyph She Who Watches at Columbia Hills State Park and learned about the historical and contemporary significance of the petroglyph from Ed Edmo (Shoshone-Bannock, Yakama, Nez Perce). Then, Toma Villa (Yakama) created a performance art interpretation of the petroglyph with students. Wearing red, students were arranged in the shape of She Who Watches and given directions by Villa. Filmmaker Woodrow Hunt (Klamath/Modoc/Cherokee) used a drone to capture the moment on film. To see video of this project, visit vimeo.com/337909437 and http://www.confluenceproject.org/library-post/she-who-watches-by-toma-villa-short-version/. Finally, during the summer, Confluence Road Trips are organized for teachers to design curriculum informed by Native perspectives as road trip participants learn about tribal sovereignty, the cultural and environmental significance of specific places, and the legacy of Native resilience.

In addition to education programming, the Confluence Project organizes Confluence Story Gatherings for the general public as "welcoming forums that feature the stories of native elders, told in their own voices, as a way to explore the interconnectedness of people and places of the Columbia River system" (The Confluence Project, 2019). The events are free and held at locations throughout the Columbia River system. The stories are recorded and can be accessed through the Confluence Story Gathering Collection available through The Plateau People's Web Portal (plateau portal.libraries.wsu.edu/collection/confluence-story -gathering-collection) or the Confluence Library (www .confluenceproject.org/library/) or the Confluence Project website (www.confluenceproject.org/library -post/story-gathering-recordings/).

If teachers are located outside of the Columbia River system or are unable to arrange a site visit, the Confluence Project offers a range of resources to complement lessons about the Corps of Discovery. These include:

- The Confluence Project website allows students to visit the installation sites from the classroom. For each installation, the website offers descriptions and links for students to learn about the significance of the Confluence Project sites (http://www.confluenceproject .org/river-sites/).

- The Confluence Library provides resources for four themes: history, living culture, ecology, and education. Resources include videos, information essays, and photograph collections—highly valuable to extend social studies curriculum (http://www .confluenceproject.org/library/).

- In collaboration with filmmaker Woodrow Hunt (Klamath/Modoc/Cherokee) of Tule Films and NW Documentary and with support from the National Endowment for the Arts, the Confluence Project produces short documentaries for teachers to use in the classroom. The series is titled *Stories from the River* and is available at vimeo.com /confluenceproject.

- After learning about the installations and initiatives of the Confluence Project, students can be challenged to respond to the same commission given to Maya Lin:
  1. Select a special place and consider it from an environmental history point of view, a community point of view, and a tribal point of view;
  2. Create a body of work that will engage the public in thinking about how they could play a role in the preservation of our cultural and environmental resources (Confluence Project, 2017, p. 3).

Students determine the best audience for presenting their recommendations for potential implementation and establishment of partnerships.

TEACHING RESOURCE 4

Honoring Tribal Legacies
An Epic Journey of Healing

As described in Elementary Lesson Plan 1: We're Still Here and Secondary Lesson Plan 6: The Bicentennial of the Corps of Discovery Role Play, the bicentennial traveling exhibit, *The Tent of Many Voices*, was significant to understanding the past, present, and future of the legacy of the Corps of Discovery from the perspective of Native peoples. Throughout the bicentennial commemoration (2003–2006), the Circle of Tribal Advisors held a steady commitment to design curriculum featuring the recorded presentations from the *Tent of Many Voices* for classroom use.

In 2014, this commitment was realized with the release of a digital collection including curriculum guides and lesson plans titled *Honoring Tribal Legacies* (blogs .uoregon.edu/honoringtriballegacies/). The resources available through Honoring Tribal Legacies are

> about embodying the reality that Tribal communities still exist despite the widespread long-term campaign to undermine their place in society. That Native people are still relevant today means we should enjoy the power of positive thinking and know that we have teachings in Honoring Tribal Legacies to promote learning among all children in America's classrooms. (http://npshistory.com/publications/honoring-tribal -legacies-1.pdf)

The digital collection includes full access to the two-volume handbook providing an overview of the project's history, curricular framework, and guide to designing curriculum centered on the perspectives of Native peoples. In addition, full access to sample units and lesson plans authored by Native and non-Native curriculum designers are available for early childhood, elementary, intermediate, secondary, and postsecondary classrooms. While the lesson plans range in topic and level,

> lying at the core of our efforts was the intent to interject healing into the learning experiences of K–12 students. We envisioned a process of healing as students and teachers came to understand themselves as part of a

place, be it a local community, Tribal homelands, and/or the Lewis and Clark National History Trail. (cpb-us-e1 .wpmucdn.com/blogs.uoregon.edu/dist/5/13162/files /2016/04/HTLVolumeTwo-147uq09.pdf)

For example, a middle school–grade unit authored by Shana Brown (Yakama) titled "A Thousand Celilos: Tribal Place Names along the Lewis and Clark Trail" is series of lessons in which students explore answers to essential questions, such as: How have relationships between people and the natural and built environment of this place been viewed? How did members of the Corps of Discovery describe and interpret this place? How did American Indian peoples describe encounters with members of the Corps of Discovery? What changes in lifeways, social interaction, and communication among peoples have occurred in this place? What does the future hold for this place? Native perspectives and excerpts from the Corps of Discovery journals are prepared as ready-to-use handouts for teaching students reading and research skills. As the unit unfolds, student research teams are encouraged to create inquiry questions about their own communities and publicly share their findings.

Through the support of the National Endowment for the Humanities, the Honoring Tribal Legacies project offered a three-week NEH Summer Institute for twenty-five K–12 teachers in 2019. The itinerary started in Billings, MT, and traveled east 550 miles along the Lewis and Clark National Historic Trail to Bismarck, ND. The "unexpected direction" of the eastbound travel set the context for the NEH Summer Scholars to gaze east, "attempting to put ourselves in the position of the first peoples here, and to some extent, imagining the oncoming march of settlers" (NEH Summer Institute and Honoring Tribal Legacies, 2019). The three weeks of presentations and excursions were facilitated in collaboration with curriculum designers from the Honoring Tribal Legacies project, Elders from the Apsáalooke (Crow), Northern Cheyenne, Mandan, Hidatsa, Arikara, and Lakota nations, faculty from tribal colleges and universities, and representatives from the

National Park Service. After the institute experience, the NEH Summer Scholars submitted lesson plans adding to the collection of teachings available through the Honoring Tribal Legacies digital collection.

With funding from the National Park Service and the National Endowment for the Humanities, the curricular offerings on the Honoring Tribal Legacies website continue to grow. The creation and use of these resources carry forward the important accomplishments of the Circle of Tribal Advisors that occurred during the bicentennial and are summarized in *Enough Good People: Reflections on Tribal Involvement and Inter-Cultural Collaboration, 2003–2006* (cms.lc-triballegacy .org/book).

CHAPTER 4

Conclusion

#DearIndigenousStudent. Do not be afraid to question a colonized curriculum. Your voice may quiver, but your truth will echo.

—Lakota Law Project (Posted on Facebook, March 27, 2017)

The purpose of *Teaching Critically About Lewis and Clark* is to provide a framework, lesson plans, and teaching resources to challenge the oversimplified version of the Corps of Discovery presented in existing textbooks and curriculum. One thing this book did *not* seek to accomplish is to offer a definitive account or reach certainty about the Corps of Discovery (aside from the certainty that its legacy has contributed to the further dispossession of Indigenous peoples). As authors, we still have many questions, about Sacagawea, her children, or about York, for example, that we did not explicitly take up. Rather, our hope was to encourage teachers and students to question dominant historical narratives that are taught uncritically in social studies curriculum, and too often accepted as objective truths by teachers and students alike.

These dominant narratives, we have argued, are embedded with colonial logics that continue to harm, erase, and further dispossess Indigenous peoples and perspectives. Existing curriculum about the Corps of Discovery often spins the tale of a military expedition into an exciting adventure story of discovery, friendship, progress, loyalty, patriotism, courage, success, expansion, and acquisition. A particular danger with celebratory narratives like this is the way in which students learn to identify with, and thus have more empathy for, explorers and settlers. As Wahpetunwan Dakota scholar Waziyatawin Angela Cavender Wilson (2006) writes of the infamous *Little House on the Prairie* series, "The whites in the story are glorified. One of the most dangerous aspects of the book, therefore, is the extent to which the reader develops an affinity with and adoration of the white characters in the story" (p. 72). This book has explicitly troubled the "affinity with and adoration of" Lewis, Clark, and, perhaps even other "pioneers." We have sought to disrupt this affinity/adoration, not by painting them as villains, but by making visible their participation within a larger structure of settler colonialism that has been foundational to the establishment of the United States, a structure that continues to exist today.

To this end, the materials we offer in *Teaching Critically About Lewis and Clark* are intended to (1) challenge the Eurocentric ways textbooks present the Corps of Discovery; (2) examine the Corps of Discovery in the context of the Doctrine of Discovery; (3) frame colonization and Indigenous dispossession as an ongoing legacy that Indigenous peoples continue to struggle with today; and (4) embed Indigenous perspectives and contemporary issues within each lesson plan. Critically challenging dominant narratives through anticolonial literacy supports more responsible social studies teaching, and we believe *all* educators should be invested in this aim. Not only does this directly support Indigenous students in our classrooms, but this broader project benefits all students. We see this book as part of the broader effort to challenge settler colonialism in social studies, and the ways such colonial ideologies have miseducated children for generations. Collective organizing and advocacy for Indigenous studies legislation and curriculum in various states is making an important difference in teaching more responsible histories, as well as critically revising the ways Indigenous peoples are represented in curriculum. It is our hope that as this movement grows, books like *Teaching Critically About Lewis and Clark* are no longer necessary. Our broader goal is to enlist teachers and students in the ongoing struggles for Indigenous self-determination and sovereignty that tribal nations continue to face today. This focus on Indigenous self-determination and sovereignty, not an overemphasis on Lewis and Clark, are what we hope becomes core content for social studies.

In her reflections on the commemoration of the Corps of Discovery, Roberta Conner (Cayuse, Umatilla, Nez Perce) felt that too little attention was given to "what else might have been happening in Indian Country in 1805–1806 besides the Expedition" (Lang & Abbott, 2004, p. 132). Although we are wary of social studies curriculum that overly emphasizes Indigenous history at the expense of Indigenous peoples' contemporary experiences, we hear Conner expressing an interest in sharing her nation's history on its own terms:

> That is something we're very much interested in telling people—what our population was, where we lived, how we lived, and the fact that much of our culture is still practiced today. This is important to us because we'd like the world to know that it's only been 199 years since our tribes became contact tribes. (p. 132)

In this quote, we recognize Conner's desire to situate contact as a relatively recent period within a much longer historical time frame. Like Conner, we look forward to a day when Indigenous histories, lifeways, and knowledge systems—what she refers to as "what Lewis and Clark missed in their hurry" (p. 133)—can be understood on their own terms. We hope educators cultivate meaningful partnerships with the tribal nations in their area so that they and their students can learn a much longer history of the place in which they live and learn; a history that begins since Time Immemorial and that is told on Indigenous terms.

We hope, too, that one day teachers take up what Conner considers her mother's "fondest desire":

> My mother's fondest desire is that instead of just traveling back and forth along the trail and doing interpretive programs, someone would actually do an inventory. If we use the Lewis and Clark journals as baseline materials, flawed as they are in terms of linguistic observations and other things, it is still the best inventory baseline we have in the interior Northwest. So, if we do an inventory of how things are faring along that route, we could look at species, what's here and what's not here anymore. We could look at languages, the diversity or lack thereof. We could look at the health and well being of the people. We could look at the health and well being of the water and the air and the landscape and the ecosystems. Whether modern travelers have any particular appreciation for a given ecosystem is not as important as whether or not it still exists. If it does not exist, then should we be doing something about that? Again, using a commemoration to look to the future to see how good a job we've done taking care of this landscape. (Lang & Abbott , 2004, p.125)

After working to critically examine and counter the colonial logics within dominant curriculum about the Corps of Discovery, our hope is that one day teachers take up this desire of transforming a colonial legacy into a restorative and decolonial future.

APPENDIX

The Standards

Six Orientations for Anticolonial Curriculum

Place	You are always on Indigenous lands.
	• Acknowledge Indigenous peoples and homelands of the places where you teach. • Include federally recognized tribal nations, unrecognized nations, traditional homelands, and urban Indigenous communities. • Move beyond acknowledgements to anchor curriculum around issues that affect local Indigenous peoples, lands, and nations. • Seek out Native place names when possible.
Presence	Indigenous people are still here.
	• Over 6 million people identify as AI/AN and there are over 570 federally recognized AI/AN nations in the United States. • Focus on contemporary Indigenous leaders, changemakers, and current events to affirm Indigenous students, challenge erasure and stereotypes, and highlight the strengths and struggles of Indigenous peoples today.
Perspectives	Indigenous perspectives challenge Eurocentrism and dominant discourses.
	• Curriculum often "faces West" (e.g., expansion, exploration); instead, consider how "facing East" (e.g., invasion, encroachment) (Richter, 2001) might reorient the curriculum. • Include Indigenous perspectives to move curriculum beyond learning *about* Indigenous peoples and toward helping students learn *from* Indigenous analyses.
Political Nationhood	"Indigenous Peoples are nations, not minorities." (Wilkins & Stark, 2018)
	• Indigenous peoples have inherent sovereignty, and while protected by civil rights, Indigenous peoples also have prior treaty rights. • Emphasize tribal sovereignty and the political status, rights, and issues that impact tribal nations as part of civics education. • Teach students that honoring the treaties is part of their democratic civic responsibility. • Consider ways that curriculum can support issues that local Native nations face today.
Power	Challenge power dynamics within curricula.
	• Challenge the ways racism and colonialism surface in curriculum (i.e., colonial metaphors like lands were "empty," or were "free" or a "prize" to be won). • Teach students about Indigenous power by highlighting examples of Indigenous creativity, agency, changemakers, and social movements. • Emphasize Indigenous power and agency to interrupt narratives that Native peoples are "damaged" or victims of oppression (Tuck, 2009; Vizenor, 1999).
Partnerships	Cultivate and sustain partnerships with Indigenous peoples, organizations, and nations.
	• Federal and state governments recognize government-to-government relationships with tribal nations and engage in tribal consultation. • Move beyond token guest speakers to sharing power and cultivating partnerships that are meaningful and purposeful. • Work to develop long-term relationships with local Native programs, organizations, or nations that are mutually beneficial (i.e., respectful and reciprocal). • Effective collaboration may include hiring a tribal liaison, creating a memorandum of understanding (MOU), or consulting early and often on decisions that impact Native students or nearby Native organizations/nations.

Source: Sabzalian, 2019; Sabzalian, Miyamoto-Sundahl, & Fong, 2019

National Council for the Social Studies: C3 Framework for Social Studies State Standards

Dimension 1: Developing Questions and Planning Inquiries

	BY END OF GRADE 5	BY END OF GRADE 8	BY END OF GRADE 12
Constructing Compelling Questions	D1.1.3-5. Explain why compelling questions are important to others (e.g., peers, adults).	D1.1.6-8. Explain how a question represents key ideas in the field.	D1.1.9-12. Explain how a question reflects an enduring issue in the field.
	D1.2.3-5. Identify disciplinary concepts and ideas associated with a compelling question that are open to different interpretations.	D1.2.6-8. Explain points of agreement experts have about interpretations and applications of disciplinary concepts and ideas associated with a compelling question.	D1.2.9-12. Explain points of agreement and disagreement experts have about interpretations and applications of disciplinary concepts and ideas associated with a compelling question.
Constructing Supporting Questions	D1.3.3-5. Identify the disciplinary concepts and ideas associated with a supporting question that are open to interpretation.	D1.3.6-8. Explain points of agreement experts have about interpretations and applications of disciplinary concepts and ideas associated with a supporting question.	D1.3.9-12. Explain points of agreement and disagreement experts have about interpretations and applications of disciplinary concepts and ideas associated with a supporting question.
	D1.4.3-5. Explain how supporting questions help answer compelling questions in an inquiry.	D1.4.6-8. Explain how the relationship between supporting questions and compelling questions is mutually reinforcing.	D1.4.9-12. Explain how supporting questions contribute to an inquiry and how, through engaging source work, new compelling and supporting questions emerge.
Determining Helpful Sources	D1.5.3-5. Determine the kinds of sources that will be helpful in answering compelling and supporting questions, taking into consideration the different opinions people have about how to answer the questions.	D1.5.6-8. Determine the kinds of sources that will be helpful in answering compelling and supporting questions, taking into consideration multiple points of views represented in the sources.	D1.5.9-12. Determine the kinds of sources that will be helpful in answering compelling and supporting questions, taking into consideration multiple points of view represented in the sources, the types of sources available, and the potential uses of the sources.

Dimension 2: Applying Disciplinary Tools and Concepts

	BY END OF GRADE 5	BY END OF GRADE 8	BY END OF GRADE 12
Change, Continuity, and Context	D2.His.1.3-5. Create and use a chronological sequence of related events to compare developments that happened at the same time.	D2.His.1.6-8. Analyze connections among events and developments in broader historical contexts.	D2.His.1.9-12. Evaluate how historical events and developments were shaped by unique circumstances of time and place as well as broader historical contexts.
	D2.His.2.3-5. Compare life in specific historical time periods to life today.	D2.His.2.6-8. Classify series of historical events and developments as examples of change and/or continuity.	D2.His.2.9-12. Analyze change and continuity in historical eras.
	D2.His.3.3-5. Generate questions about individuals and groups who have shaped significant historical changes and continuities.	D2.His.3.6-8. Use questions generated about individuals and groups to analyze why they, and the developments they shaped, are seen as historically significant.	D2.His.3.9-12. Use questions generated about individuals and groups to assess how the significance of their actions changes over time and is shaped by the historical context.

	BY END OF GRADE 5	BY END OF GRADE 8	BY END OF GRADE 12
Perspectives	D2.His.4.3-5. Explain why individuals and groups during the same historical period differed in their perspectives.	D2.His.4.6-8. Analyze multiple factors that influenced the perspectives of people during different historical eras.	D2.His.4.9-12. Analyze complex and interacting factors that influenced the perspectives of people during different historical eras.
	D2.His.5.3-5. Explain connections among historical contexts and people's perspectives at the time.	D2.His.5.6-8. Explain how and why perspectives of people have changed over time.	D2.His.5.9-12. Analyze how historical contexts shaped and continue to shape people's perspectives.
	D2.His.6.3-5. Describe how people's perspectives shaped the historical sources they created.	D2.His.6.6-8. Analyze how people's perspectives influenced what information is available in the historical sources they created.	D2.His.6.9-12. Analyze the ways in which the perspectives of those writing history shaped the history that they produced.
	Begins in grades 9–12	Begins in grades 9–12	D2.His.7.9-12. Explain how the perspectives of people in the present shape interpretations of the past.
	Begins in grades 9–12	Begins in grades 9–12	D2.His.8.9-12. Analyze how current interpretations of the past are limited by the extent to which available historical sources represent perspectives of people at the time.
Historical Sources and Evidence	D2.His.9.3-5. Summarize how different kinds of historical sources are used to explain events in the past.	D2.His.9.6-8. Classify the kinds of historical sources used in a secondary interpretation.	D2.His.9.9-12. Analyze the relationship between historical sources and the secondary interpretations made from them.
	D2.His.10.3-5. Compare information provided by different historical sources about the past.	D2.His.10.6-8. Detect possible limitations in the historical record based on evidence collected from different kinds of historical sources.	D2.His.10.9-12. Detect possible limitations in various kinds of historical evidence and differing secondary interpretations.
	D2.His.11.3-5. Infer the intended audience and purpose of a historical source from information within the source itself.	D2.His.11.6-8. Use other historical sources to infer a plausible maker, date, place of origin, and intended audience for historical sources where this information is not easily identified.	D2.His.11.9-12. Critique the usefulness of historical sources for a specific historical inquiry based on their maker, date, place of origin, intended audience, and purpose.
	D2.His.12.3-5. Generate questions about multiple historical sources and their relationships to particular historical events and developments.	D2.His.12.6-8. Use questions generated about multiple historical sources to identify further areas of inquiry and additional sources.	D2.His.12.9-12. Use questions generated about multiple historical sources to pursue further inquiry and investigate additional sources.
	D2.His.13.3-5. Use information about a historical source, including the maker, date, place of origin, intended audience, and purpose, to judge the extent to which the source is useful for studying a particular topic.	D2.His.13.6-8. Evaluate the relevancy and utility of a historical source based on information such as maker, date, place of origin, intended audience, and purpose.	D2.His.13.9-12. Critique the appropriateness of the historical sources used in a secondary interpretation.

(continued)

	BY END OF GRADE 5	BY END OF GRADE 8	BY END OF GRADE 12
Causation and Argumentation	D2.His.14.3-5. Explain probable causes and effects of events and developments.	D2.His.14.6-8. Explain multiple causes and effects of events and developments in the past.	D2.His.14.9-12. Analyze multiple and complex causes and effects of events in the past.
	Begins in grades 6–8	D2.His.15.6-8. Evaluate the relative influence of various causes of events and developments in the past.	D2.His.15.9-12. Distinguish between long-term causes and triggering events in developing a historical argument.
	D2.His.16.3-5. Use evidence to develop a claim about the past.	D2.His.16.6-8. Organize applicable evidence into a coherent argument about the past.	D2.His.16.9-12. Integrate evidence from multiple relevant historical sources and interpretations into a reasoned argument about the past.
	D2.His.17.3-5. Summarize the central claim in a secondary work of history.	D2.His.17.6-8. Compare the central arguments in secondary works of history on related topics in multiple media.	D2.His.17.9-12. Critique the central arguments in secondary works of history on related topics in multiple media in terms of their historical accuracy.

Dimension 3: Evaluating Sources and Using Evidence

	BY END OF GRADE 5	BY END OF GRADE 8	BY END OF GRADE 12
Gathering and Evaluating Sources	D3.1.3-5. Gather relevant information from multiple sources while using the origin, structure, and context to guide the selection.	D3.1.6-8. Gather relevant information from multiple sources while using the origin, authority, structure, context, and corroborative value of the sources to guide the selection.	D3.1.9-12. Gather relevant information from multiple sources representing a wide range of views while using the origin, authority, structure, context, and corroborative value of the sources to guide the selection.
	D3.2.3-5. Use distinctions among fact and opinion to determine the credibility of multiple sources.	D3.2.6-8. Evaluate the credibility of a source by determining its relevance and intended use.	D3.2.9-12. Evaluate the credibility of a source by examining how experts value the source.
Developing and Using Claims	D3.3.3-5. Identify evidence that draws information from multiple sources in response to compelling questions.	D3.3.6-8. Identify evidence that draws information from multiple sources to support claims, noting evidentiary limitations.	D3.3.9-12. Identify evidence that draws information directly and substantively from multiple sources to detect inconsistencies in evidence in order to revise or strengthen claims.
	D3.4.3-5. Use evidence to develop claims in response to compelling questions.	D3.4.6-8. Develop claims and counterclaims while pointing out the strengths and limitations of both.	D3.4.9-12. Refine claims and counterclaims attending to precision, significance, and knowledge conveyed through the claim while pointing out the strengths and limitations of both.

Dimension 4: Communicating Conclusions and Taking Informed Action

	BY END OF GRADE 5	BY END OF GRADE 8	BY END OF GRADE 12
Communicating Conclusions	D4.1.3-5. Construct arguments using claims and evidence from multiple sources.	D4.1.6-8. Construct arguments using claims and evidence from multiple sources, while acknowledging the strengths and limitations of the arguments.	D4.1.9-12. Construct arguments using precise and knowledgeable claims, with evidence from multiple sources, while acknowledging counterclaims and evidentiary weaknesses.

	BY END OF GRADE 5	BY END OF GRADE 8	BY END OF GRADE 12
	D4.2.3-5. Construct explanations using reasoning, correct sequence, examples, and details with relevant information and data.	D4.2.6-8. Construct explanations using reasoning, correct sequence, examples, and details with relevant information and data, while acknowledging the strengths and weaknesses of the explanations.	D4.2.9-12. Construct explanations using sound reasoning, correct sequence (linear or nonlinear), examples, and details with significant and pertinent information and data, while acknowledging the strengths and weaknesses of the explanation given its purpose (e.g., cause and effect, chronological, procedural, technical).
	D4.3.3-5. Present a summary of arguments and explanations to others outside the classroom using print and oral technologies (e.g., posters, essays, letters, debates, speeches, and reports) and digital technologies (e.g., Internet, social media, and digital documentary).	D4.3.6-8. Present adaptations of arguments and explanations on topics of interest to others to reach audiences and venues outside the classroom using print and oral technologies (e.g., posters, essays, letters, debates, speeches, reports, and maps) and digital technologies (e.g., Internet, social media, and digital documentary).	D4.3.9-12. Present adaptations of arguments and explanations that feature evocative ideas and perspectives on issues and topics to reach a range of audiences and venues outside the classroom using print and oral technologies (e.g., posters, essays, letters, debates, speeches, reports, and maps) and digital technologies (e.g., Internet, social media, and digital documentary).
Critiquing Conclusions	D4.4.3-5. Critique arguments.	D4.4.6-8. Critique arguments for credibility.	D4.4.9-12. Critique the use of claims and evidence in arguments for credibility.
	D4.5.3-5. Critique explanations.	D4.5.6-8. Critique the structure of explanations.	D4.5.9-12. Critique the use of the reasoning, sequencing, and supporting details of explanations.
Taking Informed Action	D4.6.3-5. Draw on disciplinary concepts to explain the challenges people have faced and opportunities they have created, in addressing local, regional, and global problems at various times and places.	D4.6.6-8. Draw on multiple disciplinary lenses to analyze how a specific problem can manifest itself at local, regional, and global levels over time, identifying its characteristics and causes, and the challenges and opportunities faced by those trying to address the problem.	D4.6.9-12. Use disciplinary and interdisciplinary lenses to understand the characteristics and causes of local, regional, and global problems; instances of such problems in multiple contexts; and challenges and opportunities faced by those trying to address these problems over time and place.
	D4.7.3-5. Explain different strategies and approaches students and others could take in working alone and together to address local, regional, and global problems, and predict possible results of their actions.	D4.7.6-8. Assess their individual and collective capacities to take action to address local, regional, and global problems, taking into account a range of possible levers of power, strategies, and potential outcomes.	D4.7.9-12. Assess options for individual and collective action to address local, regional, and global problems by engaging in self-reflection, strategy identification, and complex causal reasoning.
	D4.8.3-5. Use a range of deliberative and democratic procedures to make decisions about and act on civic problems in their classrooms and schools.	D4.8.6-8. Apply a range of deliberative and democratic procedures to make decisions and take action in their classrooms and schools, and in out-of-school civic contexts.	D4.8.9-12. Apply a range of deliberative and democratic strategies and procedures to make decisions and take action in their classrooms, schools, and out-of-school civic contexts.

(continued)

Common Core State Standards: Reading, Writing, Speaking and Listening, Grade 4

Reading: Informational Text	
Key Ideas and Details	CCSS.ELA-Literacy.RI.4.1. Refer to details and examples in a text when explaining what the text says explicitly and when drawing inferences from the text.
	CCSS.ELA-Literacy.RI.4.2. Determine the main idea of a text and explain how it is supported by key details; summarize the text.
	CCSS.ELA-Literacy.RI.4.3. Explain events, procedures, ideas, or concepts in a historical, scientific, or technical text, including what happened and why, based on specific information in the text.
Craft and Structure	CCSS.ELA-Literacy.RI.4.4. Determine the meaning of general academic and domain-specific words or phrases in a text relevant to a *grade 4 topic or subject area*.
	CCSS.ELA-Literacy.RI.4.5. Describe the overall structure (e.g., chronology, comparison, cause/effect, problem/solution) of events, ideas, concepts, or information in a text or part of a text.
	CCSS.ELA-Literacy.RI.4.6. Compare and contrast a firsthand and secondhand account of the same event or topic; describe the differences in focus and the information provided.
Integration of Knowledge and Ideas	CCSS.ELA-Literacy.RI.4.7. Interpret information presented visually, orally, or quantitatively (e.g., in charts, graphs, diagrams, time lines, animations, or interactive elements on Web pages) and explain how the information contributes to an understanding of the text in which it appears.
	CCSS.ELA-Literacy.RI.4.8. Explain how an author uses reasons and evidence to support particular points in a text.
	CCSS.ELA-Literacy.RI.4.9. Integrate information from two texts on the same topic in order to write or speak about the subject knowledgeably.
Range of Reading and Level of Text Complexity	CCSS.ELA-Literacy.RI.4.10. By the end of year, read and comprehend informational texts, including history/social studies, science, and technical texts, in the grades 4–5 text complexity band proficiently, with scaffolding as needed at the high end of the range.
Writing	
Text Types and Purposes	CCSS.ELA-Literacy.W.4.1. Write opinion pieces on topics or texts, supporting a point of view with reasons and information.
	CCSS.ELA-Literacy.W.4.1.a. Introduce a topic or text clearly, state an opinion, and create an organizational structure in which related ideas are grouped to support the writer's purpose.
	CCSS.ELA-Literacy.W.4.1.b. Provide reasons that are supported by facts and details.
	CCSS.ELA-Literacy.W.4.1.c. Link opinion and reasons using words and phrases (e.g., *for instance, in order to, in addition*).
	CCSS.ELA-Literacy.W.4.1.d. Provide a concluding statement or section related to the opinion presented.
Production and Distribution of Writing	CCSS.ELA-Literacy.W.4.4. Produce clear and coherent writing in which the development and organization are appropriate to task, purpose, and audience. (Grade-specific expectations for writing types are defined in standards 1–3 above.)
	CCSS.ELA-Literacy.W.4.5. With guidance and support from peers and adults, develop and strengthen writing as needed by planning, revising, and editing.
	CCSS.ELA-Literacy.W.4.6. With some guidance and support from adults, use technology, including the Internet, to produce and publish writing as well as to interact and collaborate with others; demonstrate sufficient command of keyboarding skills to type a minimum of one page in a single sitting.
Research to Build and Present Knowledge	CCSS.ELA-Literacy.W.4.7. Conduct short research projects that build knowledge through investigation of different aspects of a topic.
	CCSS.ELA-Literacy.W.4.8. Recall relevant information from experiences or gather relevant information from print and digital sources; take notes and categorize information, and provide a list of sources.

	CCSS.ELA-Literacy.W.4.9. Draw evidence from literary or informational texts to support analysis, reflection, and research.
	CCSS.ELA-Literacy.W.4.9.b. Apply *grade 4 Reading standards* to informational texts (e.g., "Explain how an author uses reasons and evidence to support particular points in a text").
Range of Writing	CCSS.ELA-Literacy.W.4.10. Write routinely over extended time frames (time for research, reflection, and revision) and shorter time frames (a single sitting or a day or two) for a range of discipline-specific tasks, purposes, and audiences.

Speaking and Listening	
Comprehension and Collaboration	CCSS.ELA-Literacy.SL.4.1. Engage effectively in a range of collaborative discussions (one-on-one, in groups, and teacher-led) with diverse partners on *grade 4 topics and texts*, building on others' ideas and expressing their own clearly.
	CCSS.ELA-Literacy.SL.4.1.a. Come to discussions prepared, having read or studied required material; explicitly draw on that preparation and other information known about the topic to explore ideas under discussion.
	CCSS.ELA-Literacy.SL.4.1.b. Follow agreed-upon rules for discussions and carry out assigned roles.
	CCSS.ELA-Literacy.SL.4.1.c. Pose and respond to specific questions to clarify or follow up on information, and make comments that contribute to the discussion and link to the remarks of others.
	CCSS.ELA-Literacy.SL.4.1.d. Review the key ideas expressed and explain their own ideas and understanding in light of the discussion.
	CCSS.ELA-Literacy.SL.4.2. Paraphrase portions of a text read aloud or information presented in diverse media and formats, including visually, quantitatively, and orally.
	CCSS.ELA-Literacy.SL.4.3. Identify the reasons and evidence a speaker provides to support particular points.
Presentation of Knowledge and Ideas	CCSS.ELA-Literacy.SL.4.4. Report on a topic or text, tell a story, or recount an experience in an organized manner, using appropriate facts and relevant, descriptive details to support main ideas or themes; speak clearly at an understandable pace.
	CCSS.ELA-Literacy.SL.4.5. Add audio recordings and visual displays to presentations when appropriate to enhance the development of main ideas or themes.
	CCSS.ELA-Literacy.SL.4.6. Differentiate between contexts that call for formal English (e.g., presenting ideas) and situations where informal discourse is appropriate (e.g., small-group discussion); use formal English when appropriate to task and situation.

Common Core State Standards: Literacy in History/Social Studies, Science, & Technical Subjects, Grades 6–12

	Grade 6–8	Grade 9–10	Grades 11–12
Key Ideas and Details	CCSS.ELA-Literacy.RH.6-8.1. Cite specific textual evidence to support analysis of primary and secondary sources.	CCSS.ELA-Literacy.RH.9-10.1. Cite specific textual evidence to support analysis of primary and secondary sources, attending to such features as the date and origin of the information.	CCSS.ELA-Literacy.RH.11-12.1. Cite specific textual evidence to support analysis of primary and secondary sources, connecting insights gained from specific details to an understanding of the text as a whole.
	CCSS.ELA-Literacy.RH.6-8.2. Identify key steps in a text's description of a process related to history/social studies (e.g., how a bill becomes law, how interest rates are raised or lowered).	CCSS.ELA-Literacy.RH.9-10.2. Determine the central ideas or information of a primary or secondary source; provide an accurate summary of how key events or ideas develop over the course of the text.	CCSS.ELA-Literacy.RH.11-12.2. Determine the central ideas or information of a primary or secondary source; provide an accurate summary that makes clear the relationships among the key details and ideas.

(continued)

	Grade 6–8	Grade 9–10	Grades 11–12
		CCSS.ELA-Literacy.RH.9-10.3. Analyze in detail a series of events described in a text; determine whether earlier events caused later ones or simply preceded them.	CCSS.ELA-Literacy.RH.11-12.3. Evaluate various explanations for actions or events and determine which explanation best accords with textual evidence, acknowledging where the text leaves matters uncertain.
Craft and Structure	CCSS.ELA-Literacy.RH.6-8.4. Determine the meaning of words and phrases as they are used in a text, including vocabulary specific to domains related to history/ social studies.	CCSS.ELA-Literacy.RH.9-10.4. Determine the meaning of words and phrases as they are used in a text, including vocabulary describing political, social, or economic aspects of history/social science.	CCSS.ELA-Literacy.RH.11-12.4. Determine the meaning of words and phrases as they are used in a text, including analyzing how an author uses and refines the meaning of a key term over the course of a text (e.g., how Madison defines *faction* in *Federalist* No. 10).
	CCSS.ELA-Literacy.RH.6-8.5. Describe how a text presents information (e.g., sequentially, comparatively, causally).	CCSS.ELA-Literacy.RH.9-10.5. Analyze how a text uses structure to emphasize key points or advance an explanation or analysis.	CCSS.ELA-Literacy.RH.11-12.5. Analyze in detail how a complex primary source is structured, including how key sentences, paragraphs, and larger portions of the text contribute to the whole.
	CCSS.ELA-Literacy.RH.6-8.6. Identify aspects of a text that reveal an author's point of view or purpose (e.g., loaded language, inclusion or avoidance of particular facts).	CCSS.ELA-Literacy.RH.9-10.6. Compare the point of view of two or more authors for how they treat the same or similar topics, including which details they include and emphasize in their respective accounts.	CCSS.ELA-Literacy.RH.11-12.6. Evaluate authors' differing points of view on the same historical event or issue by assessing the authors' claims, reasoning, and evidence.
Integration of Knowledge and Ideas	CCSS.ELA-Literacy.RH.6-8.7. Integrate visual information (e.g., in charts, graphs, photographs, videos, or maps) with other information in print and digital texts.	CCSS.ELA-Literacy.RH.9-10.7. Integrate quantitative or technical analysis (e.g., charts, research data) with qualitative analysis in print or digital text.	CCSS.ELA-Literacy.RH.11-12.7. Integrate and evaluate multiple sources of information presented in diverse formats and media (e.g., visually, quantitatively, as well as in words) in order to address a question or solve a problem.
	CCSS.ELA-Literacy.RH.6-8.8. Distinguish among fact, opinion, and reasoned judgment in a text.	CCSS.ELA-Literacy.RH.9-10.8. Assess the extent to which the reasoning and evidence in a text support the author's claims.	CCSS.ELA-Literacy.RH.11-12.8. Evaluate an author's premises, claims, and evidence by corroborating or challenging them with other information.
	CCSS.ELA-Literacy.RH.6-8.9. Analyze the relationship between a primary and secondary source on the same topic.	CCSS.ELA-Literacy.RH.9-10.9. Compare and contrast treatments of the same topic in several primary and secondary sources.	CCSS.ELA-Literacy.RH.11-12.9. Integrate information from diverse sources, both primary and secondary, into a coherent understanding of an idea or event, noting discrepancies among sources.
Range of Reading and Level of Text Complexity	CCSS.ELA-Literacy.RH.6-8.10. By the end of grade 8, read and comprehend history/social studies texts in the grades 6–8 text complexity band independently and proficiently.	CCSS.ELA-Literacy.RH.9-10.10. By the end of grade 10, read and comprehend history/social studies texts in the grades 9–10 text complexity band independently and proficiently.	CCSS.ELA-Literacy.RH.11-12.10. By the end of grade 12, read and comprehend history/social studies texts in the grades 11–CCR text complexity band independently and proficiently.

References

1855 Treaty Authority. (2019, January 11). Chippewa establish *Rights of Manoomin* on White Earth Reservation and throughout 1855 ceded territory. [Press release] Retrieved from healingmnstories.files.wordpress.com/2019/01/right-of-manoomin-media-statement.pdf.

Adichie, C. N. (2009, July). The danger of a single story. *TedGlobal* [Video file]. Retrieved from http://www.ted.com/talks/chimamanda_adichie_the_danger_of_a_single_story?language=enLC Interactive tour mrnussbaum.com/lewis-and-clark-interactive-tour

Agoyo, A. (2019). *Supreme Court delivers slim victory in Yakama Nation treaty rights case.* Retrieved from https://www.indianz.com/News/2019/03/19/supreme-court-delivers-slim-victory-in-y.asp

Allard, L. Brave Bull. (2016, September 3). Why the founder of Standing Rock Sioux Camp can't forget the Whitestone Massacre. *Yes!.* Retrieved from www.yesmagazine.org/people-power/why-the-founder-of-standing-rock-sioux-camp-cant-forget-the-whitestone-massacre-20160903

American Friends Service Committee & Intertribal Canoe Society. (2011). *Tribal Journeys Handbook and Study Guide.* Seattle, WA: Authors. Retrieved from http://canoeway.com/Tribal_Journeys_Handbook.pdf

Anderson, I. (2002). *Fort Clatsop: A Charbonneau family portrait.* Astoria, OR: Fort Clatsop Historical Association.

Aruchuleta, G. (2019). The Wapato returns to the Sandy River Delta [video]. Retrieved from: https://www.confluenceproject.org/library-post/greg-archuleta-wapato-returns-to-the-sandy-river-delta/

Au, W. (2012). *Critical curriculum studies: Education, consciousness, and the politics of knowing.* New York, NY: Routledge.

Baker, G. (n.d.). Interview with Gerard Baker. *Oregon Public Broadcasting.* Retrieved from http://www.pbs/lewisandclark/living/idx_6.html

Banks, J. A., Beyer, B. K., Contreras, G., Craven, J., Ladson-Billings, G., McFarland, M. A., & Parker, W. C. (1999). *United States: Adventures in time and place.* New York, NY: McGraw Hill School Division.

Banse, T. (2019, February 8.) Public art installation beside Columbia River put on hold by Yakama Nation opposition. *Oregon Public Broadcasting.* Retrieved from www.opb.org/news/article/npr-public-art-installation-beside-columbia-river-put-on-hold-by-yakama-nation-opposition/

Barton, K., & Levstik, L. (2004). *Teaching history for the common good.* Mahwah, NJ: Lawrence Erlbaum Associates.

Bears Ears Inter-Tribal Coalition. (2016). Bears Ears: A Native perspective on America's most significant unprotected cultural landscape. Retrieved from bearsearscoalition.org/wp-content/uploads/2016/03/Bears-Ears-bro.sm_.pdf

Bears Ears Inter-Tribal Coalition. (2017, August 24). Tribal leaders outraged over Zinke's effort to eliminate protections for Bears Ears National Monument. Retrieved from https://bearsearscoalition.org/tribal-leaders-outraged-over-zinkes-effort-to-eliminate-protections-for-bears-ears-national-monument/

Berson, M. J., Howard, T. C., & Salinas, C. (2012). *The United States: Making a new nation.* Orlando, FL: Houghton Mifflin Harcourt.

Betts, R. (2000). *In search of York: The slave who went to the Pacific with Lewis and Clark.* Boulder, CO: University Press of Colorado: Lewis and Clark Trail Heritage Foundation.

Bigelow, B. & Peterson, B. (1998). *Rethinking Columbus: The next 500 years.* Milwaukie, WI: Rethinking Schools.

Blumberg, R. (2004). *York's adventures with Lewis and Clark: An African American's part in the great expedition.* New York, NY: HarperColllins Publishers.

Bock, P. (2005, June 10). A meeting of minds. *Seattle Times.* Retrieved from http://community.seattletimes.nwsource.com/archive/?date=20050610&slug=pacific-pmaya12

Boyd, C. D., Gay, G., Geiger, R., Kracht, J. B., Pang, V. O., Risinger, C. F., & Sanchez, S. M. (2005). *Social studies: Building a nation.* Glenview, IL: Pearson Education, Inc.

Boyd, C. D., Gay, G., Geiger, R., Kracht, J. B., Pang, V. O., Risinger, C. F., & Sanchez, S. M. (2005). *Social studies: Building a nation* (Teacher's Edition). Glenview, IL: Pearson Education, Inc.

Bureau of Indian Affairs. (2017). Frequently asked questions. Retrieved from www.bia.gov/frequently-asked-questions

Calderôn, D. (2014). Uncovering settler grammars in curriculum. *Education Studies, 50*(4), 313–318.

Chandler, P. (2017). *Race lessons: Using inquiry to teach about race in social studies.* Scottsdale, AZ: Information Age Publishing.

Circle of Tribal Advisors. (2006). *Enough good people: Reflections on tribal involvement and inter-cultural collaboration, 2003–2006.* Grand Junction, CO: Colorado Printing Company.

City of Sherrill v. Oneida Indian Nation of New York. 544 U.S. 197. Supreme Court of the United States, 2005.

Confluence Project. (n.d). Retrieved from http://www .confluenceproject.org/

Confluence Project. (2017). Confluence in the classroom: Authentic perspectives and voices. Retrieved from www.confluenceproject.org/wp-content/uploads/CON FLUENCE_Review_Native_Curriculum_2017_.pdf

Conner, R. (2006a). Our people have always been here. In A. M. Josephy, Jr. (Ed.), *Lewis and Clark through Indian eyes* (pp. 85–119). New York, NY: Random House.

Conner, R. (2006b). We must tell our story. *Tribal Legacy Project.* Retrieved from www.lc-triballegacy.org/video .php?vid=744&query=conner

Cushman, R. L., Daehnke, J. D., & Johnson, T. A. (In Press). "This is what makes us strong": Canoe revitalization, reciprocal heritage, and the Chinook Indian Nation. In B. Erickson, & S. W. Krotz (Eds.), *The politics of the canoe: Activism and resistance.* Winnepeg, MB: The University of Manitoba Press.

Danzer, G. A., Klor de Alva, J., Krieger, L. S., Wilson, L. E., & Woloch, N. *The Americans.* (2000). Boston, MA: McDougal Littell.

Davidson, J. W. (2005). *The American nation* (teacher's edition). Upper Saddle River, NJ: Pearson Prentice Hall.

Davidson, J. W., & Stoff, M. B. (2016). *American history: Beginnings through reconstruction.* Boston, MA: Pearson Education, Inc.

Deshais, N. (2019, March 21). Neil Gorsuch joins liberals giving Yakama Nation a Supreme Court victory over State of Washington. *The Spokesman-Review.* Retrieved from www.spokesman.com/stories/2019/mar/21/neil -gorsuch-joins-liberaljustices-giving-yakama-n/

Digital Wampum Series. (n.d.). Doctrine of Discovery. [Video] Retrieved from www.digitalwampum.org /doctrine-of-discovery

Ekberzade, B. (2018). *Standing Rock: Greed, oil, and the Lakota's struggle for justice.* Chicago, IL: University of Chicago Press.

Erdrich, L. (2003). *Sacagawea.* Minneapolis, MN: Carolrhoda Books.

Estes, N. (2016, September 18). Fighting for our lives: #NoDAPL in historical context. *Red Nation.* Retrieved from therednation.org/2016/09/18/fighting-for-our -lives-nodapl-in-context/

Estes, N. (2019). *Our history is the future.* New York, NY: Verso.

Estes, N. & Dhillon, J. (2019). *Standing with Standing Rock: Voices from the #NoDAPL movement.* Minneapolis, MN: University of Minnesota.

Fogarty, C. (2019, February 8). Confluence to invest in education as Celilo Park project put on hold. *Confluence Project.* Retrieved from http://www.confluenceproject .org/news-post/confluence-to-invest-in-education-as -celilo-park-project-put-on-hold/

Garcia, J. & Shirley, V. (2012). Performing decolonization: Lessons learned from Indigenous youth, teachers, and leaders' engagement with critical Indigenous pedagogy. *Journal of Curriculum Theorizing, 28*(2), 76–91.

Giago, T. (2004, June 18). Should Indians celebrate Lewis and Clark? *Yankton Daily Press & Dakotan.* Retrieved from www.yankton.net/opinion/article_e894fec7 -5aee-574c-9fc9-4cc87593b760.html

Goudy, J. (2016). Long March to Rome: Testimonials. Retrieved from http://longmarchtorome.com/test imonials/

Grabow, C. (2010, November 11). Maya Lin and the Confluence Project. *Oregon Public Broadcasting: Think Out Loud.* [Radio broadcast] Retrieved from www.opb .org/radio/programs/thinkoutloud/segment/maya -lin-and-confluence-project/

Grande, S. (2015). *Red pedagogy: Native American social and political thought* (10th Anniversary Edition). Lanham, MD: Rowman & Littlefield.

Hart, D. (2013). *History alive! Pursuing American ideals: Equality, rights, liberty, opportunity, democracy.* Rancho Cordova, CA: Teachers' Curriculum Institute.

Herbert, J. (2000). *Lewis and Clark for kids: Their journey of discovery with 21 activities.* Chicago, IL: Chicago Review Press.

Holmberg, J. (1992). "I wish you see & know all" The recently discovered letters of William Clark to Jonathan Clark. *We Proceeded On, 18*(4), 4–12.

Holmberg, J. (2002). *Dear brother: Letters of William Clark to Jonathan Clark.* New Haven, CT: Yale University Press.

Hopfensberger, J. (2018, March 17). American Indian teens head to Vatican, hoping to overturn historic Papal decrees. *The Star Tribune.* Retrieved from www.startribune .com/american-indian-teens-head-to-vatican-hoping -to-overturn-historic-papal-decrees/477183033/

Howe, C. (2004). Lewis and Clark among the Tetons: Smoking out what really happened. *Wičazo Ša Review, 19*(1), 47–72.

Jenkinson, C. (2018). "Maney Extroadenary Stories:" The significance of the Arikara Too Né's map. *We Proceeded On, 44*(2), 23–30.

Johnson v. McIntosh. 21 U.S. 543. Supreme Court of the United States. 1823.

Kimmerer, R. (2013). *Braiding sweetgrass: Indigenous wisdom, scientific knowledge and the teachings of plants*. Minneapolis, MN: Milkweed Editions.

King, T. (2012). *The inconvenient Indian: A curious account of Native people in North America*. Minneapolis, MN: University of Minnesota Press.

King, T. (2019). *The Black shoals: Offshore formations of Black and Native studies*. Durham, NC: Duke University Press.

Kumashiro, K. (2004). *Against common sense: Teaching and learning toward social justice*. New York, NY: Routledge.

Kuruvilla, C. (2016, November 4). Standing Rock protestors burn document that justified Indigenous oppression. *HuffPost*. Retrieved from www.huffpost.com /entry/interfaith-clergy-dapl-doctrine-of-discovery _n_581cb86ae4b0aac62483d92f?utm_hp_ref=dakota -access-pipeline#comments

Kwame Jeffries, Hasan. (2018). *Teaching hard history: American slavery*. Retrieved from https://www.splcenter.org /sites/default/files/tt_hard_history_american_slavery .pdf

LaDuke, W. (1992). *We are still here: The 500 years celebration*. Retrieved from urbanhabitat.org/files/3-3 all.pdf

Lander, J. & Puhipau (Directors). (2006). Mauna Kea: Temple Under Siege [video]. United States: Na Maka o ka 'Aina.

Lang, W. & Abbott, C. (2004). *Two centuries of Lewis and Clark: Reflections on the voyage of discovery*. Portland, OR: Oregon Historical Society.

LaRocque, E. (2010). *When the other is me: Native resistance discourse, 1850–1990*. Winnipeg, Canada: University of Manitoba Press.

Lesh, B. (2011). *"Why won't you just tell us the answer?" Teaching historical thinking in grades 7–12*. Portsmouth, NH Stenhouse Publishers.

Levstik, L., & Barton, K. (2015). *Doing history: Investigating with children in elementary and middle schools* (5th ed.). New York, NY: Routledge.

Lewis, D. (2015, October 10). New University of Oregon Pioneer uniforms ignore Oregon tribes. *Indian Country Today*. Retrieved from https://newsmaven.io /indiancountrytoda

Lyons, O. (2009). The Doctrine of Discovery. [Video & transcript] Retrieved from ratical.org/many_worlds /6Nations/DoctrineOfDiscovery.html

Lyons, S. R. (2000). Rhetorical sovereignty: What do American Indians want from writing? *College Composition and Communication, 51*(3), 447–468.

Mackey, E. (2016). Unsettled expectations: Uncertainty, land and settler decolonization. Halifax, Canada: Fernwood.

Mandell, N., & Malone, B. (2007). *Thinking like a historian: Rethinking history instruction*. Madison, WI: Wisconsin Historical Society Press.

Mills, C. W. (2007). White ignorance. In S. Sullivan & N. Tuana (Eds.), *Race and epistemologies of ignorance* (pp. 11–38). Albany, NY: State University of New York Press.

Miller, R. (2008). *Native America discovered and conquered: Thomas Jefferson, Lewis and Clark, and Manifest Destiny*. Lincoln, NE: University of Nebraska Press.

Millner, D. (2003). York and the Corps of Discovery: Interpretations of York's character and his role in the Lewis and Clark Expedition. *Oregon Historical Society, 104*(3), 302–333.

Montana Museum of Art. (2005). *Contemporary Native American art: Reflections after Lewis and Clark*. Missoula, MT: The University of Montana Press.

Monte-Sano, C., De La Paz, S., & Felton, M. (2014). *Reading, thinking, and writing about history: Teaching argument writing to diverse learners in the Common Core classroom, grades 6–12*. New York, NY: Teachers College Press.

Moreton-Robinson, A. (2015). *The white possessive: Property, power, and Indigenous sovereignty*. Minneapolis, MN: University of Minnesota Press.

National Council for the Social Studies (NCSS). (2013). *Social Studies for the next generation: Purposes, practices, and implications of the College, Career, and Civic Life (C3) framework for social studies state standards*. Silver Spring, MD: National Council for the Social Studies.

National Council for the Social Studies (NCSS). (2018). Toward responsibility: Social Studies education that respects and affirms indigenous peoples and nations. Retrieved from www.socialstudies.org/positions/indi genous-peoples-and-nations

National Endowment for the Humanities and Honoring Tribal Legacies. (2019). Discovering Native histories along the Lewis and Clark Trail, NEH Summer Institute, 30 June–21 July, 2019. Retrieved from blogs .uoregon.edu/nativehistories/about-rationale/

National Park Service. (2008). A summary administrative and interpretive history of the "Corps of Discovery II: 200 Years to the Future." Retrieved from docsbay.net /a-summary-administrative-and-interpretive-history -of-the

Native Strategic Initiatives, University of Oregon. (2015, October 13). Open letter to University of Oregon Athletics and Nike: Pioneer uniforms celebrate violence and alienate tribes. Retrieved from nativestudies .uoregon.edu/2015/10/13/open-letter-to-university -of-oregon-athletics-and-nike-pioneer-uniforms -celebrate-violence-and-alienate-oregon-tribes/

Newcomb, S. (2008). *Pagans in the promised land: Decoding the Doctrine of Discovery*. Golden, CO: Fulcrum Publishing.

Nike. (2015, October 5). 10 things to know about the new Oregon Duck uniforms. *Nike News*. Retrieved from news .nike.com/news/oregon-pioneers-football-uniform

O'Briant, K. (2018). Too Né's world: The Arikara map and Native American cartography. *We Proceeded On, 44*(2), 6–15.

O'Brien, J. (2010). *Firsting and lasting: Writing Indians out of existence in New England.* Minneapolis, MN: University of Minnesota Press.

Olsen, K. (2006). Discovering Lewis and Clark. *Teaching Tolerance,* Issue 29. Retrieved from www.tolerance.org/magazine/spring-2006/discovering-lewis-and-clark

Onion, R., & Saunt, C. (2014). Interactive time-lapse map shows how the U.S. took more than 1.5 billion acres from Native Americans. *Slate.* Retrieved from http://www.slate.com/blogs/the_vault/2014/06/17/interactive_map_loss_of_indian_land.html

Oregon Historical Society. (2018). A conversation on the history and commemoration of the Lewis and Clark Expedition. Retrieved from oregonhistoryproject.org/narratives/lewis-and-clark-from-expedition-to-exposition-1803-1905/a-conversation/a-conversation-on-the-history-and-commemoration-of-the-lewis-and-clark-expedition/#.XWg4R3tlC70

Papal Encyclicals Online. (2017). *Inter Caetera*: Division of the undiscovered world between Spain and Portugal (Pope Alexander VI, 1493). Retrieved from www.papalencyclicals.net/alex06/alex06inter.htm

Patel, L. (2016, April). In E. Tuck & R. Gaztambide-Fernández (Chairs), *Grounding red pedagogy: De-centering settler-logics in education.* Symposium conducted at the American Education Research Association Conference, Washington, DC.

Prucha, F. (2000). *Documents of United States Indian policy* (3rd ed.). Lincoln, NE: University of Nebraska Press.

Red Star, W., & Zucker, S. (2018). Wendy Red Star, 1880 Crow Peace Delegation. [Video] Smarthistory. Retrieved from smarthistory.org/seeing-america-2/peace-delegation/

Richter, D. (2001). *Facing East from Indian Country: A native history of early America.* Cambridge, MA: Harvard University Press.

Rodriguez, J. (2006. Encyclopedia of slave resistance and rebellion: Greenwood milestones in African American history. Westport, CT: Greenwood Publishing.

Roewe, B. (2016). Larger faith community comes to Standing Rock in solidarity. Retrieved from www.ncronline.org/blogs/justice/eco-catholic/larger-faith-community-comes-standing-rock-solidarity

Ronda, J. (1984). "A Chart in His Way:" Indian cartography and the Lewis and Clark Expedition. *Great Plains Quarterly, Winter,* 43–53.

Rotondaro, V. (2015). Doctrine of Discovery: A scandal in plain sight. Retrieved from www.ncronline.org/news/justice/doctrine-discovery-scandal-plain-sight

Sabzalian, L. (2019). *Indigenous Children's Survivance in Public Schools.* New York, NY: Routledge.

Sabzalian, L. (2019). The tensions between Indigenous sovereignty and multicultural citizenship education: Toward an anticolonial approach to civic education. *Theory and Research in Social Education, 47*(3), 311–346.

Sabzalian, L., Miyamoto-Sundahl, R., & Fong, R. (2019). The time is now: Taking initiative for Indigenous studies in elementary curriculum. *Oregon Journal of the Social Studies, 7*(1), 6–19.

Sabzalian, L., & Shear, S. (2017). Confronting colonial blindness in civics education: Recognizing colonization, self-determination, and sovereignty as core knowledge for elementary social studies teacher education. In S. Shear, C. M. Tschida, E. Bellows, L. B. Buchanan, & E. E. Saylor (Eds.), *(Re)Imagining elementary social studies: A controversial issues reader* (pp. 153–176). Charlotte, NC: Information Age Press.

Saindon, R. (1988). Sacajawea, Boat Launcher: The Origin and Meaning of Name . . . Maybe. *We Proceeded On, 14*(1), 4–10.

Salish Sea Sentinal. (2019). Lummi Nation ramps up effort to help Orcas. Retrieved from salishseasentinel.ca/2019/06/lummi-nation-ramps-up-efforts-to-help-endangered-orcas/

San Pedro, T. (2017). "This stuff interests me:" Re-centering Indigenous paradigms in colonizing schooling spaces. In D. Paris and H. S. Alim (Eds.), *Culturally sustaining pedagogies: Teaching and learning for justice in a changing world* (pp. 99–116). New York, NY: Teachers College Press.

Sarasohn, D. (2005). *Waiting for Lewis and Clark: The Bicentennial and the changing West.* Portland, OR: Oregon Historical Society Press.

Saunt, C. (2014). Invasion of America. ArcGIS Online. Retrieved from usg.maps.arcgis.com/apps/webappviewer/index.html?id=eb6ca76e008543a89349ff2517db47e6

Shear, S., Knowles, R., Soden, G., & Castro, A. (2015). Manifesting destiny: Re/presentations of Indigenous peoples in K–12 U.S. History standards. *Theory and Research in Social Education, 43*(1), 68–101.

Shear, S., Tschida, C. M., Bellows, E., Buchanan, L. B., & Saylor, E. E. (2018). *(Re)imagining elementary social studies: A controversial issues reader* (Teaching and learning social studies). Charlotte, NC: Information Age Publishing.

Singleton, G. (2015). *Courageous conversations about race: A field guide for achieving equity in schools (2nd Edition).* Thousand Oaks, CA: Corwin Press.

Sinha, M. (2017). *The slave's cause: A history of abolition.* New Haven, CT: Yale University Press.

Skibine, A. T. (2017). The Supreme Court's last 30 years of Federal Indian law: Looking for equilibrium or supremacy? *Utah Law Faculty Scholarship, 61*, 1–38.

Spirling, A. (2011). U.S. treaty-making with American Indians: Institutional change and relative power, 1784–1911. *American Journal of Political Science, 56*(1), 84–97.

State University of New York Environmental Science & Forestry (SUNY ESF). (2017). Statement for the March for Science. Retrieved from www.esf.edu/indigenous-science-letter/Indigenous_Science_Declaration.pdf

StudiesWeekly. (2016). *Oregon Studies Weekly*. Orem, UT: StudiesWeekly.

Sullivan, G. (2000). *Lewis and Clark* (In their own worlds). Scholastic. New York, NY: Scholastic Reference.

Teaching Tolerance. (2019). Teaching Hard History: American Slavery, Grades K–5. A project of the Southern Poverty Law Center. Retrieved from www.tolerance.org/frameworks/teaching-hard-history/american-slavery/k-5-framework

Thomasma, K. (1997). *The Truth About Sacajawea (Lewis & Clark Expedition)*. Jackson Hole, WY: Grandview Publishing Company.

Tomasi, Cardinal Silvano. (2016). The Vatican responds to the Long March to Rome. Retrieved from longmarchtorome.com/march/wp-content/uploads/2012/01/TOMASI-DMK-LETTER.pdf

Tuck, E. (2009). Suspending damage: A letter to communities. *Harvard Educational Review, 79*(3), 409–428.

Tuck, E. (2013, November 7). Settler colonialism and urban schools. [Prezi]. Retrieved from https://prezi.com/xoqizhw1yrui/settler-colonialism-and-urban-schools/

United Nations Economic and Social Council. (2010). *Preliminary study of the impact on Indigenous peoples of the international legal construct known as the Doctrine of Discovery* (E/C.19/2010/13). New York, NY: United Nations. Retrieved from caid.ca/UNECS19Feb2010.pdf

Viola, H., Bednarz, S. W., Cortés, C. E., Jennings, C., Schug, M. C., & White, C. S. (2005). *Houghton Mifflin social studies: United States history—early years* (Teacher's Edition, Volume 2). Boston, MA: Houghton Mifflin.

Viola, H., Bednarz, S. W., Cortés, C. E., Jennings, C., Schug, M. C., & White, C. S. (2005). *Houghton Mifflin social studies: States and regions* (Teacher's Edition). Boston, MA: Houghton Mifflin.

Vizenor, G. (1999). *Manifest manners: Narratives on post-Indian survivance*. Lincoln, NE: University of Nebraska Press.

Washington, G. George Washington to James Duane, September 7, 1783. *Founders Online*, National Archives. Retrieved from founders.archives.gov/documents/Washington/99-01-02-11798

Washington State Department of Licensing v. Cougar Den. 586 U.S. __ 2019. Retrieved from: https://www.supreme court.gov/DocketPDF/16/16-1498/64580/20180924 115810387_36893%20pdf%20Yakama%20Nation%20br.pdf

Watson, R. (2017). *Piecing me together*. New York, NY: Bloomsbury Publishing.

Watson, R. (2018). 2018 Coretta Scott King author award acceptance by Renée Watson. Retrieved from www.hbook.com/?detailStory=2018-csk-author-award-acceptance-renee-watson

Whyte, K. P. (2019). The Dakota Access Pipeline, environmental injustice, and US settler colonialism. In C. Miller & J. Crane (Eds.), *The nature of hope: grassroots organizing, environmental justice, and political change* (pp. 320–337). Boulder, CO: The University Press of Colorado.

Willcox, L., & Brant, C. (2018). *It's being done in social studies: Race, class, gender, and sexuality in the Pre/K–12 curriculum*. Charlotte, NC: Information Age Publishing.

Wilkins, D. (2014, October 24). Deconstructing the Doctrine of Discovery. *Indian Country Today*. Retrieved from newsmaven.io/indiancountrytoday/archive/deconstructing-the-doctrine-of-discovery-vAHfau_vOkCfps7rRGPhAw/

Wilkins, D., & Stark, H. K. (2018). *American Indian politics and the American political system* (4th ed.). Lanham, MD: Rowman & Littlefield.

Wilson, W. A. C. (2006). Burning down the house: Laura Ingalls Wilder and American Colonialism. In D. T. Jacobs (Ed.), *Unlearning the language of conquest: Scholars expose anti-Indianism in America* (pp. 66–80). Austin. TX: University of Texas Press.

Wineburg, S. (2001). *Historical thinking and other unnatural acts: Charting a future of teaching the past*. Philadelphia, PA: Temple University Press.

Wineburg, S., Martin, D., & Monte-Sano, C. (2013). *Reading like a historian: Teaching literacy in middle and high school classrooms*. New York, NY: Teachers College Press.

Wolfe, P. (2006). Settler-colonialism and the elimination of the native. *Journal of Genocide Research, 8*(4), 387–409.

Wood, K. (2003). Homeland. In Circle of Tribal Advisors, *Enough good people: Reflections on tribal involvement and inter-cultural collaboration 2003–2006* (12–13). Grand Junction, CO: Colorado Printing Company.

Yardley, J., & Neuman, W. (2015, July 10). In Bolivia, Pope Francis apologizes for church's "grave sins." *New York Times*. Retrieved from www.nytimes.com/2015/07/10/world/americas/pope-francis-bolivia-catholic-church-apology.html

Yenawine, P. (2014). *Visual strategies: Using art to deepen learning across school disciplines*. Boston, MA: Harvard Education Press.

Index

About the Authors

Alison Schmitke is a senior lecturer and director of the Educational Foundations Program at the University of Oregon. She taught high school social studies and language arts for eight years. Her teaching and research focus on preparing future teachers to provide inclusive, anti-oppressive curriculum to all their students.

Leilani Sabzalian (Alutiiq) is an assistant professor of Indigenous Studies in Education at the University of Oregon. Her research focuses on creating spaces to support Indigenous students and Indigenous self-determination in public schools, and preparing teachers to challenge colonialism in curriculum, policy, and practice.

Jeff Edmundson is a former high school teacher, and recently retired after many years as director of the teacher education program at the University of Oregon.